LILIES

DEREK FOX

ILLUSTRATIONS BY
LESLIE WILKINSON

CHRISTOPHER HELM
London

© 1985 Derek Fox
First published in paperback © 1987
Christopher Helm (Publishers) Ltd, Imperial House,
21-25 North Street, Bromley, Kent BR1 1SD

British Library Cataloguing in Publication Data

Fox, Derek
   Growing lilies.
   1. Lilies
   1. Title
635.9'34324   SB413.L7

ISBN 0-7470-1008-0

Printed and bound in Great Britain by
Biddles Ltd, Guildford and King's Lynn

To my daughters

Catherine and Diana

Contents

List of Colour Plates

List of Figures, Maps and Tables

Acknowledgements

It is necessary to acknowledge my indebtedness to all those people who have, through the years, contributed in some large or small way to our understanding of the lily. Without their efforts coming before, this book could never have been.

To write a book, though, requires more than words and I would like to thank those far and wide, who, knowingly or unknowingly, have helped me in some way in putting this book together. Nearer home I would like to thank Leslie Wilkinson for his excellent drawings which show instantly and more precisely more about lilies than words can say. Finally, I have to thank my wife, Betty, who has constantly serviced the whole machine, but also seen this work through to a clear and understandable script, for which I am deeply grateful.

Derek Fox,
Hockley.

Introduction

During the last hundred years or so many books have been written about lilies. If nothing else they have varied greatly in size from the folio of H.J. Elwes' *A Monograph of the Genus Lilium* (1877-80 and onwards) — truly a monumental work — to the slender little King Penguin of Fred Stoker's *A Book of Lilies* of 1943 being some 32 pages of text with 15 pages of exquisite but small colour plates. In all the various volumes the lily has been honoured as a peer among flowers and whatever fashions may come and go this is likely to remain the attitude of all those, gardeners or not, who 'consider the lilies'.

This book about lilies is written with a number of aims in view. One is to produce a book suitable for this decade, bringing together much of the information on the subject which is relevant to today. Being written primarily for the gardener and that recent cultivar, the plantsman, it is hoped it will speak with an appropriate tongue and will provide sufficient relevant information on all the many aspects of the lily and its culture. Where too great a detail would be a burden in this book, the intention is to show where the reader, if still interested, may go in search of further information and advice.

Another aim is to stimulate a greater awareness, not only among gardeners, but amongst all those interested to some extent in plant life and in the genus *Lilium*. There is more to learned and more satisfaction to be gained in knowing about lilies than to be obtained from merely buying a bulb at the local store or the hypermarket, sticking it in the ground and watching it grow. That is not the end of it; in fact, it is hardly the beginning as will be shown.

Following upon the last thought one object is *not* to explode the myth that growing lilies is difficult and to pronounce that in some new way all is easy. No stage has yet been reached where the grower can lie back in his deck chair and contemplate the blooming glories of a lily-filled July. It is doubtful whether any real progress has been gained since, say, the 1940s in the art of growing lilies. Some methods and innovations have made cultivation easier, some pesticides and fungicides have helped combat the enemies of lilies, many lily breeders have produced plenty of hybrids amongst which are a few stalwarts that allow us perennial lilies in the garden, while we go about our ways, fussing about our particular fancies. One thing is reasonably sure and that is that we have little opportunity today of purchasing anew each year dozens of bulbs dug up from the wild. Gone are the days when we could have a dozen *L. bolanderi* for half a guinea or its equivalent. This is all to the good both for us and the remaining depleted species in their native haunts. It puts us on our mettle and, if we are to see such beauties at home, we have to learn the ways of the plants and produce them from seed through the kind agency of friends or societies. In this way not only do we gain a deeper understanding of our plants, but many friendships from people who share the same or similar interest.

Except for the lilies themselves — and they have such hardened characters one can only respect them — there are no barriers to growing lilies. It seems that gardens are forever getting smaller, but fortunately lilies, certainly some indeed, do not need a lot of room. Much preliminary cultivation may be done in the smaller recesses of the home, to the perpetual annoyance of the other partner. Boxes of lilies may be quartered on the garage roof, presumably in the belief that slugs get dizzy at heights. The person with broad acres may be at a loss to prevent the depredations of rabbits, squirrels, birds and mice, and be no better off. Which only shows that all that is required is for the future liliophile to be punctured by the next passing aphid carrying LSV (Lily Symptomless Virus) and he or she is bound up for life in the beautiful world of lilies. One other way may be in the reading of the following chapters and visualising what splendours lie ahead. Life is not just a bed of roses.

The scope of this work will be confined to *Lilium* and the small genus of *Cardiocrinum*. The three species or so involved were at one time included in *Lilium* and even today *Cardiocrinum giganteum* is often referred to as a 'lily' (what else?) and as *Lilium giganteum*. There are good reasons though for thinking *Cardiocrinum* is more closely related to *Notholirion*. It is not intended to discuss *Notholirion* and *Nomocharis* in these pages, but it may be assumed that many of the points described respecting cultivation and propagation would apply to these genera.

Having stated in the botanical sense what is the subject of this work, to clarify matters even further the following lists are of plants which commonly are known as some kind of lily but will not be treated in these pages. The first list covers plants which are close to our true lilies and are in the family *Liliaceae*, the second list covers plants which are more remote and are not *Liliaceae*, but the family to which each belongs is stated alongside, in parentheses.

List I *Liliaceae*

African Lily	*Agapanthus*
Bluebead Lily	*Clintonia borealis*
Day Lily	*Hemerocallis*
Glory Lily	*Gloriosa*
Lily of the Valley	*Convallaria*
Lily Pink	*Aphyllanthes*
Plantain Lily	*Hosta*
St Bernard's Lily	*Anthericum liliago*
St Bruno's Lily	*Paradisea liliastrum*
Toad Lily	*Tricyrtis*
Torch Lily	*Kniphofia*
Trout Lily	*Erythronium*
Wood Lily (other than *Lilium philadelphicum*)	*Trillium*

List II of other families

African Corn Lily	*Ixia* (*Iridaceae*)
Arum Lily	*Zantedeschia* (*Araceae*)
Belladonna Lily	*Amaryllis belladonna* (*Amaryllidaceae*)
Bugle Lily	*Watsonia* (*Iridaceae*)
Guernsey Lily	*Nerine sarniensis* (*Amaryllidaceae*)
Kaffir Lily	*Schizostylis* (*Iridaceae*)
Peruvian Lily	*Alstroemeria* (*Amaryllidaceae*)
Scarborough Lily	*Vallota speciosa* (*Amaryllidaceae*)
Water Lily	*Nuphar* or *Nymphaea* (*Nymphaeaceae*)

Regrettably, not all the lily species described are in cultivation. There are a number of reasons, but principally it is due to rarity, inaccessibility because of difficult terrain and because of political control. Often it is due to a combination of all these factors, added to which the species may be difficult to cultivate with little known about its special needs. Not infrequently it may seem that more and more frontiers are closing. Happily, in truth though, it is as one closes that another frontier opens. The most important frontier to open in recent years is that of China, and it is good to place on record that already one or two species have come back into cultivation, together with new stock of a few others. This will not make them plentiful; in fact, they are likely to remain very rare. Gone are the days when boxes and boxes of lilies were despatched from the vastnesses of western China often only to linger and decay on some quayside far from their place of despatch and still thousands of miles from their destination.

Where Chinese geographical names are used these are given in Wades-Giles romanisation. The lesser known names, often one feels the interpretation of guides and the transliteration of explorers, are given in what seems to represent the most authoritative form. Many places have had name changes and in recent years it has become the custom to use Pinyin romanisation, so it can be very confusing to the armchair traveller. Some of us are beginning to realise that Beijing is Peking, but few of us yet appreciate that Chang Jiang is as long and as broad as Yangtse Kiang.

The problem does not end there, because over the years the taxonomists have with increasing knowledge found it necessary to change many plant names. When we read of George Forrest's exploits we need to recognise not only the place names but the plants too. For instance between Tali (Dali) on the west side of Lake Tali (Erh Hai) and Likiang (Lijiang) he refers to *Lilium thomsonianum*, *Lilium giganteum*, *Lilium delavayi* and *Lilium ochraceum*, and it so happens that all these four are changed to *Notholirion thomsonianum*, *Cardiocrinum giganteum*, *Lilium bakerianum* var. *delavayi* and *L. primulinum* var. *ochraceum* respectively. Without trying to encumber the text with too many synonyms, additional names that may be useful are included in the index.

Chapter 1
The Importance of the Lily in the Garden

Why should the importance of the lily as a cultivated plant be discussed? Surely its place is assured, its position well nigh supreme, and so the matter can be taken as read. Or can it? In much Renaissance painting the lily was a symbol too virtuous by far to descend into contact with a vase of other flowers. Later the Dutch treated the lily more sensibly and did not place it on a pinnacle, which was all to the good. But does it not seem that the lily is similarly used in the garden? Instead of being used generously, more likely than not either only a single lily is on view or lilies are absent altogether from many gardens, where they might be freely grown. Fortunately, just around the corner another gardener, like the Dutch painter, will insist on using and growing lilies.

It is solely a question of attitude or prejudice, which like a heavy soil should be broken down. Epiphytic orchids possibly meet a similar problem for different reasons, but then they are not ordinary garden plants in that they require a unique type of compost and, for most gardeners, heated glasshouse conditions. But the lilies are generally speaking hardy plants and that encompasses most of North America. That may be so, some will say, but lilies are difficult to grow. Are they? Then why is it that few kinds of lilies, are treated as cottage-garden plants? There are the Madonna Lilies, the first hybrid, the lovely L. testaceum, and the many kinds of martagon lily. In the north even more frequently than these, the Orange Lily, L. bulbiferum croceum, will be grown. Why should these not be taken up by many more gardeners? Surely they have been found to be sufficiently adaptable.

The anti-lily brigade will at this point come back in full chorus chanting that lilies readily fall prey to disease and prove ephemeral in the garden. What plants do not suffer from pests and diseases? It is obvious in nearly every gardening book, especially in those treating of one genus or one group of plants, that a chapter on pests and diseases and how they may be

5

controlled is obligatory. Lilies do not suffer from an extraordinarily long list of troubles, no more than on average. Certainly a few may be more deadly than those afflicting other plants.

Are lilies not long-lasting plants? It is the generalisation which is the problem. Plants that are maltreated often die quickly. Lilies are more susceptible to ill treatment than most other bulbous plants. No gardener lives that has not lost plants while others have become acclimatised to their new surroundings. It is not the prerogative of the lily alone to suffer in this way. Presumably there is a greater incidence of death in newly planted lilies and this is not acceptable to buyers. They have brought bulbs and bulbs should live. It is the accepted norm. As it happens the lily bulb is somewhat different to most other bulbs and is more susceptible to troubles (it is hoped to show how these may be alleviated later on in this volume). It can be shown, though, that lilies are mostly long-lasting plants. In the RHS *Lily Year Book* (*LYB*) for 1971 some 54 pages were devoted to Lily Group members' comments on the performance of their lilies. There were over 90 instances of various species having lived for 15 years or more and 23 instances of hybrids. With the latter, of course, the members were often referring to hybrids that had, in fact, not been available for that length of time.

Accepting then that some lilies are permanent plants and treated reasonably will not be lost easily, from whom does the gardener obtain them? It is perfectly true in Britain anyway that there are few sources from which the gardener can buy bulbs, excepting for the packaged imported bulbs which, if not bought early, dry out over winter in garden centres and supermarkets. The best sources then are your friends, and particularly those you will meet or correspond with in the various Lily Societies throughout the world. The commercial sources, few though there are, are useful, but except for some small nurseries, they do not cater for the keen grower who will realise that propagation from seed is just as much a part of growing lilies as growing annuals, and in due course far more rewarding.

Despite this difficulty, lilies should still become an important part of every summer garden, for there are lilies for all situations. This means not only the largest, but also the most humble garden. Few will deny the plant its supremacy and beauty — even so, some are more beautiful than others. All that is required is a certain amount of initial courage by the potential grower. Take the plunge and wipe away the old stuffy ideas fostered for centuries that the lily is unique and therefore frail, that the lily is difficult and should be left alone solely in the care of a mythical green-fingered elite. If this book has any value, it should be in helping those with a sensible enthusiasm to choose and grow the right lilies.

In the south of England the earliest may start to bloom just before the end of May. During June there will be a number of species flowering and a few hybrids. Then will come a peak flowering time during the first three weeks of July and this will be followed by further kinds continuing the season through August. Before the month ends the amount of bloom will have tailed off very considerably, but, if Orientals can be grown, the flower may be had until the end of September. This lily season is an important period in the garden year. Being high summer, for some it is the most important period, but with less dependence nowadays placed on traditional hardy perennial plants, the garden may often lose lustre at this time. In many ways lilies can avoid this situation arising. Lilies mainly have a long growing season, and they are plants with sufficient stamina to stand up of their own accord under reasonably normal conditions. They will make an important contribution to the vertical form of the garden from the moment the stems emerge in early spring. Leaving aside the flowers, their foliage will be decorating the garden for some months until the stems naturally die down in the autumn. There is no cutting down or cutting back until the top growth withers, unless there is evidence of disease to be eradicated.

There are lilies for almost every situation. The main border is possibly of prime importance especially where there are various positions with differing amounts of light and shade. Smaller lilies are best excluded from this situation, and a place may be found for them on the rock garden where sites may be chosen giving drier or wetter conditions. In high summer we incline towards the shade and shelter of the woodland and so the garden should provide the woodland edge and glade conditions, for it is here many of the most beautiful lilies will best reside. The existence of shrubs will prevent the lateral or horizontal movement of harmful insects and provide suitable protection in periods of adverse weather (such as high wind). Tall shade of the dappled kind is good. If too dense then the lilies will be drawn and limp, and be poor flowering. Special thought has to be given to the choice of lilies when the garden is on a chalk or limy soil. A study of the list of lime-tolerant species given on p. 43 will show the opportunities are considerable and remember some of these do better when grown in alkaline rather than acid conditions. A lily in a pot or pots of lilies in a corner of a patio or along the terrace may complete the picture, but the real enthusiast knows some are best kept in the greenhouse either to exclude the worst of winter or to benefit from extra loving care.

Accepting lilies as basic to the design of the summer garden, those that should and would occupy a permanent position and not require too frequent attention in splitting up and replanting include the turkscap lilies of the martagon group, together with *L. hansonii*, *L.. tsingtauense* and their many hybrids, all having whorled leaves; the Pyrenean lilies, for early flowers, both red and yellow with their dense foliage; *L. speciosum* and its varieties with broader, bamboo-shaped leaves and late flowering habit; and for wetter situations *L. superbum* so tall and handsome, again with verticillate leaves and the beauty of flowering in August. In addition to these stalwarts, as we may call them, the gardener may then choose further species to try his hand at, or take a cross section of, newer hybrids to fit with accompanying plants of other genera. There is no intention of advocating a lily garden or border or bed as such. For a number of reasons but mainly because of pests and diseases this is not thought wise.

This fundamental concept using basic lilies (not denigrated at all because of that adjective) plus a little of what the gardener fancies may be applied in many different ways in small or large areas and in very small or very large gardens. In this way they may be considered the core about which many other lovely summer and autumn plants may grow. These will be enhanced by the beauty of the lilies.

Having discussed the form and foliage of the lily as a staple constituent of the summer garden, it is entirely wrong to ignore the flowers. First, we might consider the six-petalled flower. Strictly, it is composed of three inner petals and three outer bracts. This arrangement of threes is accentuated and so immediately noticeable in the allied genus *Trillium*. As the summer flower garden is composed mainly of 'dicots' this simple arrangement of six is uncommon, the *Amaryllidaceae* being the only other family of plants offering similar flowers at the same time.

The competition that lilies encounter from the Amaryllid family is not large. There is *Amaryllis belladonna* itself with a few uncommon varieties; there are the crinums and particularly the hybrid group *C. powellii*. The bigeneric hybrid group *Crino-donna* should also be mentioned, but at this stage we must remember the lack of hardiness in many of these plants and the need for the right situation to achieve reasonably effective flowering. As to form, these plants all flower on leafless stems, and with *A. belladonna* the foliage has completely died away by flowering time. It would be generous to conclude then that these plants do not offer competition to the lilies, but to the keen gardener would be seen as complementary and supplementing the scene with additional lily-like blooms.

Returning to the form of the lily flower again, it is interesting to try and understand why some flowers appeal more than others. Such aesthetic considerations are vital to a worthwhile appreciation of our liking for garden plants and, indeed, wild plants. The four-petalled flowers of the *cruciferae* do not provide as satisfying a shape to the eye as those with five petals. The five-pointed star is more interesting than the four-pointed. The grouping of an odd number of items is generally more acceptable than an even number. How then is the lily flower so praised with six segments? Is it the grouping of two sets of three? This seems unlikely as it demands close investigation and is not an immediate point, but a subtlety appreciated later. Certainly 'six' is not always obvious. Paintings by non-botanical artists may quite frequently show less than the true number of petals. Number, then, above five, becomes less dominant and shape and other factors take on greater importance. Simplicity and a good clean curved line accentuated by a centre keel to the petal are very telling attributes. This 'weight' of petal is lightened by those other slender parts, the usually almost colourless filaments with dancing anthers. The central often upward curving style, well proportioned, completes the picture.

Is the picture complete? There is much more for the eye to see. No word has been said regarding colour and that surely is thought to be the most important thing about a flower. Discrimination, however, may teach us that colour is not everything, and when lilies are cultivated, brilliant though they may be, they are not usually produced for the massed effect, beloved of some and abhorred by others. On the other hand colour is not to be subjugated. With lilies colour is to enrich the whole and the variety comes in the colour of the leaves and stem as well as the petals of the flower.

. . . and much for the nose to smell. To many people lilies are perfume *par excellence*, just like roses. And just like roses many lilies do not have a scent, while a few of those that do are much criticised. Such is the nature of scent that it frequently defies description, try as we may. One quality seems one thing to one person and something quite different to another. Nothing is so subjective in our appreciation or disapprobriation as a smell. Lilies usually help us overcome these problems and add with their perfume to the feast of delight which only they so handsomely display.

Chapter 2
The Lily Dissected

The plant of a lily is comprised of a number of parts:

(a) a bulb
(b) roots emanating from the base of the bulb
(c) a stem rising above ground level which may or may not have roots at its base
(d) leaves on the aerial portion of the stem
(e) pedicels attached to the upper portion of the stem or rachis which carry
(f) the flowers containing the parts for sexual reproduction, leaving the
(g) seed capsule containing
(h) seed

which will now be considered in greater detail.

Parts of the Lily

Bulbs

Amongst the hundred or so species of lilies there are many different bulbs that can be distinguished, but they all have certain points in common. Every bulb has a basal plate to which are attached scales. The scales may be considered as an adaptation of leaves and as a store of food reserves. At the innermost point, but not necessarily the centre, may be found according to season the new growing point or the base of the stem. The almost unique feature of the lily bulb — it occurs also in the genera *Cardiocrinum*, *Nomocharis* and *Fritillaria* — is that the scales are exposed having no enveloping protective sheath as is seen surrounding most bulbs. The scales of the bulb may of necessity be very young near the growing point, but the outer or end scales may be a number of years old according to the species. The colour of the bulbs is usually close to white, but a few especially when mature are distinctly yellow. When exposed to light many bulbs take on a rosy-purple coloration, but this deep purple colouring is a feature of other than very young bulbs of

10

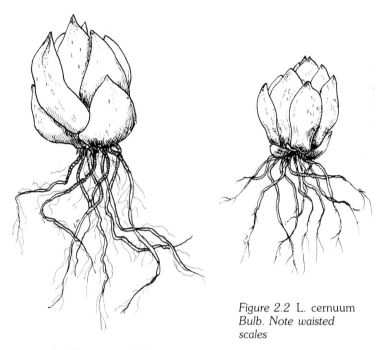

Figure 2.2 L. cernuum
*Bulb. Note waisted
scales*

Figure 2.1 L. tigrinum *Bulb*

the trumpet lilies and some of their close allies. The cardiocrinum
bulbs are this deep purple colour.

Lily bulbs take on various forms, some of which are very
distinct. The commonest type may be called concentric (Figures
2.1, 2.2) where the growing point appears to be in or near the
centre and the bulb is made up of a number of overlapping
imbricated scales varying in size, the largest being the outermost.
The scales may be broad when the overlapping will be
considerable and the bulb will appear and feel compact and look
fairly squat. If the scales are narrow the overlapping will be slight
and the bulb will tend to be more fragile. If the scales are longer
then the bulb will appear narrowly ovoid. The new growing
point will form on the basal plate within the bulb close to the
current year's stem and as outer scales wither those remaining
will cluster about the new point. Little change is seen annually
unless two growing points are formed following which two
clusters become apparent before the bulb divides. In bulbs of the
martagon group the scales may be jointed (Figure 2.3).

The next type of bulb is described as subrhizomatous and may
be linked to a concentric bulb which grows in one direction only
instead of regularly expanding throughout its circumference. The

11

growing basal plate of the subrhizomatous bulb will decline at an angle so that the mature bulb will achieve its proper depth. As previously mentioned, the scales will vary in shape according to the species, for example, narrowly lanceolate in *L. washingtonianum* (Figure 2.4) and ovate in *L. humboldtii*. Certain varieties have jointed scales.

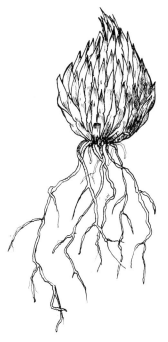

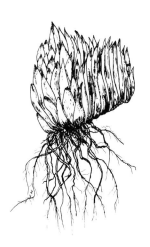

Figure 2.4 L. washingtonianum *Bulb*

Figure 2.3 L. medeoloides *Bulb, with Jointed Scales*

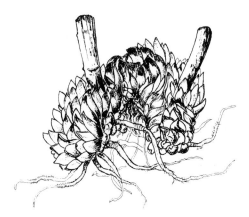

Figure 2.5 L. pardalinum giganteum *Rhizomatous Bulb*

The third type of bulb is truly rhizomatous and Western American lilies of the *pardalinum* group have bulbs typical of this form extending and often branching and making solid mats in the most vigorous species (Figure 2.5). Others which are not branching may still have the ability to form two growing points one behind the other. Scales vary from narrowly lanceolate to broadly ovate often on the same bulb and may vary in shape according to age, the youngest being the narrower, and they are paler in colour, usually white. Scales are often jointed, double jointed and, rarely, triple jointed. They are generally fragile bulbs the scales or parts of them becoming easily detached — to make new bulbs.

The next stage is the fourth type of bulb which is called stoloniferous (Figure 2.6). This kind is highly developed in the Eastern American species. The current bulb whether immature or mature extends a shaft or stolon, normally horizontally, but

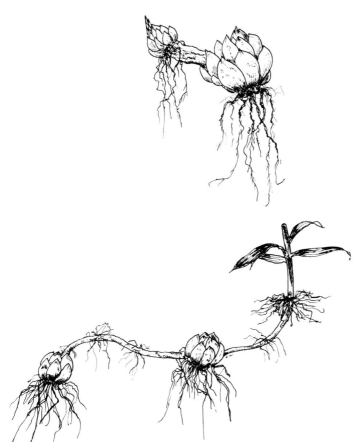

Figure 2.6
L. canadense
Stoloniferous Bulb

Figure 2.7
L. wardii *Stoloni-form Bulb*

presumably declining if an immature seedling, carrying at most a few scales. At the tip of the stolon a new bulb is formed of a conventional concentric form to provide the aerial stem for the following year. A vigorous bulb may send out more than one stolon in the season.

The final type of bulb to be discussed is that referred to as stoloniform (Figure 2.7). Correctly this should be considered in the third section dealing with stems as in fact the bulb is usually of the concentric type but it gives rise to a stem which grows somewhat horizontally underground before rising vertically to appear above ground.

Roots

Roots are usually little discussed except, perhaps, in scientific works or as subjects of research, but as we all know they play a vitally important part even though they are rarely seen at work. In the genus *Lilium* they are no less vital than for other plants, but they may tend to be overlooked or ignored as this attitude is fairly common where all bulbs are concerned. If a lily does not grow the second season after planting, and this is often heard as a general complaint, then one cause may be that the bulb as received and planted had no roots or only dead ones and therefore failed — because the ill was more deep seated — to produce roots afresh during the following season. The result being that the plant lived on its resources in the bulb and when they became used up the lily expired. Root growth and the ability of the bulb to make new root growth is vital to the health of the plant.

The roots of lilies vary as do the bulbs (Figure 2.8). In fact there is an obvious link, the roots having a number of functions other than the basic one of supplying nutrients to the plant. Roots hold the plant in its position, but besides that they may need to position the bulb in the ground as it grows or as its environment changes. Environmental change may take place if soil is washed off from the surface or silt or detritus is deposited over the bulb. The concentric bulb as it grows from a seedling soon exhibits a strong root system often out of proportion to the size of bulb. Amongst the new roots will usually be some fat roots, somewhat caterpillar-like and somewhat concertina-like. These are contractile roots which can work to bring the young bulb down to a suitable depth. The rhizomatous bulbs do not have these contractile roots, as they find their proper depth by depression of the extending basal plate. Their roots are wire-like with little branching. Likewise the stoloniferous bulbs do not require contractile roots as the new growing stolon may incline or

14

Figure 2.8
L. szovitsianum
Bulb with Good
Basal Roots

decline in the soil according to need. The roots are generally more wire-like and even less branching and possibly growing more horizontally in the soil like thin stolons rather than penetrating deeply as the roots of the other bulbs. The roots of bulbs having stoloniform stems often have very fibrous root systems with a mass of thin threads frequently branching. This rooting would seem suitable for a light humus-rich soil that most stoloniform lilies require. A great deal more study could be done on this subject, so generally neglected, and it should be appreciated the comments made are formed from garden conditions rather than what would be far better, those in the wild.

Stems

It is possible to consider the stem of a lily in two parts: that which is below ground and that which is above. In many species the subterranean portion plays a vital role in the active growing cycle of the plants. The stem may rise vertically to break the soil surface immediately above the bulb (Figure 2.9), or, as has been mentioned already under 'Bulbs', a stoloniform stem may wander some distance, as much as 45 cm, before rising to the surface. There are some species which send up bowed stems, and this

15

may be an adaptation to provide greater strength against the wind or animals. These may be considered intermediate between the two extremes. Often the function of the underground stem is to provide a second root system to feed the plant during its most active period. The vertical stem will provide a mat of roots above the bulb usually feeding on a rich humus layer. The wandering stem will also provide a secondary root system, the roots usually issuing from 'nodes'. A further function of the underground stem will be to initiate small bulblets which will first grow on the stem and later, as they send out roots, separately as the stem withers. This is a common clonal method of increase which is of consequence to amateur propagators.

Figure 2.9
L. martagon *Bulb with Stem Roots*

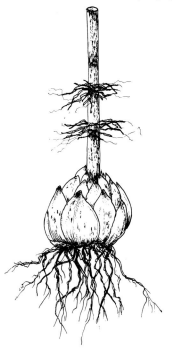

The aerial portion of the stem is commonly familiar. It may vary from as little as 10 cm to as much as 3 m, allowing for the inflorescence. The stem has sufficient strength to hold itself correctly against the natural forces it is designed to combat. Only in the garden might stems need to be staked. If, as herbaceous plants often need to do, they take the protection offered by shrubs, it is to survive against marauding animals, rather than to hold themselves erect. Other than providing a framework for the foliage and the flowers the stem in a few species will produce bulbils in the leaf axils, yet another useful and easy means of propagation. Bulbils also appear on the lower, usually leafless,

16

portion of the stem of a few species inhabiting warmer climates. These bulbils go into leaf quickly, which suggests that in nature perhaps the plants are growing through a moist verdant layer.

Lily stems suffer from two related negative characteristics. These are common to many but not all monocotyledonous plants; neither is unique to them. First, the stems have no method of branching. Branching only occurs in the inflorescence. Secondly, if the growing point is severed from the stem growth virtually ceases for that season. So no secondary growth from the base or branch is possible to complete the life cycle. Frustrated for that year the plant puts into reserve what it can to try again the following year.

The bulb will sometimes send up what looks like an exceptionally vigorous shoot, terminating in a galaxy of often ill-arranged flowers. This usually proves to be a fasciated stem or two stems conjoined with the stem not being round, but often with a flattened imperfect shape. It is most likely caused by the bulb wishing to divide, it being mature and vigorous enough, and so providing two growing points the previous season, but, at a delicate stage in this process, conditions deteriorate, such as the overdrying of the soil, and the task of division is not fully completed.

Leaves

The leaves of lilies are found in some species either scattered up and round the stem (Figures 2.10, 2.11) or in others placed in a whorl or whorls at specific heights around the stem (Figures 2.12, 2.13). These latter leaves are said to be verticillate and are often associated with scattered leaves, usually smaller in number and size, either above or above and below the whorls. The plants have to be of a certain maturity before the whorls are manifest and this is particularly obvious in some Western American species. At one time it was thought that whorled-leaved lilies preceded the scattered-leaved in the course of evolution, but this view is not usually held today as the reverse can be shown to be more logically the case.

To the untutored eye the leaves of lilies all look very similar and it is true that many do appear very similar. One failure in producing hybrids is the dominance of the flower to the excessive subordination of all other parts. The distinctness of foliage soon disappears in hybrids and this is not unique to the genus *Lilium*. It can be witnessed in the quite different genus of rhododendrons where individual species are often noted for the excellence of their foliage. This is rarely the case with rhododendron hybrids.

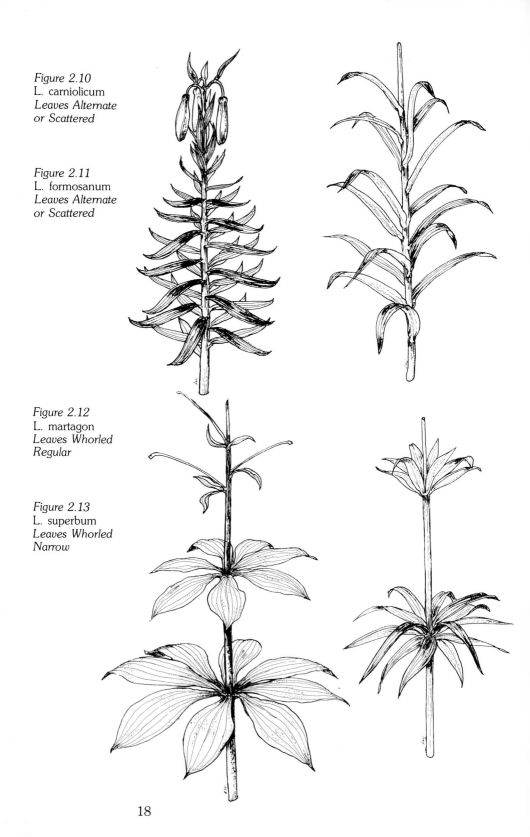

Figure 2.10
L. carniolicum
Leaves Alternate
or Scattered

Figure 2.11
L. formosanum
Leaves Alternate
or Scattered

Figure 2.12
L. martagon
Leaves Whorled
Regular

Figure 2.13
L. superbum
Leaves Whorled
Narrow

18

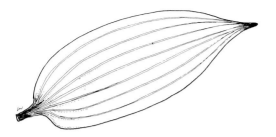

Figure 2.14
L. speciosum *Leaf
Petioled*

All lilies have leaves varying in length usually the shortest being the lowest and the uppermost, but the variation is as great as seen in the pinnae of fern fronds. The width of leaves varies considerably between lilies, but they are all 'parallel'-veined, the number of veins definite being as low as one to as many as nine. The leaves are basically flat in section, not recurving along the edge and usually without petioles. In those few species having petioles they are short (Figure 2.14). As with the density of foliage the poise of the leaves is also very important for aesthetic considerations. Many, especially those with whorls of leaves, will hold their leaves horizontally, but frequently with the tips dipping (Figure 2.15). Other species especially those with reasonably broad foliage will hold their leaves towards the upright (Figure 2.16) whereas those with long narrow leaves often hold them pendent. The leaves may be a fitting 'backcloth' and decoration to enhance the display of the flowers, but they are there to work to perform the task of photosynthesis. Their fitness to do this job is beyond doubt as through evolution and natural selection they are proved the most efficient in their rightful habitat. When seeing a lily or any plant for that matter in its habitat for the first time it is worth pondering upon the years of development and numerous generations that have brought it to this peak of perfection after millions of years.

Nobody thinks of lilies as a hairy tribe. They are most often glabrous plants, but some have a distinct hirsute quality that sets them apart. Such are the buds of *L. martagon*. The narrow leaves of L. *pomponium* are noticeable for their silver sheen produced by the ciliate margins. After many years L. *ciliatum* was defined and set apart from its neighbours partly by the long hairs on the leaf margins (Figure 2.17), so clearly seen when looking down on the young growing stem.

The leaves of the members of the genus *Cardiocrinum* are quite distinct from those of *Lilium* and this is one of the principal characteristics separating the two genera. The leaves are broad

Figure 2.15
L. tsingtauense
Leaves Whorled
Broad

Figure 2.16
L. chalcedonicum
Leaves Alternate
Ascending

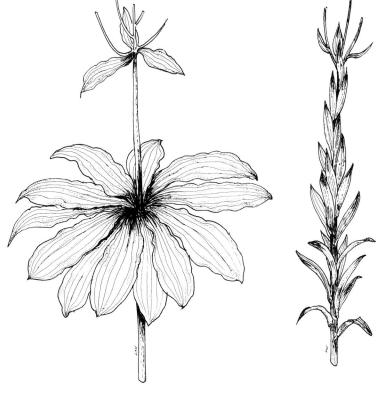

Figure 2.17
L. ciliatum *Leaves*
Margined with
Hairs

Figure 2.18
C. giganteum *Leaf*

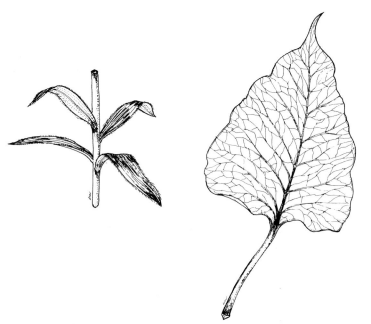

and cordate with long petioles (Figure 2.18); they are net-veined and rolled along their length (not flat) as they emerge. In the more commonly known and very stately species *C. giganteum* and its variety *yunnanense* there is a basal ring of foliage followed up the stem with spirally arranged leaves. However, in the two other closely related species there is a bare lower stem before an apparent whorl of leaves — not a whorl in any true sense — followed up the stem by a few smaller scattered leaves. An adaptation which looks as if it did not quite make it, but it gets some marks for trying!

Pedicels

These are the stalks upon which the flowers stand or hang. They are mentioned here not because of any particular botanical peculiarity, but because in their great variation from species to species and hybrid to hybrid they have a profound effect upon our judgement of any lily. Some lilies have great elegance, some much less, and this character in lilies can be seen to depend to a considerable extent on whether the pedicel is short or long, at what point and angle it breaks from the stem, its straightness or its curvature and the path of that line compared to the whole. To take one example, the upright flowering lilies with their short stout often closely clustered pedicels, despite their dominance and directness in distributing their flower to the beholder (see Figure 7.4), never can show the quality and grace that comes with the pendent bells of *L. canadense* where pedicels and flowers are so complementary (Figure 7.2).

Flowers

The flowers of lilies vary one species from another as much as any other part may vary within the genus. As there is shape, size and colour to consider not only of petals but of filaments, anthers, style, stigma and ovary then doubtless the variation in the flowers is greater. Certainly it is more obvious, as it is to the flowers, like the bee, we are drawn.

The flower (Figure 2.19) consists of what looks like six petals, but are found to be made up of three true petals and three sepals which lie immediately behind the petals. The sepals are sometimes narrower and envelop the petals when in bud, so it is the casing of the sepals that is seen at this stage. The petals and sepals may be referred to as tepals, which is nothing more than a useful anagram, or as perianth segments. At the base of a segment is the nectary furrow and this furrow is in some species bordered by knobbly projections called papillae. These papillae are most obvious in some species like *L. henryi* and *L.*

21

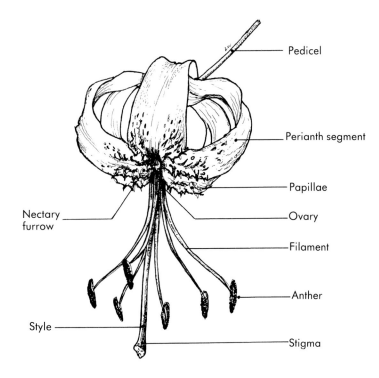

Figure 2.19
L. henryi *showing flower parts*

Pedicel

Perianth segment

Papillae

Nectary furrow

Ovary

Filament

Anther

Style

Stigma

speciosum where the petals are strongly recurved. The recurvature of the segments and their size greatly affects the form of flower.

Within the tepals and from near the base of each arise the six filaments. These are generally long and slender and are loosely attached to the tepals. At their ends are held the anthers, which, at dehiscence revealing the pollen, in many species become obviously versatile (or pivoted at the centre), so that moving freely at the slightest touch the other end will move towards the 'body' of an insect entering, leaving or hovering before the flower. The pollen-sacs and pollen are distinctly coloured and with the filaments are often helpful in distinguishing one lily from another.

At the centre of the flower will be the style at the end of which is the tri-lobed stigma. At a time when the stigma is ready to accept pollen it becomes sticky. The style (and stigma) which may be dark, but is usually pale in colour, is attached at its base to the end of the somewhat cylindrical and usually green ovary, which in its turn is formed at the end of the pedicel in front of the tepals.

The shapes of lily flowers are usually distinctive so that most can be categorised. However, there are still numerous gradations, mainly concerned with the recurving of the tepals and from where that recurving commences along the length of the segment, that make a clear-cut description difficult.

Shape. The first shape of note is characterised not so much by the petals as by the pedicels, which assert that the flower should look upright, as in *L. dauricum* (Figure 7.4). These lilies are sometimes referred to as crocus-flowered, but although this may seem suitable in most cases it is not really a happy idea as it can lead to confusion to describe one flower by another. The upright-flowered lilies may have their tepals widely open at 120° or more (see Figure 7.13) or they may be at 90° or slightly less, but this is frequently not distinctly described, likewise the curvature of the tepals. Such points are more vital in pendent flowers. The segments of upright lilies are often clawed along the basal portion being little wider than the nectary furrow. This allows one to see through the flower, but as the nectary furrow is supposedly full of nectar, any rain or moisture running down the tepals would topple down over the flush furrow to the ground beneath and not be entrapped in the flower to damage it. The tepals may also be narrow or widely spaced adding further to the openness of the flower.

The commonest pendent flower shape is the turkscap, as in *L. martagon*, (Figure 7.7), where the tepals are usually tightly recurved and the stamens and stigma are prominently exposed below the recurving perianth segments. The tips of the segments may curve over the pedicel or on to the base of itself. Where the tepals are less recurved as in *L. szovitsianum* the flower may be referred to as funnel-campanulate (Figure 7.12). If the curving becomes less pronounced as in *L. canadense* then the term campanulate is appropriate and when even less, as in the related species, *L. grayi*, then funnel-shaped is a suitable term. These words express and convey an idea where no illustration is available, but unfortunately mean slightly different things to different people. They try to do justice in a difficult medium.

Another basic flower shape is the trumpet for which *L. regale* may be used as the type (Figure 7.11). The tube of the trumpet may be extended as in *L. formosanum* or shortened as in *L. nepalense* (Figure 7.8). In this trumpet shape the ends of the tepals may recurve to a greater or lesser extent, but the effect on this larger-sized flower is, although important aesthetically, not so pronounced. Most of the trumpet-flowered lilies are not pendent but incline downwards. One to break the rule looks upward and this is *L. nobilissimum*.

If the tube of the trumpet is taken away completely then there is only the bell remaining, and bell-shaped may be thought suitable, but to avoid comparison with 'campanulate' the term bowl-shaped is generally used. This may be applied to *L. auratum* (Figure 7.1). If then instead of the tips of the segments being recurved nearly the whole length of them is recurved, a flower like that of *L. speciosum* or *L. henryi* is obtained. There is no good name for this shape and in basic outline it is like the original turkscap, but this term is certainly unsatisfactory. As the two lilies mentioned have prominent papillae then the phrase recurved papillose lily is usable.

Size. It is not necessary to say a great deal on the size of lily flowers. It is well known that they are often large and spectacular, but others are relatively small. The largest species do not, perhaps, have the largest flowers but often what is lost in size is sometimes gained in quantity. The end result is procreation of the species and this has to be done with the greatest efficiency and expediency possible. To achieve a good production of fertile seed adequate cross fertilisation is essential. This may even be so in those lilies known to be self-fertile, if the strongest offspring are to germinate and mature.

Without doubt *L. auratum* has flowers of the largest diameter being 25-30cm across. The longest trumpet blooms must come from *L. neilgherrense* although rarely seen these days, as apparently they can exceed 25 cms in length. If the prize were to go to the lily producing the largest flower in relation to the size of plant, then it would have to be awarded to the diminutive *L. formosanum pricei* which may be only 15 cm high when its single trumpet flower is 10 cm long. The largest turkscap flowers may be found on *L. humboldtii* var. *ocellatum* (Figure 7.5) when growing at its mighty magnificence, and then the total inflorescence and mass of plant growth will generally exceed that of other lilies. The smallest flowers on Pacific Coast lilies especially related to plant growth will be found on *L. occidentale*. *L. parvum* will be a close second (Figure 7.10). The opposite number to *L. formosanum pricei* across the Pacific in the diminutive class is the dwarf form of *L. maritimum* flowering at 15 cm high with a normal-sized bloom for the species. A most attractive plant for the cultivator with suitable conditions. Other smaller-flowered species are, to our eyes, generally happily in proportion. Some, however, do not make the grade very well. Too often *L. pyrenaicum* is a fine mass of foliage topped with one or two somewhat pallid yellow blackish-streaked turkscap flowers, only the vivid red pollen exciting the eye of the beholder. On the other hand the Himalayan *L. nanum*, which by name one expects to find small, looks fully in proportion bulb to stem to leaf to flower. Again it holds no brilliance or vividness, but to the plantsman appears correct and well-fashioned and conjures up those ethereal plants with which it naturally cohabits. Could it be that *L. pyrenaicum* on the edge of the lily's range by adaptation has learnt to live on the fringe (and be an amenable plant in cultivation) but become no real beauty, while *L. nanum*, perhaps close to the centre of the lily's world, has still retained the essence of the original lily and to the gardener an intransigence to any marked modification of its habit.

Colour. The colour in garden flowers is all important. Nobody denies that, but neither gardeners nor anyone else are very good at describing colours. The use of a fancy name, such as 'Tangerine Orange' may be helpful and meaningful to many readers and yet another, 'Flamingo', may convey very little to most people except a suggestion of redness, although two colour charts used this name, surprisingly for the same shade! It was partly because of the difficulty of expressing colours by words that the RHS Colour Chart resorted to numbers alone within the named basic colour groups. It seems that many of us, even before we get old, suffer to some extent from a degree of colour blindness. And yet we attach a great deal of attention to colour and will continue to do so.

Like most flowering plants, but by no means all, lilies draw attention to themselves by colour or the lack of colour; the latter, of course, refers to the white lilies. There are no blue lilies and never will be, for there is no true blue colouring (delphinidin) in the make-up of lilies. The colours are provided by the anthocyanins, the anthoxanthins and the plastid pigments.

The anthocyanins supply the red colours to lilies. They are colours which with sugar are dissolved in the sap of the perianth segments. The colours are mainly derived from pelargonidin or cyanidin. Pelargonidin gives the orange-scarlet colours. If it is based on a white ground it will appear like *L. davidii unicolor*. If it is on a yellow ground it will be like *davidii* red forms and *L. amabile*. In many lilies we see pelargonidin in a diluted form and we may call the colour apricot, where it is on a yellow ground, and fawn, where it is on a white base. There are, of course, one thousand and one variations and these are found amongst the numerous Asiatic hybrids. The other anthocyanin in lilies is cyanidin which gives the true reds and not the orange-reds. It is the red seen in Oriental and Western American lilies which come as pink in the diluted form. The red is as a strong colour on *L. auratum rubro-vittatum* or often very pale on *L. japonicum*.

25

These are both on a white ground. On a yellow ground it appears on *L. pardalinum*, but in a dilute form on a white ground in *L. kelloggii*. Variations in shade and tone are not just dependent on the strength of the pigment, but also occur because of the chemicals with which it is associated, sugars and sap pH. These factors change during the flowering period. All lily growers know how the fresh rich wine-red changes to muddy purple in old age. The 'bluing' effect, which is also a dulling of the colour, is caused by additional hydroxyl groups in the pigment. It may be witnessed in the diluted pink of *L. cernuum*. More than usual brightness is caused by methylation where the methyl radical replaces an hydroxyl.

The anthoxanthins are similar to the anthocyanins but provide colours ranging from the deepest yellow to palest cream. The pale pigments, such as apigenin, are referred to as flavones and the darker, such as quercitin, as flavonals. These pigments appear in most lilies such as the throat coloration of many trumpet species, the 'recessive' colour of certain forms of Asiatics such as *L. leichtlinii* and *L. amabile luteum*, and the basic colouring of *L. szovitsianum*; but those lilies lumped together as Orientals, would seem to be devoid of these anthoxanthins.

There remain now the plastid pigments which are different to those already discussed in that they are insoluble in the sap but, being microscopic particles, float in the cells. The yellow plastids are called xanthophylls and the orange carotenes. These plastids provide a background effect and a strengthening or building up of the colour provided by the anthocyanins and anthoxanthins.

It is useful, especially to hybridisers, to appreciate that other plants have a similar range of colouring to lilies. The chrysanthemums are a case in point where after so many years of cultivation, the reds still do not come to match the like of *L. pomponium*. The rhododendrons have the ability to achieve a better 'blue' effect. The paeonies achieve with peonidin an outstanding red rarely witnessed in lilies.

Recalling again the poor colour often seen as a flower fades, only reminds us that the flower, however long-lasting or ephemeral, is not a static object but constantly changing through one phase to another, if we wish to tabulate or categorise the progress. Those who have grown Western American hybrids in which the somewhat garish background colours have been eliminated will have noticed how the remaining colours change not only through the life of the flower, but because of variations in temperature and light intensity. It would seem that it is the anthocyanins which are most noticeably affected and in these lilies at least, apparently the cyanidin is contained in cells close to the surface. This variation in shade and tone of colour can have a most pleasing appearance when seen on a large inflorescence as so many beautiful tints are found together, or on a single flower when throughout its life from tip of tepal to the base the subtle changes are watched from time to time like the rising of the sun and its going down.

Reproductive Parts of the Lily

The filaments and anthers of lilies are an important and vital aspect of the visual display of the lily flower. The practice in floristry of denuding the flowers of their anthers and therefore of the pollen, though often a necessary one, must be abhorrent to genuine lovers of lilies. The filaments are thin, delicate, often gracefully bowed, faintly coloured green, even diaphanous. Although appearing lengthy they are normally shorter than the style which is stouter. Except in some European turkscap lilies where they are inhibited and stay-at-home, the filaments usually splay out and allow the anthers to hang versatile. This is an excellent arrangement whereby any nectar-seeking flying insect is bound in the course of its endeavours to come in contact with the pollen with wing or abdomen and may easily deposit some of it on the protruding stigma of the same or another flower. Most of the pendent turkscap lilies have the pollen-bearing anthers on the same plane as the stigma. With the Oriental lilies and the trumpet lilies the style extends well beyond the anthers. In the smaller funnel-shaped or campanulate lilies it seems that insects, not necessarily being on the wing, are enticed into the perianth as they inadvertently gather pollen, as the anthers are often set further back inside the flower, behind the stigma.

While it is receptive of pollen the tri-lobed stigma exudes a viscose fluid to aid the retention of the pollen. This is an added precaution for the heavy pollen of lilies itself adheres to all but the shiniest of surfaces. This is well known to those who have handled lilies and to children who having learned of the smell of lilies walk out of botanic gardens with yellow or russet brown noses. The stigma may be pale green, whitish or stained purple according to the species. If stained purple then this colouring may extend back along the style, otherwise this is usually whitish or pale green.

The ovary behind the style is no dominant feature at flowering time. It is nicely protected behind the enwrapping basal portions of the perianth segments. Needless to say the ovary may be damaged should small birds attack the unopen buds in search of nectar. Once the tepals have fallen and presuming the ovules to have been fertilised, the ovary will start to enlarge, but unless the

Figure 2.20
L. dauricum *Seed Pod*

lily is upright-flowering, when little adjustment is necessary, the pedicel will react to the fertile ovary and adjust itself in order to bring the future seed capsule into a vertical position, that is with its apex uppermost. The ovary is in three sections, having three carpels, and in each section there are two rows of ovules, later to become seeds. When the seeds are ripe the seed case dries and splits into three sections and a vertical pile of seeds is seen to be positioned either side of the central keel. A fine net of fibres usually still connects the three sections so that the seeds are not dispersed by falling out of the capsule. Only the top of the capsule allows the free exit of the seeds, so it would seem dispersal is under the best circumstances carried out by the wind. As the seeds in the capsule dry sufficiently, the wind carries the topmost out of the capsule. As more than a light breeze is required to move other than chaff, the ·plump seeds once airborne are likely to carry a metre or so. Although referred to as plump the seeds are flat in section, like slices of bread cut from a bloomer! Typically they are slightly winged, but varying according to species and in regard to their position in the capsule, so that the winged effect may be wholly lost.

Seeds of Cardiocrinum

In the genus *Cardiocrinum* the seeds are thinner for their size and distinctly winged. The seeds as they dry are not entrapped like the lily seeds by the fine netted web between the sectional casing, but by long pointed teeth that are formed on the edges of the sectional casing. It should be appreciated that the seed from a stem of *Cardiocrinum giganteum* may take many months to dehisce. These giants live under the canopy of Himalayan oaks aside such stupendous large-leaved trees as *Rhododendron grande*, with bamboos and a close jungle where the winter winds are calm. Once on the wind these large winged cardiocrinum seeds would travel further than the lily seed before dropping on to the leaf-laden floor. Only when having penetrated to the humus layer would the seed be in a position to germinate. Meanwhile the lily seed higher up the valley is no better off! Still in its dry capsule even yet unopened it is dried each autumn day by the sun and the valley airs moving up and down. At night it is frozen. As winter approaches it will be enveloped in snow and perhaps become broken at the stem. As the sun rises higher in the early spring the pod will be freed from the snow, alternately washed and dried, and in semi-disintegration, if not already completely disintegrated, it will free the seeds, which will wash into the granitic sand or be caught by some root-bound humus. With sufficient warmth the seed will germinate.

Figure 2.21
C. giganteum
Seed Pod

Until now we have been dealing with the morphology of the lily, or what it looks like to the human eye. It is now time to look under the skin so to speak and say a few words about the cells and cytology of the lily. Over fifty years have gone by since the first studies were published on the chromosomes of lilies by Masayosi Sato, and in 1934 a three-part article entitled 'The Chromosomes of Lilium' was published in the RHS *Lily Year Book* No. 3 and this gave us the work of Mather, Sansome & La Cour. All the then available lilies, except one, were found to be diploids having a chromosome count of 2n = 24. The exception was *L. tigrinum* only known at that time in the triploid form where 2n = 36. The cardiocrinums were known as lilies in those days and they were seen to possess the same number, 2n = 24. It is significant that no comment was made on any uniqueness of the cardiocrinums. In 1946 Stewart discussed 'The Morphology of Somatic Chromosomes in Lilium' having included *C. giganteum* in his studies. The ideogram of the karyotype does not appear so distinct nor does it call for any special comment by the author. So whereas we can see obvious morphological differences between *Cardiocrinum* and *Lilium* they are not so apparent at the chromosome level. The ideograms placed in order to show similarity of chromatin distribution put *C. giganteum* between *L. auratum* and *L. tsingtauense*! It took *L. grayi* away from its natural position amongst the morphologically similar American lilies of the Eastern States and placed it between *L. tsingtauense* and *L. japonicum*. One species *L. auratum* was found to have three karyotypes. Four different species were found to have the same karyotype and not surprisingly these four species were Western American lilies. Soundly Stewart states that: 'There is no direct evidence to be obtained from a study of somatic chromosome morphology as to the method of origin of the variation between karyotypes', and that the usefulness of chromosome morphology is limited by the independent occurrence of karyotype variation in indicating differentiation of species. It would seem, therefore, that study of the chromosomes of lilies has proved more useful to those seeking steps to solve further problems away from lilies than to the lily enthusiast wishing for clues to solve the evolution of the genus and desiring in his search for order out of chaos to classify the members of the genus to his satisfaction. It is known that the chromosomes of *Fritillaria* and *Cardiocrinum* (? and *Notholirion*) are very similar to *Lilium* and that they are very stable. Comparison may be made with the genus *Crocus* in the family *Iridaceae* where the chromosome count varies between 2n = 6 and 64.

Cytology of the Lily

One sphere in which chromosome examination has been most useful is in the determination of hybrids particularly of the F_1 group involving the species. In 1944 it was shown that the parents of the first European hybrid, *L.* × *testaceum* were *L. candidum* and *L. chalcedonicum*. In 1948, after the original suggestion that *L.* 'T.A. Havemeyer' was a cross between *L. sulphureum* (*L. myriophyllum* as it was known) and *L. tigrinum*, it was shown that the second parent with *L. sulphureum* was, as suspected, *L. henryi*.

Now it is known that some lilies are apomictic and when used as the female parent rarely produce anything but their own kind. *L. regale* is notorious in this respect. If apomixis is suspected in what should be a hybrid batch, then it can be well worthwhile testing the seedlings in the early stages to see from the chromosomes whether both parents are involved in the karyotypes. The full procedure was described by Dr A.B. Wills at the 1969 Lily Conference held in Scotland. It may be found in the RHS Lily Year Book Vol. 33 for 1970. Dr Wills stated that the only specialised equipment required was a microscope having a good objective of about × 40 magnification; very high magnification not being necessary because lily chromosomes were relatively large. The diagram in the article, however, shows the chromosome complement of a *L. lankongense* × *davidii* hybrid magnified 700 times (*LYB*, 1970, p. 176).

Having looked at the chromosomes and realised that they still withhold more knowledge from us than they impart, it is obvious the next stage might be to tackle the genes carried within the chromosomes. It is these that hold the keys to the hereditary storehouse of lily characteristics. Unfortunately that is not possible here and it will be necessary for most of us to pick up shreds of evidence as we are allowed to see them. It is in the field of interspecific fertility particularly where we may expect to gain most.

Chapter 3
Cultivation

Cultivation truly starts with the placing of the seed in the right soil and, one might add, at the right time. This, though, is dealt with under propagation, so here we will concentrate on how the mature bulbs may be cared for and grown to produce the best possible flower stems, whether outdoors or under glass.

If the bulbs are to do well, the prerequisite is that they should be healthy and undamaged. The second point is that they should be available at the right time, fresh, that is, not long out of the ground, firm not flaccid and, according to the type of bulb, supplied with roots. The nursery or the source must be responsible for the health of the bulbs and likewise damage in transit, unless it is of an exceptional nature. If the purchaser is not satisfied he should go elsewhere or even do without. If there is a bulb-merchant as intermediary and, perhaps, even another as retailer then it is highly unlikely any or very few of the preconditions will be met. This is a sad situation, but too often true. Many bulbous plants, especially those with outer protective skins, are far better able to reach the gardener as and when he wants them. Lilies kept out of the ground for months boxed with others in wood shavings are likely to be almost dead, dried and desiccated when finally a customer is found. Frequently moulds will have started to administer the last rites.

As long as the bulbs are not too bad certain treatments may be offered them. First, they should be cleaned of any fungus-infected scales. Dip them for an hour or two in a solution containing a systemic fungicide. Detach two or three scales on which to grow fresh bulblets. Place the bulbs in damp peat in cool conditions around 7°C (44°F). If all is well the bulbs will be fresher and firmer after a fortnight, while possibly showing the tendency to throw new basal roots. Assuming this is still not the time to plant outdoors, then the bulbs should be potted and grown for a while in cool conditions under glass or suitable cover. When favourable conditions apply outside then permanent planting may take place at the earliest opportunity. On no account should poorly rooted or weak bulbs be planted into cold conditions to over-winter.

When is the correct time for planting lily bulbs outdoors? The answer is at any time when there is sufficient warmth in the soil for active growth to take place below ground. It goes without saying that soil conditions should be suitable too. This means from some time in spring until mid autumn or fall. It may seem surprising to include summer and the flowering season, but this is quite acceptable as long as it is practical. Often it is not practical, as long stems must go with the bulbs, and because evaporation and dehydration can be very rapid at this time demanding transfer having to be accomplished quickly. The gardener who knows what he is about can achieve this happily and to his advantage. So we are left with spring and autumn. Spring is an excellent time as long as fresh bulbs from the ground or pots can be obtained at this time. Certainly growing roots should be handled even more carefully than the bulbs and not allowed to dry out. The lily grower who raises a lot of his own stock will be able to do much at this season.

This leaves the season following flowering which is an extended autumn. Its length is dependent upon where you live. Flowering time is variable too, well into August with both hybrids and species. If you are fortunate to be able to grow the softer plants then September must be included too. This leaves the big grower and his bulb-merchant or agent just a few weeks, very few weeks indeed, to lift, clean, sort, package, ship, resale and retail, and a host of other things beside so that the gardener may have his bulbs in time. Nine times out of ten it is not possible. If you do know a grower who can let you have the bulbs in good time in autumn while the ground is still warm enough to encourage root action then that is excellent. Otherwise, it is a case of making the best from not such good circumstances. It is because of failure from bulbs arriving too late that so many gardeners become disheartened and disenchanted. The really keen ones go on to grow their own.

Planting Outdoors

Presuming the bulbs are available at the right time, how should we go about planting them? Whether you have one of a kind or many the procedure should be similar. Lilies may be grown in groups and look best in this fashion, but all kinds should not be grown together, in fact, rather the reverse. Planting at intervals in beds or borders interspersed by shrubs, other herbaceous plants and medium to dwarf conifers can be very satisfactory. If the vectors of disease are going to be with us sooner or later then we should not make it too easy for them and natural barriers in the form of other substantial plants seem highly satisfactory. Sufficient separation should, therefore, be aimed for between groups.

The soil should be a well-worked deep loam. The depth of top soil can hardly be too deep, but few of us are lucky enough to possess too much of such a valuable commodity. Much can and should be done to improve the subsoil below, while at ground level we can add frequent mulches. The main concern though should be the drainage. If this is naturally very good so much the better. Make sure nothing is done to hinder the drainage even where no lilies are growing at present. If the drainage is fair, then doubtless ways can be seen to improve it by adding coarse material into the sub-soil, but remember all the time that the excess water must move away vertically or laterally, preferably both, as readily as it arrives. It is far too easy to make a sump and that is the worst that can happen. Always bear in mind — how can we help to move the water away?

On sloping land the answers are relatively easy to find, but on flat surfaces it can be very difficult and it may be necessary to lay sloping drains below the top soil.

Once good drainage is assured the top soil can be improved or altered according to our needs. Usually grit would be added to allow free movement of moisture within the compost and humus, with its flexible bulk, to ensure that the compost retains sufficient moisture and does not dry out too rapidly. The humus, especially in the form of natural leaf soil, is particularly attractive to the finer roots and especially the stem roots of lilies. To ensure there is an adequate food supply to the roots and that at no time are the bulbs' resources being exhausted, a general fertiliser should be added with a reasonably slow release of nitrogen. In seeking perfection a natural site should be chosen where the acidity of the soil is just sufficiently below neutral, say pH 6, to be suitable for most lilies, but to which acidic peat can be added to please the bog and calcifuge lilies or chalk or limestone to charm the calcicoles. Unless it is really warranted there is no need to take drastic action to achieve a particular acid/alkaline reaction of the soil. Over the years the soil can be coaxed in the right direction. If grit is to be added and the soil is too alkaline then obviously granite chippings are preferable. If the pH is to be increased then limestone grit is the kind to use. Likewise grades of peat vary in their acidity, while leaf soil from alkaline regions will follow that reaction. Much then can be done in the normal course of soil improvement to achieve the desired end.

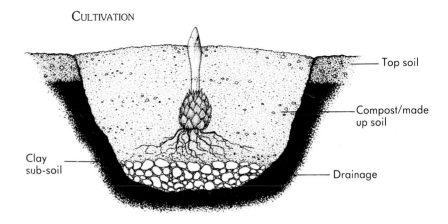

Top soil

Compost/made
up soil

Clay
sub-soil

Drainage

Figure 3.1 Unsatifactory Drainage. There is nowhere for the water to go, so it builds up and around the bulb

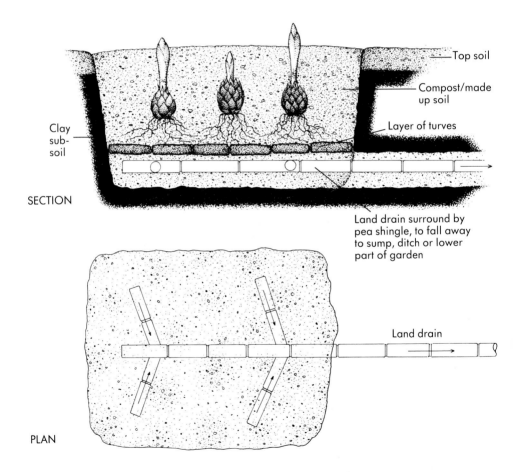

Top soil

Compost/made
up soil

Layer of turves

Clay
sub-
soil

SECTION

Land drain surround by
pea shingle, to fall away
to sump, ditch or lower
part of garden

Land drain

PLAN

Figure 3.2 Satisfactory Drainage. Water moves away freely via the land drain

34

Shallow-planted Bulbs

Actual planting may now proceed. With a few exceptions lily bulbs appreciate deep planting. The main exception is *L. candidum*, the Madonna Lily, which is different too in that it produces a growth of leaves in the autumn that last through the winter. The bulbs should be out of the ground for the least possible time and that during August, not really any later. They should be no deeper than to allow a light covering over the bulbs. If the soil is acidic add lime and growth will be stronger. Although in many gardens clumps stay untouched for years, easing out over-growing bulbs after flowering and sprinkling with fertiliser or mulching round with manure is very beneficial. All varieties of Madonna Lily may be treated alike. *L.* × *testaceum* and similar hybrids may be shallowly planted with 2-4 cm of soil over the nose. The other parent *L. chalcedonicum* in nature sticks to no hard and fast rule as in places it may be found almost on the surface while in others well below.

The other surface-planted bulbs are the cardiocrinums. They have no relation to *L. candidum* nor in nature do they have any preference for lime, rather the reverse. It is said *C. giganteum* will grow in an alkaline soil, but they are forest dwellers living in a thick humus layer. Additional peat or leaf soil should be mixed in and the bulbs planted into the loam with it pressed around them so that the noses are just at ground level. This may be done in early autumn with large-sized bulbs likely to flower the following summer, but small bulbs as long as they are not dried out may be dealt with at any time when the season and weather is convenient. A generous layer of tree leaves may be scattered over the bulbs, but not such as will matt or cake on the surface. Even so these may be loosened and others added with light cypress branches or similar placed over the top with the coming of spring in order to protect the precocious emerging leaves from sharp frosts. Where necessary slug bait should be applied early, as the slimy creatures can quickly make a sorry mess of the broad leaves. Otherwise the tattered remains stay as a constant reminder of a battle lost and a further year required before the monocarpic bulb will burst into flower.

Deep-planted Bulbs

The remaining bulbs to plant fall into three categories; the directly rising stem rooted, the rhizomatous and stoloniferous bulbs which may or may not root from the stem, and the stoloniform species, where the stem wanders underground before arising erect to break the soil surface. All require a deeply-worked soil, but room for lateral growth is more necessary for some, *particularly the last mentioned*. Knowing that soils and their depth vary a great deal, it is no good advocating planting 20-30 cm deep if it means the basal roots searching into the most unfriendly conditions, or, more likely, having to grow upwards! Most bulbs are adaptable, in fact, in nature are constantly adapting, even if slightly, to changing circumstances. The bulb is born on or close to the surface and has by differing means a way of reaching a desired level underground. It may then be a better tactic for us to plant young bulbs, putting them from 8-15 cm below the surface and letting them find their own final position. Remember that well-worked soils may be very puffy and will in any event sink a good deal.

This leaves an opportunity for further mulching. Where the soil is obviously too shallow then raised beds will have to be made, ensuring that although well drained, the rain will not run quickly off the surface.

It will be noticed that most stem-rooting species with concentric bulbs have fleshy basal contractile roots by which they can draw the bulb lower. These roots should be carefully spaced out while planting. The stoloniferous bulbs of species like *L. canadense* do not seem to demand a very fixed level in the ground, but they have the ability to send the new stolon at an angle to allow the new bulb to be higher or lower. The rhizomatous bulb can also adjust its level somewhat, even appearing to grow on top of itself in order to become nearer the surface. The roots are mainly lateral and not necessarily deep-delving.

One important point to realise, of course, is the physical problems the lilies may have in keeping a 2 m high stem with fully open flowers vertical during windy weather. Staking can and should be resorted to where necessary, but it is never very much better than unsightly and everything should be done in correct planting and siting to help the lily stand on its own one foot.

The lilies with wandering stems cause no worse problems than demanding living room. Usually they like light friable humus-rich soil through which to send their relatively weak stems. Particularly deep planting is not essential and 10 cm would normally be sufficient. Often as the stem turns to rise erect stem-rooting occurs, as at earlier nodes, and this gives extra rigidity.

Two further points in planting should be mentioned. The first is placing the individual bulb on a bed or cone of sharp sand. This can be useful in two or more ways. It ensures perfect drainage immediately below the base of the bulb; being virtually inert it is unlikely to harbour deleterious fungal spores; and the sand will be a helpful barrier against underground slugs and soil-borne larvae many of which find lily bulbs nutritious. Once the bulb is placed in position it should be covered in sharp sand if these pests are particularly troublesome. Means to eradicate them should be taken prior to planting. The other planting suggestion applying mostly to concentric bulbs is to lay the bulb on its side. This may be advantageous initially especially when the bulb scales are fairly open and not tightly imbricated. As years go by the new scales will form as the lily wants them to be and doubtless will right itself.

Before the bulbs are finely covered they should be carefully marked where planted either in their circles, squares, triangles and rectangles, or individually, by small sticks such as light bamboo, being not too conspicuous. They should also be adequately labelled preferably showing the date of planting. If the bulbs are going to need staking later on little twigs inserted appropriately may indicate, at least initially, where the canes may be inserted at a later date without running spikes directly through the precious bulbs.

Aftercare may include mulching with leaf soil with grit added; not using worn out disease-harbouring old potting compost, but including fresh wood ash and charcoal if available. Most lilies will like a little extra potash and the charcoal helps to keep things sweet and prevent clogging by the fine ash. Weeds must be kept at bay. The top surface may be most attractive to germinating seeds and not only perennials, but weeds such as annual grass and chickweed must be ruthlessly exterminated right from the start, otherwise they will ruin much of your good work. As the lilies grow a check should be made for early signs of pests and diseases, not waiting before acting just because the signs are few and small. Do not wait for the epidemic.

Having taken the trouble to ensure perfect drainage, it may be found that our usually inadequate rainfall has failed entirely. Few of us live on the sides of mountains with three months or even three weeks snowmelt to work on. Few of us garden in rain forests or even on the edges of them. Most of us will want to water our plants and our lilies from time to time. While a few species are acclimatised to summer rain, the majority are used to copious supplies of water early in the growing season followed by a relatively dry atmosphere (even though the soil is wet) before flowering until the early or even late autumn. Watering then should be aimed at the soil and the roots where it can be effective rather than the foliage where it may invoke disease. Where it is going to be essential annually, trickle irrigation at ground level discreetly arranged would seem to be the answer.

37

At the other end of the scale the top surface should be kept such that it is always permeable to water from the watering can rose and not be seen to run off, a most frustrating aspect of watering in a drought.

Growing Lilies in Pots

There are a number of good reasons for growing lilies in pots and they may be best appreciated set out as follows:

(a) not being hardy they may be kept at certain times in a controlled environment
(b) they may be forced indoors to flower earlier
(c) they may be moved easily while in full growth and used on terraces, patios and in courtyards, etc.
(d) they may be grown and exhibited or displayed without cutting
(e) they may be given unique conditions of compost, etc. unattainable outdoors, and
(f) the soil conditions, prevalence of pests, etc. outdoors may be unsuitable to a particular lily or to lily culture in general
(g) they may naturally flower later than the first autumn frosts
(h) they may be required for pollination at a specified time
(i) they may need an improved environment to ripen seed
(j) they may be given to friends or sold to would-be lily enthusiasts on garden open-days.

Not surprisingly there are a few problems arising from growing lilies in pots:

1. they are more trouble to look after
    (a) needing special compost and feeding
    (b) individual and frequent watering
    (c) being more prone to disease
2. and more expensive to maintain
    (d) demanding glasshouse space for part of the year
    (e) supplementary heat
    (f) requiring containers.

Although the advantages outweigh the disadvantages gardeners should not embark on this method without first appreciating what is entailed. Glasshouses may be bought and their environment by various devices automatically controlled. To some extent this may be applied to watering, but it is unlikely this can be taken much further than the growing-on stage. Assuming large pots of lilies being grown for display, these do entail expending a great deal of time in careful watering. One thing with lilies is that they are susceptible not only to overwatering, but also to underwatering and so the happy mean must be kept up over long periods.

Even so lilies in pots are very effective and an extension of our interest and so very much worthwhile. Many lily growers will use what glass they have for raising young bulbs and seedlings in the initial stages. They must be kept healthy at all costs and so doubtful bulbs or even susceptible species or varieties should be kept well away — but some less hardy kinds may be easily taken on in the general run of things.

Compost should be adjusted where necessary to the particular lily. This may mean more humus or more chalk or such a variation to meet its needs. Drainage once again has to be particularly thorough and the compost itself free draining. If in doubt add more grit to the compost. What is lost in the richness may be made up with liquid feed. Apart from potting up poor and rootless bulbs for initial improvement and planting out later, time, pots and compost should not be wasted on anything but first-rate bulbs.

Presuming reasonable facilities are available these may be potted at any time during the supposedly dormant period, but bulbs must spend the least possible time out of the pots. In the ordinary way bulbs must not be crammed into pots, neither must the pots be too big for little bulbs whose roots will not fill them. Three *L. concolor* fit neatly into a 15 cm pot; one large *L. auratum* hybrid or three *L. chalcedonicum* will go into a 23 cm pot; and three to four medium-size *L. auratum* hybrids could go into a 30 cm pot. If deeper than average pots are available so much the better. Where cheaper hybrid bulbs are used for 'once off' decoration and the bulbs are to be considered expendable then much tighter conditions could be used filling 15 cm pots.

Whether clay or plastic pots are used a generous amount of drainage material in the form of sherds and dustless large chippings or similar should be used. Dress the sherds with grit before adding the first layer of compost. If the bulbs are stem-rooters then place them midway up the pot and cover them lightly with compost. When the stems begin to grow the pots may be gradually filled with a rich compost, ensuring as best as possible that it will still be free draining even with a mat of stem roots. Non-stem-rooters may be placed near the top of the pot to gain as much below-bulb area for the roots. It should, however, be seen that the stems perched up and exposed may become rather fragile.

Where tubs, half-barrels, urns and similar containers are to be used on terraces and at suitable vantage points, it is soon appreciated that these are not easily moved about, let alone brought in under glass from late winter till spring. The easiest practice here is to grow the bulbs initially under glass in 15 cm pots and at a suitable time after, say, spring bulbs are finished bring them out to refill the containers. Old compost should be discarded and the pots replenished with new and, if loam is used, it should be sterilised as with normal potting composts.

Lilies under Glass

There are a number of lilies which are best grown under the shelter of glass. According to where we live this number may cover just two or three of the southernmost lilies or a whole bevy of species. The colder the region the less practical it becomes to attempt growing plants from within the tropics. All kinds of difficulties and snags arise, but these are not impossible to overcome if the will is there and the means available.

As lilies are herbaceous and as those generally concerned come from the hills or the mountains no great temperatures are required at any time. The house may be allowed to drop a degree or two below 0°C (32°F) in the winter and need never be above 36°C (90°F) in summer. The difficulty in continental areas where it will be cold in winter will be to restrict temperatures from rising too high in summer. This problem arises with most plants and not just lilies.

The species that benefit from glass are the following:

(a) in milder temperate regions

alexandrae	* neilgherrense
arboricola	* nepalense
* bakerianum	nobilissimum
brownii australe	poilanei
catesbaei	* primulinum
iridollae	sulphureum
longiflorum	* wallichianum

(b) in colder temperate regions
all those mentioned above and

candidum	parryi
formosanum	philippinense
leucanthum	pomponium
maritimum	sargentiae
occidentale	speciosum

* Those so marked are stoloniform and not suitable for normal pot culture.

40

The two lists are offered as a guide. Hard and fast rules are not possible. The conditions in maritime Britain are quite different to those only a few miles inland. The same may be said for Boston, Mass. by the coast and Northampton, Mass. inland. Some of those mentioned come from a wide area and a range of altitudes and so may vary in hardiness within the species. Regretfully a few mentioned are presently unobtainable and others very difficult to find, but we live in hope that such will not always be the case.

Having scrutinised the lists, it is possible to divide the lilies into two further groups. There are those whose stems rise directly from the bulb, like L. *longiflorum* and L. *formosanum* and those, like L. *nepalense* and the others marked with a *, where the stem is known to wander underground. Where the stem rises directly, and this may include L. *primulinum*, suitably large, preferably deep, pots will be quite satisfactory.

Those with wandering underground stems of the stoloniform type should be accommodated in the greenhouse border, if this is possible. Otherwise specially broad boxes should be employed having ample dimensions to accommodate the awkward stems. Although it may be thought that the stoloniform stem may be constricted within the walls of a pot as are the roots, performance is obviously hindered and so it is necessary to give them as much room as possible. These lilies are lovers of leaf soil so much humus must be incorporated in the compost. They are also accustomed to the monsoon rains in summer so like plenty of water and humid conditions at that time. Nevertheless they still demand good drainage.

With the facilities of a greenhouse it is possible to force lilies into flower out of season. The lilies that will do this readily are those which are not so dependent on hard seasonal changes. The lilies most used are Ll. *longiflorum* and *speciosum*. They have been florists' lilies for a great many years and there were times when they were greatly in fashion. Asiatic hybrids of many kinds may also be used for this purpose. Unfortunately the quality often seen out of season is sufficiently poor to give the lily a bad name. The amateur who wishes to extend the flowering season may do so quite readily using some slight heat in the greenhouse to bring on the cultivars well before those outside commence. Choice of varieties of L. *speciosum* alone will ensure flowers in October and possibly November.

Bulbs may be dug up from outside in January if conditions are likely to be suitable. Potted up immediately in fairly rich compost they will have their roots in good condition and will respond readily to the extra warmth, say, minimum 8°C (45°F). The compost should not be too wet at first, so water sparingly. When growth is well commenced watering should be increased and liquid feed given too. When the flower buds change in colour, feeding should cease.

The control of pests under glass should be ruthless and there should be no waiting for aphids or other pests to turn up. A spraying programme could be laid down from the start. The control of fungus diseases and botrytis is helped enormously by maintaining a fresh and buoyant atmosphere, but it would be a good thing when growth had well commenced to spray with a broad-based organic fungicide and again in the bud stage with a copper-based fungicide even though nothing particularly trouble-some was obvious. Should symptoms arise then again immed-iate action is warranted. *Botrytis* is best controlled by a copper fungicide.

Composts should depend to some extent on the particular lily — and hybrids may follow their parents or forefathers — but most should be based on a sterilised loam with coarse sand/grit and peat/sterilised leaf soil, following the formula for the John Innes composts. To these should be added plenty of extra grit to satisfy the need of free drainage — so many supposedly good loams are too sticky and heavy — and where the lily is a real humus dweller this may be added liberally to the final mix. If loam and leaf mould is used with a proper proportion of general fertiliser then the lilies should not suffer from any nutrient deficiency, expecting that the natural materials will contain all and sufficient quantities of the necessary trace elements. If soilless peat-based composts are used then these must have the necessary trace elements added artificially. In addition care must be taken to give the correct liquid/foliar feeding throughout growth. There is no buffer in these artificial composts as is the case when using loam.

Besides those lilies requiring the protection of glass the following lilies may also be grown in pots in the greenhouse:

Asiatic hybrids	*japonicum*
Oriental hybrids	*mackliniae*
auratum and varieties	*maculatum* and varieties
brownii	*philadelphicum*
bulbiferum	× *phildauricum*
chalcedonicum	*pumilum*
concolor	*regale*
dauricum	*rubellum*

The exclusion from these lists of any species or any kind of lily does not mean that it cannot or should not be grown in pots.

Alpine and rock gardeners in particular, many of whom are skilled in pot culture, may wish to grow the following under controlled conditions if only for exhibition:

cernuum	sherriffiae
duchartrei	formosanum dwarf form
nanum	maritimum " "
oxypetalum	pitkinense " "

and some others of greater rarity should they become available.

Lime tolerance

Many lilies, perhaps most, grow on acid soils, others on hard limestones. Some are on alkaline and acid soils. Some of the preferences are referred to under the individual species in the survey, but to give an easy indication the following is a list of those which are or which are thought to be tolerant of lime or chalk:

amabile	henryi
bolanderi	humboldtii
brownii ?	langkongense
bulbiferum	leucanthum
callosum	longiflorum
canadense var. editorum	martagon
candidum	monadelphum
carniolicum	pardalinum
cernuum	parryi
chalcedonicum	pomponium
concolor	primulinum
dauricum ?	pyrenaicum
davidii	regale
duchartrei	sulphureum
hansonii	szovitsianum

The inclusion of a species suggests that its varieties and its hybrids may be lime-tolerant. Some of the rarer lilies have not been tested. There are indications that more of the Western American species are tolerant than was originally expected. At least some of the hybrids are showing this.

If it may be any encouragement to those gardening on lime who often feel penalised, some lilies do not flourish on acid soils. This includes *L. henryi. L. candidum* and many trumpet hybrid lilies do not build up to vigorous mature bulbs. These are personal observations and there may be more instances.

Further points on cultivation are given throughout the survey of the species where appropriate to the lily concerned.

Chapter 4
Propagation

In general terms there are no difficulties in reproducing lilies, their hybrids, and cardiocrinums. It has been said before that there are many ways in which lilies may be propagated and that Nature has been bounteous in this respect. If Nature has been bounteous then usually she has had good reason to be and so we may assume there is some agency at work by which lilies suffer, particularly on their way to maturity. There is no panacea offered in these pages, but perhaps some benefits may accrue when readers put this guidance and their own understanding and common sense into practice.

The general principles are put forward here, but special points are made where necessary under the individual species in Chapter 7. These may also be thought appropriate to related hybrids where they exist. It takes some time to understand and assimilate all the whims and fancies of these plants, especially when many are inconstantly available, but fortunately for most matters many species and their hybrids fall into quite definite categories and this is most helpful.

Germination — Lilies

Propagation by Seed

The most important method of propagating lilies is by seed. Since the earliest days of the RHS Lily Group some fifty years ago, seed has been advocated as the primary method of raising lilies. To those many gardeners who are accustomed to purchasing hyacinths and tulips as bulbs this may seem strange, but it has proved over the years to be a most sensible method, in fact, in many ways essential. In days gone by most lilies were dug in their native haunts and shipped across the seas to the relatively few gardeners who could afford the luxury, cheap though they were by today's standards. This source of supply is virtually closed. Conservation demands and in many cases sheer rarity decrees that seed is used by those enthusiasts who grow the species. Seed is more readily available, easily transportable, subject to little, if any, restriction between countries and usually

45

inexpensive. The great added advantage is that lily seed is not known to carry the virus diseases of its parents, so that, at least initially, a new healthy lily is born with each germinating seed. Disadvantages are that seed does not continue a clone, but produces a new and original being, so that where it is desired to maintain a particular quality or where a unique hybrid needs to be multiplied only vegetative and not sexual means of reproduction is available; and a mature bulb usually, but not necessarily, takes longer to produce from seed than by other means.

As lilies span the globe in the northern hemisphere and are found in many various climatological zones it is not surprising to find that they exhibit differing characteristics. The most important of which to the present discussion is that there are two different forms of germination, one described as hypogeal and the other as epigeal, and seed of a particular species exhibits one form only. When hypogeal germination takes place the cotyledon stays below ground, at the end of which a tiny bulb with a root is formed. In some species the cotyledon may be 1 cm or more long and the bulb grows at some distance from the seed casing, but in a few species the cotyledon is so short that the bulb may seem to be growing inside a bulging and splitting seed case. The first leaf seen above ground of a hypogeal germinating lily is a true leaf. When epigeal germination occurs the cotyledon is brought above the surface of the soil often with the seed casing still adhering to the tip. The bulb is usually insignificant at this stage and the first true leaf appears above the surface later, following an increase in bulb size and root length (Figure 4.1).

Associated with these methods of germination is a time factor which is of considerable importance both to the lily in the wild and the grower at home. Germination is often further described as immediate or delayed. Immediate is when given adequate heat, moisture, air and light germination commences and becomes continuous through all stages, while the expected conditions permit. Delayed is in most cases meant to suggest that germination commences in the normal way, but when a certain stage of development is reached further growth is inhibited until a seasonal period (usually cold) is passed, following which growth recommences. It can also mean a period before germination commences and, in practice, this means inbuilt prevention of autumnal germination.

Immediate conditions are usually associated with epigeal germination. The seed dehisces during unacceptable conditions for germination, but with the coming of spring activity commences, leaves are produced above ground and growth

46

Hypogeal Germination of Seven Different *Lilium* Hybrids and Species

*Figure 4.1
Germination
Diagrams*

3. *L. martagon* seedling at
   stage undergoing cool
   period.
4. *L. szovitsianum* seedling
   at a similar stage

1. Western American hybrid seedlings, February 1982
2. Actual size

5. *L. bolanderi* starting to
   grow first true leaf in
   February 1982; sown 21
   September 1981. Cool
   temperate conditions
   throughout

6. *L. washingtonianum
   purpurascens*

7. *L. washingtonianum.*
   Both sown 21 September
   1981. No visible 'spring'
   growth mid-February
   1982. Cool conditions
   throughout

8. *L. parryi* sown 27
   November 1981. Most
   seedlings showing
   'spring' growth mid-
   February 1982. Cool
   conditions throughout

Two Types of Germination of *Lilium*: Left, Hypogeal; Right, Epigeal

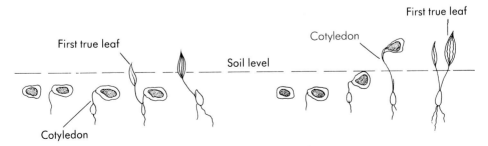

First true leaf

First true leaf

Cotyledon

Soil level

Cotyledon

Hypogeal

Epigeal

continues while conditions allow. Delayed epigeal germination may seem to give the same set of circumstances, but it is necessary to appreciate the seed being sown at the natural time, that is, autumn, when the conditions may be suitable for germination, but the period of time for the small bulbs to mature for over-wintering is too short. In the case of *Lilium pomponium* germination takes place in cool conditions, suggesting its attachment to the Mediterranean climate, so that, in effect, seed falls to the ground in late summer and awaits the winter rains when it germinates, continuing its growth through the spring until summer conditions make further progress impossible.

Delayed conditions are usually associated with hypogeal germination. Once again germination takes place in the spring, but all growth is below ground in forming a bulb, that, without the aid of photosynthesis, will withstand the following winter before growth above ground commences. As an illustration this is how lilies of the *martagon* group start their existences. There is an important exception to this procedure. In the case of Western American or Pacific Coast lilies time of germination seems to be strictly controlled and there is no definable delay period. The basic procedure is that following the ripening of the seed it falls on to moist cool conditions, where it either immediately or very shortly germinates, that is, a minute bulb is formed. This takes two to three months by which time winter has settled upon the ground and, according to location, virtually no further growth is possible until spring. However, even under the snow, conditions may be quite temperate, or should the lily be close to the sea the winter may be normally mild, so that, in both instances slight growth is possible and the first leaf shoot is ready to emerge with longer milder days or the melting of the snow. The Pacific coast favourable to lilies stretches from British Columbia to the Mexican border and covers about twenty degrees of latitude. Some variation must be expected to cover this circumstance despite the overall maritime influence. Similarly the coastal cliffs, the Coast Ranges and the Sierra Nevada all attract differing conditions and allowance has to be made for this. The most noticeable deviation from this 'Western type' germination is seen in lilies coming from the southern end of the range. *L. parryi*, for instance, will frequently show germination in the spring, if sown at that time, whereas the seed of the majority of Western American lilies will lie dormant until the autumn and will not be induced to germinate earlier. The southern lilies, perhaps in a stage of transition, are losing their dependence on northern strictures gained during their original migration from northern Asia.

Table 4.1 indicates the type of germination that might be expected from the various species. There are a few doubtful areas of knowledge and this is particularly so where rare and difficult species are concerned.

Table 4.1: Epigeal and Hypogeal Germination

EPIGEAL

Immediate			Delayed	Autumnal/ Winter
amabile	henrici	philadelphicum	carniolicum	pomponium
arboricola	henryi	philippinense	chalcedonicum	
bakerianum	lankongense	primulinum	ponticum	
brownii	leichtlinii	pumilum		
callosum	leucanthum	pyrenaicum		
candidum	longiflorum	regale		
catesbaei ?	mackliniae	sargentiae		
cernuum	maculatum	sherriffiae		
concolor	nanum	sulfureum		
dauricum	neilgherrense	taliense		
davidii	nepalense	tigrinum		
duchartrei	oxypetalum	wallichianum		
formosanum	papilliferum	wardii		

HYPOGEAL

Delayed		Immediate		Autumnal/Winter
* alexandrae	martagon	iridollae ?	bolanderi	pardalinum
auratum	michauxii	koknese (form	columbianum	parvum
bulbiferum	michiganense	of martagon)	humboldtii	pitkinense
canadense	monadelphum	medeoloides ?	kelleyanum	rubescens
ciliatum	* nobillisimum	parryi	kelloggii	vollmeri
distichum	polyphyllum		maritimum	washing-
grayi	rubellum		occidentale	tonianum
hansonii	speciosum			wigginsii
japonicum	superbum			
kesselringianum	szovitsianum			
ledebourii	tsingtauense			

Note: * Recent evidence suggests that these two species, which enjoy a maritime climate, do not have traditional spring germination followed by a cold delay period. Germination appears best treated as autumnal and, following a low temperature period equivalent to mild temperate maritime winter, will produce the first true leaves in the spring. Germination is therefore rather similar to that of the Pacific Coast American species.

49

Germination — Cardiocrinums

Apparently, unless cardiocrinum seeds are sown immediately they are ripe, their germination is delayed at least by one year. The obvious visible signs of epigeal germination become apparent in late winter or early spring — February in southern England. It is, perhaps, worth noting that the 'claws' on the seed capsules prevent the speedy dehiscence of the seed and as there is little strong wind in their native haunts during autumn it is worth speculating that seed is distributed over a period of many months and that the delay factor is a common agency in the reproduction of plants which take seven or more years to mature.

Methods of Raising Lilies by Seed

The two species, *L. martagon* and *L. pyrenaicum*, are naturalised in Britain. It may be assumed that they regenerate by seed, both producing viable seed and in quantity. In a few British gardens a third species, *L. szovitsianum*, reproduces itself easily from naturally scattered seed. *L. regale* and a few other lilies may do likewise in suitable situations elsewhere. Certainly hybrids of Western American lilies have occurred naturally in the author's garden over many years. This suggests that the first method is broadcasting seed in the wild garden. Although some success may come of this it is not to be advocated, the wastage being enormous and the time taken for the bulbs to mature — the few that do — considerable. What is a sound proposition is sowing the seed in rows in a suitable part of the vegetable garden. Those lilies, like *L. regale*, which produce good seed in quantity may be produced in plenty by this means. Choose a site where it will be convenient for the seedlings to remain for two growing seasons and, unless they are definitely lime-tolerant, where the friable and presumably well-drained soil has not been recently limed. A drill 2.5 cm deep will be suitable, along which the seeds should be scattered thinly so that no thinning later is required. If after two years the bulbs happen to touch one another there is no harm in that, and that is how sowing thinly may be interpreted. Sowing should be done in the spring, say mid-April, for immediate epigeal kinds, when things are definitely warming up. Early autumn is in order for delayed hypogeal kinds, when it is essential that Western American types are sown. Care should be taken to keep the rows clean and free of slugs. Any sign of aphids should be dealt with speedily and in the usual way. Assuming the ground has been well fertilised previously, little more needs to be added other than a booster of general fertiliser, not too high in nitrogren, at the start of the second year. At the end of the second season, while the soil and air temperatures are still warm, the bulbs should be transferred to a new site; those large enough but not necessarily sufficiently mature to flower going to their permanent place in the garden. The seedlings should not be lifted until the new site is ready, when they should be transferred without delay, great care being taken to lift as much root as possible undamaged.

Open ground conditions are not really suitable for very many lilies and may be used only where quantity is required or early losses can be acceptable. However, those having garden frames available may wish to adapt the method to these better controlled conditions. A greater range of lilies could be grown over a longer season. Sowing could take place with considerable benefit earlier in the spring and, as long as temperate conditions are preserved throughout the summer with no drying out, growth should be maintained well into the autumn. Many species show a desire to grow over a particular length of time and have, perhaps, an inbuilt mechanism controlling this period. So it is that some kinds die down early, others late, some very late, but the seedlings and immature bulbs, like those of many other genera, have a wish to grow away early and carry on later, if conditions are suitable, possibly being less active at mid-year. Besides care in watering and extra vigilance being maintained for aphids, which are most easily controlled by a systemic insecticide, fungus diseases may readily appear, especially in the autumn, so that leaves die down prematurely. *Botrytis* is best controlled by a copper fungicide, but for other purposes a systemic kind, such as benomyl should be used, particularly to control *Fusarium* rot. The latter may prove very troublesome, upsetting and disappointing for the grower. To mitigate this it is important to use either a sterilised compost or at least one (or any of its constituents) which has been known not to have grown bulbs or corms of any kind previously. Very good drainage is another essential and it is highly recommended that the compost is one that will crumble readily or be washed out readily from a mass of lily roots, that will then be less tangled when the bulbs have to be separated. It is very important to try to preserve the young lily roots from one growing medium to the next. Not only does this reduce the risk of inducing disease, but it helps the young plant in the next growth stage. Energy stored in the tiny bulb does not have to be consumed in restoring a root system. It may be assumed that the seedlings will remain in the frame for two years, but the more vigorous will be quite sizeable after one year when they might be moved. However, do not hurry too much to move the babies on, because they are so easily damaged when young. It is far easier and better for good results to handle a more sizeable bulb later on. If the seedlings look too crowded too soon, it is due to sowing them too thickly. Beneficial effect could be had by using a liquid feed during the main periods of growth, and the strength of the fertiliser should be balanced with the age and vigour of the plants.

Many gardeners will intend sowing lily seed as they do most of their other more specialised plant seed in pots, pans, boxes or trays within the reasonably controlled conditions of a frame, glasshouse or conservatory, perhaps using the additional facility of a thermostatically-controlled propagator. The value of the latter for lilies is marginal. The ordinary seed tray is obviously too shallow for lilies. At the other end of the scale the full size pot of 12.5 cm diameter and over is initially too deep and wasteful of seed compost. What is required at a later stage is a deep pot holding a fresh and richer compost, so a compromise can be set where the seeds are sown in half pots and are later transferred *en bloc* — the roots holding the compost together — to a deep pot having a good layer for drainage below the new well-fertilised compost. A larger diameter pot might also be used to give extra elbow room for the outer circle of seedlings. Either plastic or earthenware pots may be used. What is necessary is that a more open compost should be used in the plastic pots above a layer of granite chippings to give sharp drainage. Later on it will be found that the granite chippings will fall out of the mass of roots fairly easily, allowing the seedling bulbs to be separated with most root intact. Normal procedures should be adopted for sowing the seed on firmed moist compost, but the question arises as to the value of sowing the seeds individually. It may be thought rather fussy to do this and to set them upright, but it cannot be bettered. Whatever else may be achieved excellent spacing is assured and this means the seedlings continuing undisturbed in the pot for the longest possible time. For spring sowing March is early enough unless there is heat available. If unavoidable, sowing as late as May will still allow satisfactory growth to be made in the first year. The period of germination will depend on the species or cultivar and the temperature, but whereas *L. formosanum* may germinate in under a fortnight given sufficient heat, all kinds may take up to two months in a cool spring. That refers to epigeal germinating kinds; hypogeal lilies will not be visible until the following year.

It is because of this tiresome wait that people have experimented with other ways of germinating these lilies. Originally it was glass jars, which proved rather cumbersome, but today it is the polythene bag and the twist tie which make up the basic equipment of the hypogeal germinating lilygrower. It helps greatly if the seed can be obtained in the autumn, for then the seed is the freshest and the time saved the maximum, but this is not essential. The bags most suitable and easily obtainable are those sold on the roll approximately 18 × 23 cm. They should be fairly thin and so allow the passage of gases through the plastic medium which is beneficial to the seeds and young bulblets. In order to keep the seeds moist and generally separated from each other a mixture of moss peat and grit should be placed in each bag. The mixture should be sterilised to ensure all harmful fungus spores are killed off; likewise the seed should be dusted by a suitable fungicide. With the peat-grit mixture looking well moistened, but not showing free liquid in the bag, pour in the seed, seal the bag and shake up the seed in the mixture. Label adequately adding the date. Leave room for a further date to be added when the bag is removed from the warm cupboard (21°C, 70°F), which is when seedling bulbs are well formed and are to be transferred to the salad compartment of a domestic refrigerator. The bulbs, still in their polythene bag untouched, should remain cool for three months. A precise timing is unknown and may vary with the species and be generally less than the three months stipulated, but it would be foolhardy to bring the bulbs out too early. A point to bear in mind is that some lilies, notably Orientals (*L. auratum*, etc.) will commence growing their first true leaf in the cool chamber if they are kept there too long. Although growth is slow, it will be detrimental to the bulb and could make handling more difficult.

The following stage is to pot up the tiny lilies, separating them delicately from each other. A soft, fine, easy-running, sterilised compost is ideal and the pots may be immersed in water afterwards to ensure a close adhesion between the fine hairy roots and the compost. The first growth is usually noticed within a few days. A most careful touch is essential when handling these seedlings, and to make things easier it is a good thing to use a grey stone grit rather than a white spar, so that the white bulblets and their roots stand out clearly. If seeds are not obtainable until the spring, the grower will have to decide whether there is much to be gained by this procedure. In fact, often quite useful growth is achieved during the autumn, but a careful watch on timing is required. It is no good bringing the batch of seedlings out of the refrigerator at a time when there is no growing weather left in the year.

The procedure just described is suitable for the martagon lilies, the Caucasians and the Orientals. A slightly different procedure applies to the Western American lilies. Seed should be sown as already described in the autumn: as late as November is usually all right. If it is sown earlier, say, in spring or summer it will lie dormant, but come to no apparent harm. The polythene bags are kept cool from the start, not in the refrigerator, that is possibly too low, but about 7°C (45°F) should be satisfactory. The writer in southern England often uses a cloakroom window ledge on the north side. No doubt the various species differ in their exact requirements, but germination presumably takes place in the temperature range 4°-10°C (40°-50°F). The position mentioned could cool further in the winter months, whilst the bulbs fatten and the roots lengthen, but with the coming of longer days, if there is a little light, green shoots will start to emerge from the bulbs. It is at this time that they should be transferred to pots or deep boxes. Autumn sowing in the conventional manner could be adopted as long as the correct temperatures can be conveniently maintained. However, using the polythene bag method the seed takes up less room, the grower has a clear idea of what is going on, and he only has to pot on seed that has germinated, leaving the remainder another year or discarding it as desired. It cuts out having many seed pots around, in which little or nothing may be happening although these lilies usually produce seed with a very high percentage of germination.

Vegetative Propagation

Lily bulbs lend themselves to rapid multiplication and this is especially obvious when compared with the conventional methods of increasing narcissus bulbs. Scaling of bulbs is a simple matter and any person who buys or otherwise acquires a bulb should learn the practice. It is not, perhaps, well known enough that a fresh young bulb will establish itself better in a garden than a 'bought in' product. Producing a few new bulbs from a couple of scales is the best way of keeping the plant for years to come. How often it is heard of purchased bulbs that they lasted but one season!

Scaling of Lily Bulbs

In order to generate the growth of new bulbs at the base of the scales, scaling may be done at any time of the year, but the best and usually the most convenient time is during the months of August, September and October. The outer scales of the bulb are snapped off the base in succession. If required the bulb may be completely descaled. Care should be taken in snapping them off as many scales on a concentric bulb are awkward. The aim is

54

for them to break as close to the base as possible. Scales may be taken off the stoloniferous shoot of bulbs like *L. canadense* and scales are easily (often too easily) plucked off the rhizomatous bulbs of many Western American lilies. In the case of the latter it will be found that old yellowing scales produce new bulblets just as readily as new white scales, so it seems better to take off older scales and leave the new to furnish the next season's growth. Many Western American lilies have jointed scales and, although it is right to break these up in order to obtain as many new bulbs as possible, it will generally be found that top scale sections work least readily and basal sections most readily. On double jointed scales it is possible to find a bulblet growing at both ends of a centre section. The new bulblet forms on callus which itself grows on the broken edge of the scale. This callus forms more readily on tissue close to the basal plate. It is often possible to increase the number of bulblets by cutting into the basal section of a broad scale with a razor-sharp blade. For instance: a scale with a base 2.5 cm long may be given three cuts 5 mm deep. Four bulbs may then be formed instead of one or two. Great care should be taken in removing the bulblets from the scale. Some may be as big as peas while others are very tiny. These latter may be left to grow on and be dealt with a few weeks later. Roots may at times remain on the scale as they have grown on the callus, which is not immediately part of the basal plate of the new bulblet. If this tends to occur on particular types it may be as well to remove a portion of the scale with the bulblet to ensure the root is taken. Small scales of rhizomatous bulbs generally, but not always, produce one bulblet and it may be found convenient to grow on the bulblet with the scale still attached. They are more easily handled that way.

It may at times prove possible to retrieve a rare bulb that is on its death bed of *fusarium* rot. The better scales should have the bad portion removed by use of a sharp sterilised blade and the remaining pieces treated with benomyl. There is a chance that bulblets will form on these treated scales. Sterilise the knife again afterwards.

Figure 4.2 Bulb Scale of L. 'Orange Wattle' with Bulbils. Scaling done on 17 November 1983; drawn 11 March 1984

The manner of dealing with lily scales will depend on the quantity prepared, the numbers of types of lily being used and the facilities available. A compost of 50 per cent coarse sand and 50 per cent moss peat similar to that used as a cutting compost could be suitable to adopt for propagating frames, boxes and deep trays. What is required is a mixture that easily breaks loose, but is also sufficiently moisture-retentive. In plastic pots this compost would do just as well, but in earthenware containers a larger percentage of peat may be required. In plastic bags it becomes more a question of individual taste, but moist peat mixed with coarse grit is very satisfactory. How they should be treated depends on the lilies concerned. It is as well to remember how they would react were they seeds. Do they grow well in the heat, or do they like the cool? Do they like a delay period before moving to the next growing phase? To ignore these points learnt with the seed is to throw away good knowledge and enjoy frustration. Mentioning but two: the martagon must have its cool period whether naturally or in the refrigerator, and the Western American lily scale should grow its bulb in the moderate cool (not the refrigerator) of an autumnal environment and grow away slowly as the year turns. Those lilies with particular idiosyncrasies as seeds will generally react similarly as scale bulblets.

Propagation by means of stem bulbils

Stem bulbils formed in the leaf axils (Figure 4.3) is the most familiar method of propagation as it is the simplest available to gardeners. Unfortunately, only a few species produce stem bulbils and this method is really only possible with these and their hybrids which copy the practice. *L. tigrinum* produces stem bulbils plentifully and it has passed this quality on to many hybrids. Again, unfortunately, there is a tolerance to various virus diseases carried by this species and commonly passed on as a parent to its hybrids. The simple nature of bulbil propagation fosters the spread of the diseases wherever lilies may be grown throughout the world. *L. sargentiae*, a trumpet lily and not a turkscap as *L. tigrinum*, also freely produces stem bulbils, but again it is prone to virus disease. Its progeny generally does not produce bulbils liberally, but this may be due to disease, as there are indications that plants carry fewer bulbils once disease-infected. *L. suphureum* is known to make aerial bulbils, but, despite this ready means of increase, appears to have died out once in Western cultivation. *L. bulbiferum* produces bulbils in certain forms. Some lilies are at times seen to carry one or a few bulbils at or near the apex of the stem usually when flower formation has been frustrated, or the plant is too young to flower. Within this category of plants producing stem bulbils above ground may be included certain Oriental lilies. Typical of the kind is *L. alexandrae* which in late summer will make a few bulbils along the lower part of the stem. These bulbils often go into leaf quickly while on the green stem. In nature it is probable the stem grows through a moist grass or moss layer.

The bulbils should be collected as soon as sufficient number are

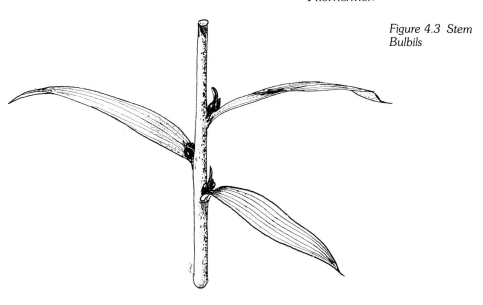

Figure 4.3 Stem Bulbils

large enough to handle, that is, about half pea size or thereabouts. There is nothing to be gained in allowing them to remain on the plant even though the stem may be green. If some are too small let them stay and, if there is enough growing time left in the season, perhaps, they will fatten further and some of a second crop grow, so that another picking may be taken later.

As with seeds the bulbils may be planted outdoors or indoors. The main thing is not to delay their planting, because, although they survive much drying out, they get off to a flying start making much root in the autumn if so allowed. Outdoors a prepared bed should be made up with the plentiful addition of leaf soil or peat, working the soil and humus into a good friable tilth. The bulbils may be planted in drills 2.5 cm deep and spaces 2.5 cm apart along the row. Cover the bulbils with humus-rich compost and water well, if conditions are on the dry side. Keep free of weeds from the start. Close weeding the following year, even with due care, will otherwise damage a high proportion of the large single leaves making up the row. The bulbs may normally stay undisturbed for two seasons, but should be fed with a general fertiliser not too high in immediately available nitrogen. If outdoor conditions are not suitable — a close guard must be kept on slugs and snails — then it is easy to plant the bulbils in frames or in pots or boxes of adequate depth. However, the more restrictive the conditions the more closely must the subsequent growth be watched and, in any case, one season in the pots or boxes undisturbed will be sufficient.

Propagation of Lilies by Stem Bulblets Formed Below Ground

This is another ready means of increase available to the amateur with many kinds of lilies. The Asiatic group are often particularly fruitful in this way and also to be included are those lilies with a stoloniform stem wandering underground before emerging such as *Ll. duchartrei* and *nepalense*. Many growers will find the increase by this means sufficient without using other methods. All that is required is for the lilies, which are presumed to be growing well, to be well nourished and being stem-rooters, as they are likely to be, kept heavily mulched with a compost comprising a high percentage of leaf soil. As the mulch is to be kept moist it should contain coarse sand and remain porous even when sun-dried in summer, so that there is little or no run off when watered. The addition of bone meal and wood ash mixed in the mulch would be beneficial. There is no desire to disturb the young bulblets until the stem of the parent has withered in the autumn. Then the top soil with the decayed stem may be removed, leaving the main bulb intact beneath. The bulblets should be separated out, graded if desired, and grown on much as described for aerial bulbils. Care should be taken not to damage the very fragile roots that some will have entwined with the decaying fibres of the mother plant. Replanting should take place without delay to save any drying out, otherwise ensure the bulblets are kept moist and in the cool.

Propagation of Lilies by Division

Division may be resorted to from time to time with many species and hybrids. It must be appreciated, though, that some species do not divide naturally and, if they do, especially excessively, then they may be considered diseased. Division of the natural increase of bulbs may be dealt with in the autumn when it has been decided to replant. This task should not be left so late that there is little warmth in the soil or sun in the sky. Lilies do better by being shifted when still active. They acclimatise to the new surroundings and many commence new root growth before the onset of winter. This allows them to grow away well in the spring without putting too great a strain on the resources of the bulbs themselves.

To mention certain lilies specifically: *L. candidum* should be dealt with in August preferably before growth of the autumn crown of leaves. Most American bulbs divide easily. Lilies of the Eastern States, like *Ll. canadense* and *superbum*, are stoloniferous, so stolons may be broken off the mother bulb and replanted. The rhizomatous bulbs of many Western American lilies divide in most hybrids and some species but not in all, and produce great clumps of bulbs in the most vigorous, demanding separation. *Ll. columbianum* and *kelloggii* are not rhizomatous and seem rarely to divide.

One of the features of the genus *Cardiocrinum* is that the mother bulb expires in the season of flowering. Left at the base of the plant are some bulblets of a year's growing, which may be separated and transplanted either into a nursery bed for a couple of years, or a new permanent position. Seed is normally generously produced and recommended as the basic means of reproduction. Plants in the Savill Gardens (in Windsor Great Park) were always raised by this means, as it was said the resulting specimens were much grander than those coming from bulblets.

Other Methods

Other methods of reproducing lilies have been described from time to time, being usually concerned with means of inducing the production of bulbils or bulblets on the stem. There seems little more than curiosity value in some of these ideas. The most important method not described here is that of tissue culture, which presently remains within the confines of the laboratory in the hands of the scientist rather than the plantsman. However, for those wishing to try it, it may offer new challenges and opportunities. The necessary materials are available. The main disadvantage seems to be in obtaining at an acceptable cost to the amateur, a sterile working chamber. Unless completely aseptic conditions can be obtained inside, say, plastic sheeting, the disappointments are likely to be numerous and frustrating.

Chapter 5
The Troubles of Lilies

Like other living things lilies have their share of pests and diseases. Some would say they have more than their fair share. This is not necessarily so, but it does indicate the seriousness of some diseases and the menace of certain pests which are difficult in some situations to control or eradicate.

I Pests

Animals

As man has found lily bulbs a useful food, it is not surprising that many lesser animals find lilies good to eat.

If the garden is exposed, even temporarily, in the spring, to *deer, hares* and *rabbits* they will quickly devour young growths. This kind of nuisance depends much on the situation of the garden and it will not only be lilies that suffer. Rabbit-proof and deer-proof fences that are adequately maintained in perfect order throughout the year are the best means of defence. Chemical controls, and trapping or shooting will not solve the problem. Others of the species will rapidly move into an unpopulated or depopulated area where there is a welcome food supply.

Rats and mice can be a real garden menace where there is poor control of their numbers by other animals. They will attack bulbs in the ground and in store — not that lilies should be in store under normal conditions. Trapping must be relentlessly pursued where predators are scarce.

Grey squirrels are known to be troublesome at times. The writer is currently watching a situation with some trepidation where there has been a build-up of these rodents over recent years and now has come a season where there are no acorns. There could easily be a food crisis in the spring with dire results.

Slugs and Snails

Although the animals so far mentioned can cause a great deal of trouble often in a short space of time, *slugs* can be a persistent major problem both below and above ground, according to the

60

species. If keeled slugs are known to be in the ground, and these are the kind that do much damage unseen, then lilies should not be planted there. The ground should be drenched with liquid metaldehyde. Constant disturbance or cultivation and prevention of all plants or weeds for a season is a good plan thereafter. Marked pieces of potato may well be planted to attract the slugs when they may be dug up and the pests destroyed. The potato will also indicate the degree of infestation. Some protection can be given to the bulbs by planting in coarse sand and grit, pots may be plunged in sharp grit and chippings. These are deterrents, but will not stop slugs for long. The surface-feeding slugs, which may be found lurking in all kinds of nooks and crannies, under dead leaves and all manner of plant debris should be baited by slug pellets of methiocarb or metaldehyde. It may be better to ring the changes and use both kinds alternately. *Snails* should be treated in the same manner. There is still much to be said for taking a turn in the garden at night with a torch, especially after rain. The slugs may often find the lily before the bait. With this method the gardener may find the slug first. Slugs are hermaphrodite and lay clusters of round white jelly-like eggs in little niches in the soil. It is deeply satisfying destroying these eggs and frequent cultivation of the top inch or so of the soil will bring them to light or expose them to birds.

Birds

A few species of *birds* may from time to time cause damage to flower buds by pecking for nectar before the flowers open. Later they may attack and eat your best seeds in drying capsules. It is a sporadic custom and may occur more frequently during dry spells. The advantages that may be had by encouraging birds considering the pests they consume, be they insect eggs, larvae of many kinds, caterpillars, aphids, etc., far outweigh the disadvantage of their intermittent depredations.

Aphids

Those lilies, having survived the first major onslaught of the slugs, will most likely next come under attack from *aphids*. These, the greenflies, etc., are the most dangerous pests. Not only do they debilitate the plants and cause twisted leaves and damage to buds, the end result being unsightly and worthless, but the aphids are the most important vectors in spreading virus diseases. Control of aphids is not difficult by spraying at regular intervals with malathion or other suitable systemic insecticides. The insecticide may usually be incorporated with a fungicide to control *botrytis* and similar disorders. Total control of aphids like most other troubles not being possible, isolation, or rather, separation of lilies in the garden can be a major factor in limiting virus diseases. The use of shrubs particularly of thick-leaved evergreen kinds seem particularly useful as separators. Remember that under glass aphids may be around all through the year, and a close watch must be kept on young shoots at soil level and the young and old leaves of seedlings during the winter months.

Lily Beetle

The *Lily beetle* has been a nuisance in certain areas in the south of England for many years, but recently it has become much more troublesome. Both the larvae and the adult beetles feed on the leaves and the upper parts of lilies, and on a number of other liliaceous plants, including *Convallaria*, *Polygonatum* and *Fritillaria*. The larvae — humped, dirty yellow with dark heads — are very repulsive covering themselves with dark slimy excrement. They are up to 10 mm long when full grown. The beetle is bright scarlet with black legs and antennae and up to 8 mm long. Because the beetle and the larvae are so easily visible control is said to be simple. This has not stopped gardeners being caught unawares. Their voracious appetites can soon make a mess of lilies. The larvae should easily be killed by both contact and systemic insecticides and possibly the beetles, but it is understood they can be readily caught between the fingers by the incensed gardener. The mature larvae live just under the soil surface in the winter. Those whose lilies have suffered attacks should try to ensure they do not move them around when replanting. The original beetles in England came from imported bulbs. Grateful recipients of bulbs from gardens that have had the beetle should be on their guard. The eggs are laid on the underside of the foliage, the little that is left remaining.

Lily Thrips

Lily thrips attack the bulbs only and particularly the bases of the scales. Both the adults and the larvae live out their lives in the bulb. Larvae are salmon-pink and adults shiny black insects. Their feeding seriously weakens the bulbs (the scales go flabby and break away) and allows the ingress of bacteria and fungi. Eventually the bulb rots away. Control for amateurs includes hot water treatment at 44°C (111°F) for one hour, dusting with BHC and thoroughly spraying or washing with malathion. Although no one knowingly sends out infested bulbs, it behoves all gardeners to inspect all bulbs coming into their possession for a variety of reasons, not just those mentioned above.

Leatherjackets, Wireworms and Millipedes

There are a number of other underground pests that can cause losses to lilies and other plants and crops. The *leatherjacket*, the larva of the crane fly or daddy-long-legs is common in grassland, but may be found in new gardens, flower beds or unsterilised loam. *Wireworms*, the larvae of click beetles, can be a nuisance in newly cultivated ground. BHC dust and Bromophos can be useful controls. The latter insects and *millipedes* can be baited with pieces of potato and other cut pieces of root vegetable placed in the cultivated soil.

Nematodes

Leaf-lesion nematodes and *root-lesion nematodes*, also called *eelworms*, are microscopic pests which have caused much trouble with lilies in some countries. They are serious pests of many food crops. The leaf-lesion nematodes may be treated by the roguing of infested plants. Bulbs may be given hot water treatment at 44°C (111°F) for one hour. The main type of treatment for the control of root-lesion nematodes is soil fumigation with chemicals like methyl bromide. If the lily grower suspects infestation then he should seek proper qualified advice from the appropriate horticultural or agricultural authority.

Bulb Mite

In the past *Bulb mite* has been considered a very troublesome but secondary pest, attacking many kinds of bulbs besides lilies, after some initial damage has taken place. Recently in Australia where previously little known among lily growers, this mite has become a very devastating pest capable of destroying whole crops if left unchecked. It has also proved very difficult to control with modern insecticides. The adult mites are about the size of a pinhead, yellowish-white, often tinged pink, and usually present in great numbers particularly just above the basal plate between the scales. But they are now reported to be attacking roots, basal plate and higher up the scales and into the centre of the bulb. Badly infested bulbs should be burned and the remainder given hot water treatment as advocated for eelworms. In the past effective control has been possible by fumigating dry bulbs with paradichlorbenzene spread over the floor of an airtight container at the rate of 4 g per litre of space for 120 hours. Dusting the bulbs with flowers of sulphur has also been recommended. Precisely what means of control proves to be most efficacious in Australia remains to be seen.

II Diseases

A little understanding of the diseases that attack lilies is necessary to the cultivation of lilies, otherwise ignorance might lead to despair. Many have given up growing lilies not understanding why their bulbs have died. Although this can happen far too often and far too soon, if certain precautions are not taken it is wrong to consider that a plant, because it is a bulb, should live forever. As it happens some lilies are long-lived, others are not.

Botrytis

The first trouble the new lily grower is likely to see on his plant is some dying foliage. It may or may not be caused by the fungus *Botrytis elliptica*, commonly called *botrytis*, or *blight*, or in the past, the 'Lily Disease'. The disease shows itself first as dark oval spots on the leaves. The leaf tissue in the spot dies leaving a purple rim. The spots can spread rapidly in the damp conditions suitable to the proliferation of the fungus spores and soon all the lower leaves will have died. The blight will continue up the stem, and into the stem, and up to the flower buds, which will prove useless. Useless either because the fungus will attack them like the leaves or the leafless plant will not be able to sustain them. The worst does not always happen, but it is far better to control this disease, which in bad seasons can be very upsetting. Sprays made up from Bordeaux Mixture or colloidal copper can be very effective, more so than the organic fungicides. The first application should be made when the stems are about 25 cm high and if there have been attacks previous years it should be seen the ground underneath is thoroughly wetted. Two repeat sprays most likely will be needed at fortnightly intervals, but much depends on the weather conditions and the effectiveness of the spray when applied.

It can, of course, happen that in the early stages of spring growth the young leaves can be weakened by frost and damaged by rough weather. This can give us a plant looking as if it had *botrytis*. It has often been said that *botrytis* has to serve for many ailments. In any case damaged tissues can lead to other fungus troubles attacking the plant and timely preventive spraying can limit these from getting under way.

Basal Rot

Whereas *botrytis* weakens, it seldom kills our lilies, as it rarely penetrates below ground. This is not the case with *Basal Rot*, *Fusarium oxysporum*, which attacks the scales where they join the basal plate. Within a short time the bulb can have disintegrated and rotted away. The fungus contaminates the soil and it is not safe to plant more lilies in the area for some years unless it has been treated with 2 per cent formalin (40 per cent commercial Formaldehyde) or other suitable sterilant. The trouble usually comes into the garden from infected bulbs, so once again the gardener should be very careful of what he accepts and plants out into permanent positions. If any bulbs are under suspicion, they should be cleaned up, any rotted material burnt, and the remaining bulbs dipped in 0.5 per cent benomyl for one hour. The bulbs might then be planted in pots or suitable containers for growing on for a season before being ruthlessly scrutinised again prior to permanent planting. Lilies may also develop this disease while in store. Some lilies are more susceptible to this rot than others, but as there is more than one variety of the disease it is possible that where one lily may be tolerant of one variety it may be susceptible to another. It should go without saying that any rotted or rotting bulb tissue should always be carefully collected from the soil, potting compost or wherever it happens to be and destroyed by burning. If soil sterilisation is impractical, then contaminated soil or compost should be removed to a safe place.

Blue Mould

Of course, not all fungus diseases that attack lily bulbs are kinds of *Fusarium*. There are those belonging to *Penicillium*. *Blue mould* occurs as a storage rot. It starts as sunken brown spots on the scales and as these enlarge they become covered with white fungal growth. The spores produced on this turn it the bluey-green, which we know is not confined to lily bulbs. Benomyl has been used too much on these moulds and one or more strains are now resistant to this fungicide. Where the attack is in the early stages and the basal plate is unaffected, infected scales may be detached from the bulb and destroyed.

Rhizoctonia

Another soil-borne fungus which may attack lilies is *Rhizoctonia*, living normally as a saprophyte on dead and decaying material. Most likely the fungus attacks old withering bulb scales, roots or some damaged portion of the lily below soil level before engaging the healthy areas. Treating the plants with a systemic fungicide may be as much as can be done other than keeping lilies away from the contaminated soil which is usually light and sandy.

Phytophthora

Phytophthora may attack the basal portions of the lily plant, roots and stem. The cause may be poorly drained soil or exceptional wet weather conditions. Attacks may occur on both young and old and control is difficult. They may be more serious on woody subjects rather than lilies.

Damping Off

Seedlings even germinating after months since sowing usually stand up very well to *Damping off* if sown in free-draining sterilised compost. Scale bulbils and seeds germinated in reasonably sterile conditions of polythene bags should also be planted into sterilised compost. If the losses are going to occur they will probably do so between this stage of immaturity and a year or two ahead and sterilised compost can act as a reasonable insurance, at least for a start.

Lily Rust

There is also a *Lily rust* which occurs from time to time in Britain particularly on *L. candidum*. Small brown powdery pustules are to be seen on the undersides of leaves and the stems. Colloidal copper would possibly be the best fungicide to use as a spray.

Virus Diseases

There are many *virus diseases* found in lilies, but only about five of them cause defects, some very noticeable and very serious. The viruses are usually transmitted by airborne aphids, but it has been reported that soil-borne pests can also be the vector in carrying disease. If this is the case the real solution is the glasshouse with the lilies in sterilised composts in pots all living in an aphid-toxic atmosphere. Dr North has suggested that all the disease problems discussed above are of little importance or would prove of little concern, if our lilies were virus free. It is only when they have a virus disease already that the fungal diseases of *botrytis* and *fusarium* achieve such devastating importance.

Lily Mottle virus is one of the more important viruses well known in tulips for the broken colour it produces, especially in Rembrandt tulips. If one is even going to try and keep lilies healthy, they should on no account be grown near tulips. It may be said that it is very rare to see broken colour in the flowers of lilies. Often it is the leaves with their streaked appearance which are most noticeably affected. However, the flowers may show broken colour and be smaller in size in *L. martagon* and its hybrids. The plants markedly deteriorate and eventually die.

Cucumber mosaic virus is equally serious. Again the leaves are first to show the disease and will be streaked and mottled and, if the lily is one of the more susceptible kinds, the leaves may also be distorted and curled irregularly. The flowers in these cases will usually be misshapen; trumpets, for instance, breaking apart. *L. formosanum* exhibits all the symptoms of virus disease most readily and is, if you want that kind of thing, a good indicator. Growers will readily banish such plants to the incinerator before they die.

Lily symptomless virus may be combined with other viruses or alone. It is usually symptomless, but that is not to say the plants act as vigorously as they should. We tend to accept our plants as we see them not knowing they might be twice the size were they healthy. This may happen with a great many Asiatic hybrids which contain species like *L. tigrinum* and *L. bulbiferum* which are noticeably tolerant of virus diseases. They do languish and die out if not suited, but they do have sufficient stamina to function reasonably well and multiply if grown well. These tolerant lilies, beneficial though they may be to most lily growers are not the answer to the problem. What are required are virus resistant lilies. Lilies which will not fall a prey to the diseases and so will not be in a position to transmit disease to susceptible kinds.

Lily rosette or *yellowflat* was the first virus disease to be recognised among lilies and that was in the commercially important *L. longiflorum*, which at one time was extensively grown and highly fashionable. Nobody was married or died without it! Many other species are highly susceptible. Plants become stunted, leaves crowded, curled downward, yellowed and sometimes reddened, the flowers, if buds are produced, not opening properly. Another virus of *L. longiflorum* is *Necrotic fleck* where pale flecks, the tissue later dying, occur between the veins. This brings about the stunting of the plants. No amateur should buy bulbs of *L. longiflorum* unless their provenance is impeccable, because they are usually stock that has served its time and may be expected to be riddled with disease. Seed should be his source of supply.

Brown ring formation was a virus which the Dutch found with *lily symptomless virus* in *L.* 'Enchantment', which besides being the commonest Mid-Century Hybrid in gardens is also grown plentifully for the florists' trade. The smaller bulbs have shorter usually more open scales with concentric brown rings around a centre becoming necrotic. Shorter, lighter coloured plants result which die-back earlier in the season.

There are no cures for virus disease. It is something that all the time, whatever we are doing in the way of cultivation, has to be prevented, and with many species, for instance, *L. auratum* and *L. speciosum*, at any cost. However, there is no need to give up growing lilies, there is no need or even occasion for despair. Few are the lilies in the wild that die of virus disease. Over twenty years ago seed came to me from New Zealand taken from some of Dr Yeats' beautiful *parkmannii* hybrids (Plate 18). They germinated marvellously and it looked as if I was in for great riches, but the aphid vector worked between infected *L. longiflorum* and those seedlings. Within a couple of years my many had been reduced to a few. Yet some of those few are still growing today. When it is appreciated that the oaks and birches overhead swarm with aphids, that the ants cannot chase up the trees fast enough nor the honeydew — what a lovely name! — fall thicker, it is surprising any lily survives. If there is a reason, then it is a horizontal one. The aphids fall down and fly up, but possibly do not fly round natural barriers like cypresses, rhododendrons and camellias quite so readily.

Any lily known to have virus disease of some kind should in the ordinary way be dug up and destroyed by fire. This advice has long been given, but it is not entirely practical if the garden contains what we may call 'many well-known hybrids'. It is highly unlikely they will all be as pure as the driven snow — and that's not very pure — even if they show no obvious signs. Should a gardener raise most of his own lilies from seed, then he should be extremely careful as to what he allows in otherwise. Bulbs from any source, including those from friends, should be grown in isolation for a season. Tulips, especially garden forms should be kept apart from lilies, and likewise any variegated *Liliaceae* with distorted or crinkled leaves. *Polygonatum hybridum* 'Variegatum' should definitely be considered suspect and green- and white-flowered forms of *Trillium grandiflorum*.

A lily with virus disease may be used to produce healthy seed, if it is still capable of the task, as the disease is not carried into the seed. Special precautions should be taken to see that the lily does not infect other lilies before being cast on to the funeral pyre.

Only three of the diseases discussed above are likely to trouble most lily growers. They are *botrytis*, *fusarium* and virus diseases, but even so, from time to time lilies may look unhealthy for other reasons.

III Other Disorders

There are a few temporary *disorders* that gardeners should know about, if only to save them from further worries. First, some lilies come up early in the spring, while some of our gardens suffer from late frost. Most lilies will suffer a lot of cold even after rising many centimetres clear of the ground. Their stems bend over and snow may weigh them down. Usually they return to normal

68

unscathed, but now and again they are badly caught and the resulting damage looks similar to virus infection. Some years flowers are nipped in the tiny buds nestling in the foliage.

Sometimes a lily grows up well in the spring, but at flowering time or thereabouts the would-be green foliage becomes overcast with bronzy streaks or flecks and the flowers are small and poor in quality. The cause is usually a lack of basal roots with the bulb constrained to give its all. A number of factors may have brought this about from drought to root rot due to excessive wet. No further harm will be done by digging up the bulb even in midsummer, cleaning it and giving it a close and careful examination.

Chlorosis may occur to those acid-loving lilies planted in an alkaline soil. More obvious may be the overall lack of vigour. It is not easy suddenly to drop the pH of any soil, particularly while in use. Peat or an acid-reacting leaf soil may be added in quantity, with the addition of some powdered sulphur, but truly this should be done beforehand; likewise the incorporation of trace elements. Chelated iron may be watered into the soil for some immediate benefit.

As with many other plants from time to time fasciation of the stem occurs in lilies. It is as if two or more stems are strapped together. With excessive fasciation the effect is usually rather horrible with too many leaves and too many flowers, none of which is up to size or well-placed. This fasciation lasts only for the season's growth, returning to normal the following year. The reason may be due to a physical impediment on the growing point of the bulb when being formed the previous season or due to damage incurred by an insect or animal.

With many American hybrids and L. pardalinum giganteum if no other West Coast species, when the stem has grown about half its height leaves in the growing point appear to become translucent and lose their ability to unfurl readily. The pressure exerted by the fluids rising up the stem upsets the tissues of the growing point and a rot sets in. This is soft at first but blackens and hardens over the top and no further growth is possible. If the trouble is spotted early enough, the leaves that cannot unfurl may be carefully peeled apart, and when all or most are freed, then the stem may continue to grow and flower normally. Usually at best some damage ensues particularly to the leaves. The reason for this disorder seems to be unknown. It may be due to bad weather which seems unlikely. It may be a breakdown in the plant itself, but why? The effect is casual, not happening to the same plants each year. Further it is not a sign of weakness as usually it is the strong stems that suffer.

Chapter 6
The Geographical Distribution of the Species

When looking at the world distribution of the genera *Lilium* and *Cardiocrinum* some interesting facts emerge. They in turn generate ideas and various hypotheses and it is from these that we begin to have a feeling not just for the flowers and their aesthetic appeal, or even the plant as a whole, but for the lily's way of life and how it has been cast for millions of years. From looking at distribution we may see there is a story to tell. It is not just lilies that can do this. It applies to other important genera. Lilies, however, are as good as and, for our purposes, better than most. For one thing there are neither too few of them, nor too many.

The family *Liliaceae*, to which lilies obviously belong, covers the whole globe, except for the poles, and so is found represented in every major continent. The genus *Lilium*, however, is restricted to the northern hemisphere (Map 6.1).

In the extreme north of this range is *L. martagon pilosiusculum* on the boundary of the forest zone at 68°40′N. This is in Siberia on the River Khantaika. A little further east the second most northerly species, *L. dauricum*, is found at 64° 30′N on the Lower Tungusk River. In Europe the most northerly station would appear to be under 60°N for *L. martagon* in Estonia. In North America these latitudes are not reached and only *L. philadelphicum* and possibly *L. columbianum* in the west would be beyond 51°N.

The most southerly lily is *L. neilgherrense* just holding on to its isolated location in the Nilgiri Hills in southern India. This is at a latitude of 11°30′N. Another isolated lily much further to the east is *L. philippinense* in northern Luzon at 17°40′N. But the southernmost lily found in the complex and botanically important region of continental S.E. Asia is *L. primulinum burmanicum* near Chiang Mai in Thailand at 18°55′N.

Already it is apparent that some species are widespread while others have only a small niche and but a slight hold on this world. *L. martagon* undoubtedly has the largest range with a

Map 6.1 Distribution of the Genera *Lilium* and *Cardiocrinum*

spread from Portugal through Europe and Asia to east of Lake Baikal at 124°E, some 9,000 km. This lily like no other has shown its adaptability to many differing climates, but although it shows variability has not lost its basic identity. Under modern-day pressures it is difficult to assess whether it is gaining or losing ground naturally. It can hardly spread further west. Man has been responsible for seeing it naturalised to the north of its range in Europe. Perhaps he will be responsible for its further movement eastwards where it might meet with other species of its group from which it has at some time in the distant past become detached.

One of these other martagons has, being a single island dweller, one of the smallest distributions. It is *L. hansonii* inhabiting Ullung off the east coast of S. Korea. It shows a willingness to grow in our gardens, so has to some extent an in-built adaptability. At some stage it became broken off from the rest of the world, lost in its island home with no opportunity to spread abroad. Other island dwellers lead a very precarious existence; they include the species *L. alexandrae* and *L. nobilissimum* both from south of Japan. The first has its main seat on an island with only a 16 km coastline, the second inhabits the cliffs overlooking one bay on a smaller island of the Ryukyu archipelago. Neither species has shown a real keenness to live outside its native environment, so we may well assume that their hold on life is very slight. Unless we are careful they are likely to be lost.

As some species are locked in by the sea others may be locked in by the land. This isolation may take a number of widely differing forms. Mountains are possibly the most obviously significant. *L. regale* had, despite its ability to grow under many conditions, found no way out of the confines of the Min River valley in Szechwan until Ernest Wilson released it in 1903. Whether this is to the ultimate good of the species remains to be seen. It has yet to show a willingness to naturalise even though it produces lots of good seed which germinates easily. Deserts and too arid conditions prevent the spread of lilies. On the plains the competition is doubtless too fierce, while the lily easily falls prey to grazing animals. Where man uses the plough only a limited number and type of bulbous monocotyledons can hold sway — no situation for the lily with its easily damaged bulb.

So the lily is left with a restricted number of habitats. Some of these may be described:

(a) In the forest at the mercy of the trees. They may only survive because from time to time the forest is thinned by fire or some other disaster.

(b) At the woodland edge where they must compete with shrubs and other strong vegetation and be more prone to animal grazing.

(c) In scrub with some protection and sufficient light, but often prone to grazing and that the scrub will turn to forest.

(d) On hill or mountainsides where the effects of farming are not so great. Cattle and goats again are the great problem, but there are:

(e) Cliff edges, ledges and narrow troughs between boulders and rocks.

(f) By the sea protected by scrub, sand and rock. In a way the extreme weather found by the seashore and the salt-laden atmosphere may be a form of protection to those plants that can survive it.

(g) In marshes, by ditches and running streams, but such marginal habitats are still vulnerable to many predators and there is the risk of flood and wash aways.

(h) And a combination of a number of these habitats.

In times past the lily has been a very successful genus. It may even be thought successful today in a limited sense, but it seems to have known better times. Without getting too deeply involved we may like to assume that the first lily, perhaps a mutation of a kind from *Fritillaria*, evolved in central Asia. Over the years it grew in numbers and spread in a limited way. But great upheavals in land and climatic changes over the course of millions of years pushed it around, sometimes nearer the equator, sometimes nearer the poles. During all this time many species evolved, possibly many more than we know today. Various populations became isolated, others were left free, but more vulnerable. When times were good a species (or more than one) expanded or even became nomadic. Those that went north as ice receded did not necessarily move back on the same tracks when inevitably pressed south again.

If we now look at the world with the true martagons removed (Map 6.2) it is possible to see clusters of lily species in various communities. There is the main centre based in China with an outstretching tentacle along the Himalayas to Afghanistan, another sweeping around the Japanese islands to Sakhalin and Kamchatka, and another broader zone northwards into northern China, Korea and Siberia. To the west we note the stronghold of the Caucasian species. Did they come from northabouts or southabouts? As there are two similar but distinct lines, i.e. *L. szovitsianum* and its relations and *L. ponticum* and its relations, they may have advanced by different routes. The Balkan group

Map 6.2 Distribution Without the True Martagons of the Genus *Lilium* in Europe and Asia

further to the west seems separate again, but it contains *L. rhodopeum* closely allied to *L. szovitsianum*, and *L. carniolicum* closely allied to *L. ponticum*.

The differences are no greater than the distances between the communities might suggest to be warranted and with north-south movements as well as east-west movements their relevant positions might easily be explained. The remaining turkscaps of Europe scattered westwards in the Maritime Alps and the Pyrenees seem to fall into place without creating undue problems. But what of the upright lily, *L. bulbiferum*, how does that fit in? We tend to look at such lilies as being quite different. Yet all they do is look up at us, or announce their sexual parts to insects overhead. During the last war Cooper, at the Royal Botanic Garden, Edinburgh, with a great deal of luck and good fortune obtained a good quantity of viable seeds from pollinating *L. bulbiferum croceum* with *L. monadelphum*. The results were not too startling in many ways, but the cross was achieved, as a number of the hybrids were fragrant. It proves, if anything, that there is a connection and suggests that the *szovitsianum* group, including *L. candidum*, had with *L. bulbiferum* a common ancestor, and undoubtedly red in colour. It may easily have been wiped out at some early stage while living half-way across Asia. Might one suggest between the North Pole and the new Himalayas?

What of the martagons (Map 6.3) so happily removed from Map 6.2. With their further adaptations, vigorous tendencies and ability to hybridise amongst themselves, it would seem they came in at a later stage and swept through northern Asia and Europe when a void was already created for them to fill.

The sweeping went eastwards too and some martagon-like forms moved into North America. Presumably this happened via the Aleutians and Alaska when the Poles were warmer. With the return of a cold age the lilies were pushed south. Conditions were obviously suitable along the western seaboard 'and north-south movements accompanying changing climatic conditions were not difficult. Upheavals in land masses made more radical changes, separating once and for all some species and varieties. Those that travelled furthest south tended to stay put and became less dependent on their original characteristics and gradually adapted to new conditions. This process is continuing, or is, at least, still incomplete. Those lilies that travelled further east across Canada were similarly treated to changing climatic conditions but less to land upheavals. Both were subjected to the dominance of the forests which gave them protection. Those in the east that moved furthest south became more under other

75

Map 6.3 Distribution of the True Martagon Lilies, *L. martagon*, *L. medeoloides*, *L. distichum*, *L. tsingtauense* and *L. hansonii*

influences, like those in the west, and adapted to more moderate seasonal changes, less dramatic climatic changes and a more even day length. Competition was fierce and to find sufficiently open conditions bogs and marshes had to be exploited. The detachment from whorled leaves has been achieved totally with *L. catesbaei* and significantly with *L. philadelphicum andinum*, while both have reverted to immediate germination. Other partial reversions are noticeable in a number of the American species and the most obvious are found in the more southerly species.

The concentration of lilies in communities is in most cases more apparent than real. That is, in those areas where lilies exist, they are by no means dominant plants and still have to be searched out, especially when not in flower. It would be an interesting and yet painstaking exercise could it be done to map the locations of lilies in western Yunnan. The phrase 'concentration of species' may appear to be most appropriate. Yet the difficulty of the terrain is such that we are unlikely to see more than one species, if lucky, in a day's march, however well arranged. Looking at the Caucasus, again the concentration is there (Map 6.4) but the mountainous terrain is the controlling influence. Mainly the various species are stretched out along the mountain range both to the north and to the south. Only in that particular corner of N.W. Turkey to the east of Trabzon are we likely to meet a complex of species. Japan has a high concentration of lily species, about 14 plus many varieties out of 3,700 species in their total flora. Shimizu mapped eight areas where three or four species may be found growing together. The United States is vast compared with Japan, but the latter may be likened to the Pacific Coast, which holds another concentration of the species. Taking in southern British Columbia, Washington state, Oregon and California they are stretched from 51°N to 31°N, and California with the most species is a vast area and the site of lilies are mere dots on the map. There is one area though at least where many species do congregate and that is on the California-Oregon border, and a little way south where nine species may be found. If the area is expanded a little more we can count another two.

The distribution of the genus *Cardiocrinum* is conventional. The species follow a pattern seen with many other plants forming an arc within S.E. Asia, from Sakhalin in the north through Japan, China and along the line of the Himalayas (Map 6.5).

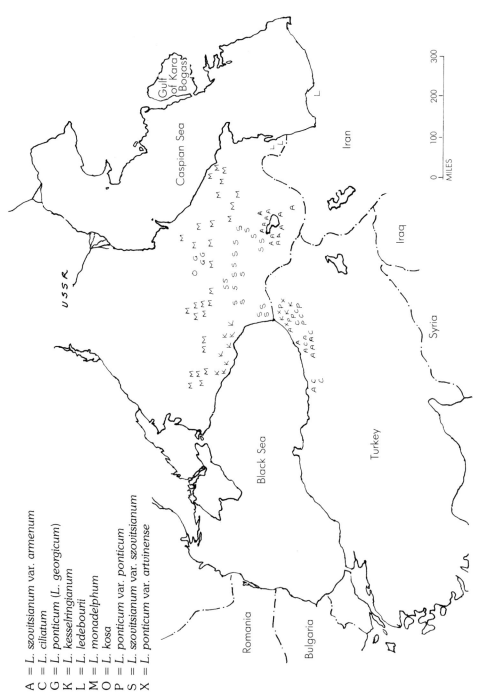

A = *L. szovitsianum* var. *armenum*
C = *L. ciliatum*
G = *L. ponticum* (*L. georgicum*)
K = *L. kesselringianum*
L = *L. ledebourii*
M = *L. monadelphum*
O = *L. kosa*
P = *L. ponticum* var. *ponticum*
S = *L. szovitsianum* var. *szovitsianum*
X = *L. ponticum* var. *artvinense*

78

Map 6.4 Caucasian Lilies (excluding *L. martagon caucasicum*)

Map 6.5 Distribution of the Genus *Cardiocrinum*

Chapter 7
The Genus *Lilium* and its Family Connections

The genus *Lilium* contains all the species of lilies which are discussed in the survey to follow. According to whether some lilies are considered species in their own right or subspecies or varieties of species, the number of species varies between ninety and one hundred or thereabouts. *Lilium* belongs to the family Liliaceae, which comprises about 200 genera and approximately 2,000 species. *Cardiocrinum*, the only other genus dealt with in this book, is closely allied to *Lilium*, and the species concerned were considered within *Lilium* at one time. *Cardiocrinum* is, of course, one of the genera within Liliaceae, and other closely allied genera are *Notholirion* and *Nomocharis*. Both of these genera are almost totally confined to mountains of south-east Asia in their distribution. *Notholirion* contains species which were once considered as lilies, and *Nomocharis* is now much reduced in numbers as some species have been returned to *Lilium*. Some stability now reigns in this regard and the criteria used have over the years gained in their validity. The problems, however, surrounding 'What is a species?' bubble as if in a fiery cauldron, while the splitters and lumpers go about their business!

Another genus within Liliaceae closely related to that of *Lilium* is *Fritillaria*. Lilies may have evolved from a primitive form of *Fritillaria*. The distribution of *Fritillaria* shows many similarities but equally strong dissimilarities with that of *Lilium*. Like *Lilium*, *Fritillaria* is only found in the northern hemisphere and covers Asia, Europe and western North America, not stretching into the eastern half of that continent as do the lilies. The main concentration of *Fritillaria* is more western in Asia, whereas lilies are more eastern, and the climatic conditions that many species sustain are quite distinct. Yet it is interesting to note how both lilies and fritillarias do come together. In Sikkim in the Himalayas at the feet of Kanchenjunga under the canopy of a very heavy monsoon live both *Fritillaria cirrhosa* and *Lilium nanum*. Under the Mediterranean sun in the Maritime Alps *Fritillaria tubiformis* lives cheek by jowl with *Lilium pomponium*. In the Californian

Sierra Nevada where brush and woodland join, *Fritillaria recurva* may be close to the fragrant and uncivilised *Lilium washington-ianum*.

Looking aside to other *Liliaceae* a very broad range of plants is found, that may come from either hemisphere. From the east come aspidistras and hostas noted for their excellent foliage, both indoors and outside. From the south come plants as diverse as *Tulbaghia*, so onion-like, from South Africa, and *Astelia*, so symmetrical but individualistic, from New Zealand. From the west come the trilliums, with the reminder that all lily flowers are built in threes (or should be!), and the erythroniums, like lilies in miniature and just as beautiful. Some genera climb like *Bowiea* and *Rhipogonum*, others are shrubby like *Ruscus* and *Philesia*. Some bathe in the sands of the desert like *Yucca* and *Aloe*, and the *Narthecium* has its roots in the bog.

Outside the *Liliaceae*, of especial interest to gardeners are the *Amaryllidaceae* which, because the division between the two becomes more difficult to find as time passes, should, according to some authorities, be rightly absorbed into the one family of *Liliaceae*. Not so the *Iridaceae*, which is more happily enclosed within its parameters. With many other families as well, including the sedges, rushes, grasses, palms, aroids, gingers and orchids, the lily family is united to make up the great class of monocotyledons.

L. alexandrae Wallace (Plate 2)

Survey of the Species in Alphabetical Order of the Genera *Lilium* and *Cardio-crinum*

Western botanists and gardeners have contributed much in the past to the confusion of this species with the closely related *L. nobilissimum* and other Japanese species. Lack of true material and adequate information were partly to blame. Even though both lilies remain rare, the position is adequately clear today thanks to the Japanese, and in particular Shimizu, seeing the need to clear the veil from Western eyes.

This species is found in a few tiny islands in the Ryukyu archipelago. The main island (and this has a coastline of only 16 km) is called Uke-shima, from which the Japanese name for the lily, Uke-yuri, is taken. Two other islands are Kakerama-shima and Yoro-shima and it may be found on one or two more. This is N28° 10' E129° 25' and on the map will be seen to be among Amami Gunto. It grows in valleys, fields and at the foot of hills and blooms there in mid to late May.

There are a number of distinguishing points between this species and *L. nobilissimum*, but the two most obvious, when in flower, is that *L. alexandrae* has a horizontal or slightly upward turning bloom with brown pollen, and *L. nobilissimum* has

81

upright flowers and yellow pollen.

The seed is up to 7 × 5 mm medium brown and gives hypogeal germination tending to occur under cool or coolish conditions, but usually requiring a protracted period of months before the first true leaf is produced. There is no specific cold period delay. The white bulb is globose, up to 15 cm across, but outer scales tend to be larger and taller than the inner ones, lanceolate and acute. The rooting green stem grows stem bulbils both below and immediately above ground level and rises to 1 m or slightly more. The leaves are broad-lanceolate to ovate-lanceolate, 3-5 veined, short petioled, up to 20 cm long by 4 cm wide. The fragrant flowers may be solitary to 4, horizontal to slightly upright, open funnel-shape, white, green at the base and at extreme tips, rarely pinkish along the outer keels of the tepals. The flower diameter is 16 cm and depth 10 cm when the tepals are 17 cm long, inner 4.5 cm wide, outer 3 cm wide. (Exceptional measurements recorded = 23 cm dia., depth 16.5 cm, tepal 18.5 cm, inner 6.9 cm, outer 4.0 cm.) The stamens are much shorter than the pistil, anthers purplish brown, pollen reddish brown. The long style is pale green at the base curved upward with purple-brown tri-lobed stigma. Flowering in southern England mid to late July. Seed capsule is oblong 5 cm long.

There is one variety, more strictly a form, var. *rosea* Bonavia which occurs rarely. The colour is very pale pink. Whether this is consistent or the colouring varies from plant to plant is not known, but one colour form is mentioned above in the description.

It is suggested that this lily is one of the most difficult in cultivation, but this is not really warranted, though it cannot be put in the easy class. It should be treated like a less than hardy *L. auratum*, which by virtue of its native low latitude makes it want to grow slowly during the winter period. This is particularly so of young bulbs. Propagation is not difficult. Once a bulb is acquired stem bulbils, not many, are obtainable from low down on the stem. They usually throw a leaf or two while still adhering and may be detached with a small root, so growing on is immediate. The bulbils should only be used if the plant is considered or appears to be free of virus. Seed takes a long time to mature, but this is of little concern. The plant is self-fertile. The seed may be sown as soon as ripe and kept reasonably cool, and the first leaves may emerge in the spring or not until late autumn. Older seed may take longer. Large pots are required for mature bulbs and particular attention should be given to the drainage and the free-draining quality of the acid compost. If the bulbs can be top-dressed with fresh compost then the stem roots will improve the size of the plants and flowers. In fact good treatment pays dividends. Partial shade, at least, should be given and temperatures kept to moderate levels.

There is an opportunity awaiting for someone to make the first strong hybrid cross with another Oriental species, or what would seem possibly easier or more satisfactory, one of the complex hybrids containing not only *auratum-speciosum* blood but also that of *Ll. japonicum* and *rubellum*.

L. amabile Palibin

This Far Eastern species is confined to Korea and possibly due to this has caused little trouble in its naming. It has only one synonym, *L. fauriei* Léveillé & Vaniot from a collection by Père Faurie on Cheju-do (then Quelpaert Island) but it was originally collected by Kalinosky near Seoul in 1886 and it was from this that Palibin described the species. Nakai united the two together.

It is well distributed over the Korean peninsula, but on Cheju-do Lighty found it in flower in mid-July at 1400 m under the crater of Mount Halla in a moist meadow with the well-aerated soil almost entirely comprised of coarse volcanic material. Wilson found it abundant on granitic soils near Pukchin in North Korea. He also found it plentiful on palaeozoic slates and limestone, and considered it liked a gritty loamy soil with good drainage and the company of grasses and dwarf shrubs.

The seed gives immediate epigeal germination. The white bulb is ovoid-elliptic up to 4 cm high and 3 cm across with numerous broad tightly-overlapping scales. The stem is strongly rooting and rises directly to 75-100 cm high. The scattered leaves absent near the ground becoming numerous towards the top are lanceolate, 3-veined, up to 9 cm long. The racemose inflorescence may have up to 5 (more in cultivation) grenadine-red, dark purple spotted, turkscap flowers, but poor coloured plants are known. The tepal is up to 5.5 cm long, clawed with a papillose nectary furrow. The anthers are dark chocolate brown and the pollen cinnabar-red. The lobed stigma is large, reddish chocolate. Scent is thought unpleasant and the flowers open in late June and July. The seed capsule is obovoid 3 cm long by 1.8 cm across.

There is one named variant var. *luteum* hort. of a clear yellow with dark spotting. This originated in Holland from imported seed and has occurred at times since. Cross pollinated yellow-flowered plants yield fertile seed from which this variety is best kept in cultivation.

This may not be a sparkling species with top-star rating,

although the yellow form is very handsome, but it is very amenable in cultivation. Easily raised from seed the bulbs soon mature. It takes to most reasonably cultivated soils accepting either acid or alkaline conditions, as long as they are well drained. Full exposure amongst companion plants is as acceptable as is some shade, but once the latter becomes too dense the bulbs decline in common with most other species.

As a parent this species may be overlooked, but it has many admirable qualities for the hybridiser. It should be remembered that var. *luteum* provided the yellow shades in the highly successful Mid-Century Hybrids, and that *L*. 'Cardinal', a first cross with *L. tigrinum*, has a stalwart constitution we might wish for in other hybrids.

L. amoenum Wilson

This dwarf pink lily was collected by Augustine Henry in 1897 at Mengtz in Yunnan, but it was not seen in cultivation until 1936 when bulbs collected near Likiang were grown to flower in 1938. Unfortunately these bulbs died without setting seed and the species has not since been reintroduced. This lily grows lower down in the valleys between 1800 and 2200 m and must not be considered hardy in temperate climates. It is closely allied to but distinct from *L. sempervivoideum* Léveillé.

The small white bulb is ovoid 3 cm high and less broad with ovate scales. The slender, glabrous rooting stem may be up to 30 cm tall and carrying up to 15 scattered very narrowly elliptic distinctly 1-veined leaves up to 5.5 cm long by 8 mm wide. There are 1-3 somewhat pendulous, bowl-shaped deep pink, red spotted flowers. The tepals up to 4 cm long recurving slightly at the tips have a green glabrous nectary furrow.

A new introduction of this choice little lily is to be welcomed and may it happen soon.

L. arboricola Stearn

Described as an epoch-making plant when first introduced in 1954, because it was epiphytic and not quite like any lily known, it really made a stir. This was short-lived, like the species' short spell in cultivation. When there was no chance to make a second collection from the wild, the enthusiasm faded and it became a rare piece of botanical history. Kingdon-Ward and his wife found it in The Triangle near to Sumprabum in north-east Burma. It grew in trees mixed with other common epiphytics and was apparently unknown to the local population. Growing at only 1400 m altitude it stands no chance of being hardy. The habitat is quite dry in winter and there are a few light frosts. Its closest relation may be its nearest other species, *L. primulinum*, but the differences are many and distinct and it does seem on the evidence that this lily is an adaptation to its extreme habitat. That is not to suggest it could not exist on the ground.

The seed is extremely light, semi-circular in outline 7-9 mm long with an unusually broad wing around the 2.5 mm-long body of the seed. It has immediate epigeal germination. The bulb somewhat flattened above and below, 3 cm tall by 5 cm across has thick broad yellowish-white scales. The rooting stem grows from 70 to 120 cm high. The alternate dark green leaves are relatively few, subpetiolate, narrowly lanceolate up to 25 cm long, 4-5 cm wide. Bulbils grow in the leaf axils. The small, pendulous fragrant, unspotted, soft apple green flowers have strongly recurved tepals. Filaments spreading outwards are pale green; pollen is deep orange; style 2.5 cm long, stigma small scarcely wider than the style. Seed capsule is oblong, about 4.5 cm long.

Needless to say much thought will be given to this remarkable species' special requirements when next it is tried again in cultivation.

L. auratum Lindley (Figure 7.1)

This, the Golden-rayed Lily of Japan, caused nothing less than a sensation when first exhibited in London in 1862. The introduction of this species to a world which was already accustomed to *L. speciosum*, engendered a wave of enthusiasm and fashion for all lilies, but particularly a demand for this one. The Japanese produced the bulbs, millions of them, but few of them survived more than a season or two. Even today of those who take to growing lilies, there are only one or two who do not succumb to trying, or gambling with their chance of success, to grow such imported bulbs. Of course, now we can belong to the wise and know all about virus diseases. We can seek out the *parkmannii* hybrids or rather their successors and can choose our source of supply. If we still doubt the good health of the bulbs, or have more patience than money in our pocket, we can obtain seed of a good hybrid strain or the species or one of the varieties.

The main sphere of distribution covers most of the island of Honshu except the south-west area. Shimizu suggests that the sites in south-west Hokkaido, Shikoku and Kyushu are escapes from cultivation from the grounds of feudal castles. It is seen to grow with *L. japonicum* in central Honshu and in the north with *L. rubellum*. Wilson described the eastern central sites where the lilies grew in black volcanic soil, among coarse herbs and shrubs,

Figure 7.1
L. auratum

on the margins of copses and even in thin woods. In places there
was a thin covering of humus, but usually nothing but volcanic
ash and lava debris on the steep hillsides. Much to the north
behind Sendai they grow on friable grey sandstone in association
with coarse herbs, shrubs and trees. Although called the
Mountain Lily, Yama-yuri, it is not an alpine or sub-alpine plant
in truth, although it may be found up to 1250 m. It belongs to
steep, lower hill slopes and ravines even down to sea level. For
plants at the higher and more northerly levels there is a thick
covering of snow in the winter. There is heavy rain during the
summer, but about the time when the species begins to flower
the weather becomes more settled and the autumn is fine and
sunny.

The seed is 11 × 9 mm and gives hypogeal germination in
warmth and is then delayed until near the end of a cold period.
Occasionally seedlings will grow away without the cold spell, so
maybe there is some variation depending on the source of the
seed. The yellowish white bulb is subglobose up to 10 cm across

with ovate-lanceolate and lanceolate scales. The strong rooting purplish green stem rises directly to 90-240 cm high and is clothed with many scattered, leathery, petioled, narrowly- or broadly-lanceolate leaves up to 22 cm long and 3.5 cm wide. The very fragrant bowl-shaped flowers as much as 30-cm across may be up to 6 in the wild, or up to 30 or more in cultivation, and racemosely and generally horizontally disposed. The tepals up to 18 cm long, are white, streaked yellow down the centre, spotted carmine or crimson on raised fleshy papillae on the lower half, the tips strongly recurved. The spreading filaments have long versatile anthers with chocolate-red pollen. The curved style has a capitate stigma hardly protruding. The seed capsule is up to 8 cm long.

There are a number of varieties known in the wild. The most important is var. *platyphyllum* Baker which is found growing on the islands of the Izu archipelago mixed with the type. It is a very fine plant with broader leaves and relatively larger flowers for a shorter stem. Also the tepals are broader and the spotting concentrated more to the base. In var. *pictum* Wallace the flower is heavily spotted crimson and the tip of the gold band is flushed crimson too. Var. *rubro-vittatum* Duchartre has the gold band changing to crimson towards the tip, the spots larger, highly coloured and the anthers bright red. Var. *rubrum* Carrière is where the band is wholly crimson. Var. *virginale* Duchartre is an albino in that the crimson spotting has become pale yellow or non-existent, but the gold band remains. It is dwarfer and less vigorous. These and a few others have all resulted from the wild. The red kinds and the albino are all rare, but are known to exist as regularly occurring aberrant forms.

To write down in just a few words how to cultivate this lily when it has been a continually recurring problem to thousands of gardeners for over a hundred years is an unenviable and exacting task. First, there is no point in growing a particular bulb unless it is healthy. It should soon show its unhealthiness by obvious symptoms. If the scales are loose and flabby it may be unhealthy or just too long out of the ground. To plump it up put it in moist peat for a week or so. Should it be firm and clean take off two or three scales to propagate a few fresh bulblets. If the roots are poor, cut off or just died back do not plant into cold wet soil, but pot up in a large well crocked pot with a very loose gritty peaty sterilised compost fractionally covering the bulb, having previously immersed it for a few hours in a systemic fungicidal solution. Keep moist and cool. When the stem starts to grow, do not cover with more and richer compost until assured that good basal root growth has been achieved. At this stage careful outdoor planting could be effected if conditions are reasonable. Like many Japanese species this lily will take and enjoy abundant moisture as long as the drainage is excellent. Depending on this it may be planted deeply and a good mulch of grit and leaf soil provided for the stem roots. Shrubs and suitable herbaceous plants may be used as shelter and screening from other lilies. In the right climate where the sun is not too intense full exposure may otherwise be given, but the more 'continental' the climate the greater will be the need for some shade.

In recent years less interest has been shown in growing the species. This has been amply compensated by the enthusiasm for growing the Orientals or *parkmannii* hybrids or whatever name you may tend to use. This is a just reward to those few in New Zealand, Australia and the USA who spent years producing new shapes and colour forms for our delectation and, at the same time, perfecting the qualtties which make these lilies more easily adaptable and more tolerant to a range of garden conditions. No longer do we need to seek out a dubiously healthy var. *rubro-vittatum* with diligence and difficulty, but can more than likely buy a named clone or one of a similar strain of dependable quality at our local supermarket.

The crosses not just with *L. speciosum*, but with a mixture of *japonicum-rubellum* blood, have broadened the range of flower type and colour and extended the range of plant size and flowering period. These and other qualities may still find improvement and as long as we retain our curiosity to produce afresh from seed we will have excellent lilies in days and years to come.

L. bakerianum Collett & Hemsley

To the lily enthusiast this is not so much a single species, but a complex group of lilies, which in Woodcock & Stearn's *Lilies of the World* was clearly defined from the plants named *L. lowii, L. yunnanense, L. delavayi, L. linceorum* and *L. bakerianum* var. *aureum* into five varieties *typicum, yunnanense, rubrum, delavayi* and *aureum*. To-day none of these lilies is more than vaguely known and, although there may recently have been a new introduction of one variety, no one of these has apparently flowered in Britain for many years except for var. *typicum* in the early 1960s.

The typical variety was first collected by Collett in 1888 from the Shan Hills of eastern north Burma. It is also found across the border in N.W. Yunnan and in W. Szechwan as far north as Kangting (Tatsienlu). The collections of this lily have usually been fairly tender ones from Burma, and Wilson's from the north were unsuccessful in Britain and proved not hardy in Massachusetts. The var. *delavayi* comes from N.W. Yunnan and S.W. Szechwan. It was originally collected by Delavay, and later by Forrest on 22 occasions. It grows in open dry stony country with grasses and shrubs at altitudes between 2600 and 3500 m. Delavay also collected var. *yunnanense* at Tapintze in 1887. Forrest collected this variety on several occasions. Var. *aureum* was a Forrest collection from north of Lake Tali (Erh Hai). The most eastern variety is *rubrum* collected by Bodinier & Martin in 1897 from near Gan-Pin in Kweichow. It occurs again at Mengtsz where Henry collected it at 1820 m. The most southerly site returns to var. *typicum* which grows near Loilem (20°N, 98°E) in eastern Burma. Collected by Charlotte Cuffe, the lily was growing on the edge of a wood facing north on limestone at 1500 m.

The seed has immediate epigeal germination. The bulb of var. *typicum* is broadly ovoid to almost globose 5 cm across with firmly imbricated ovate-lanceolate white scales becoming tinged rose-purple on exposure. The rooting basal stem is stoloniform and emerges to grow 30-90 cm high with scattered, tri-veined linear or lanceolate glabrous leaves up to 10 cm long and 1.5 cm wide. The fragrant, pendulous, bell-shaped flowers may vary in number from 1 to 7 opening greenish and becoming creamy white variably spotted with reddish brown within. The tepals are up to 7.5 cm long and the tips recurve. The stamens are within the bell, the anthers brownish and pollen orange. The large green stigma protrudes beyond the anthers. The seed capsule is obovoid 4 cm long by 2 cm across.

Var. *delavayi* has flowers pale greenish yellow or dull olive green to olive-brown with reddish purple spotting.

Var. *yunnanense* has a shorter stem (20-60 cm), shorter leaves and more horizontal flowers pure white or rose tinted with tepals 7.5 cm long sometimes minutely speckled maroon.

Var. *aureum* has rich golden-yellow flowers minutely speckled purple on the inside from the base to the tips of the tepals.

Cultivation has been a problem with every introduction. Some growers have had considerable success but usually for just a few years. It seems doubtful that any bulbs grown in cultivation have reached the stage of being established. One problem is the tender nature of many of the forms, but that apart, it does not seem right that plants from rocky dry situations at 3500 m in N.W. Yunnan cannot be found a small niche in some of our gardens. Following after E.B. Anderson's success in 1960, perhaps, if the introduction was by fresh seed rather than dug bulbs the difficulty of establishing a freely seeding group might be eased. Very rarely do bulbs imported from the wild last but a short time even of the easier species. With our thoughts on conservation the idea of digging bulbs in plenty as was done in the past fills the mind with dismay and disgust.

L. bolanderi S. Watson

This is one of the most charming and desirable of the Pacific Coast lilies and it is the pride of every lily enthusiast to grow and flower. Usually though it does not last many years in cultivation and so needs to be raised continually from seed which is not too easily obtained.

The range of distribution is relatively small from Humboldt County in N. California into S. Oregon at elevations from 150-800 m in the Siskiyou Mountains. It may be found south of Brookings away from the coast, between Patrick and Shelley creeks and along the old Gasquet Road in Del Norte County. The habitat is one of open pine woods, oak scrub and manzanita where the drainage is good and as such it is a 'dryland' bulb. Often it is on reddish clay soil amid rocks. The rainfall is 125-190 cm per year and with snow cover part of the winter. Wayne Roderick said it takes 'full sun in open areas of chaparral where it gets a few summer rains'. It rarely grows 'through brush, although sometimes gaining the protection of the edge of shrubs'.

The seed germinates hypogeally in the late autumn in cool conditions and shows the first true leaf above ground with the coming of spring. The ovate bulb up to 5 cm tall has numerous lanceolate scales and may be found 8 cm below ground. The stem emerges directly changing from burgundy to green and grows from 45-90 cm high, rarely more. It is clothed in whorls of about 9 oblanceolate upturned leaves up to 7.5 cm long, usually more glaucous than any other lily. The umbellate or racemose inflorescence may have 3-7, exceptionally more to 18, vinous-red or brick-red velvety campanulate flowers, heavily spotted dark crimson into the throat which is yellowish. The exterior has a glaucous sheen, green at the base. The actual coloration may depend on the degree of exposure to the sun. The outward-facing to nodding flowers are hung on pedicels arching towards the end. The tepals are somewhat spreading only partly recurved at the tips, up to 4.5 cm long. The stamens are shorter than the tepals and the pistil, the pollen orange. The protruding straight style has a purple tri-lobed stigma.

The cultivation of this lily, with that of L. kelloggii which inhabits the same general area, is a baffling and perplexing problem to many would-be growers. This may suggest the species' lack of adaptability outside its own niche rather than an enforced incarceration in a restricted enclave. This being so the best tactics may be to copy the natural conditions and only deviate where circumstances demand. In parts of Britain this may not be too difficult, but in many areas of the lily-growing world the problems could be insurmountable. Although a 'dryland' bulb, that is, not coming from the bogs, this species must have plenty of moisture particularly through to flowering time. Grove said it was intolerant of a dry sub-soil and suggested some form of subterranean irrigation for this and other Californian lilies. He also thought it lime-tolerant, so those gardening on alkaline soil should not be deterred. More West Coast lilies may be tolerant than was once supposed. Certainly many of the hybrids of mixed parentage are doing as well on chalky and limy soils as on acid soils and are not showing the deterioration associated with some Oriental lilies in similar circumstances.

L. bolanderi has played an important role in the making of Pacific Coast hybrids initiated by Mayell with a cross using *L. pardalinum*. This was followed by bringing in *L. kelloggii* × *parryi* putting the four species together. One of the resulting seedlings, pink in colour, pollinated *L. pardalinum giganteum* and produced my own Bullwood Hybrids – another good starting point. Some of the Monterey Hybrids also show the influence of *L. bolanderi*. The rich coloration, the bizarre spotting and the almost non-recurving tepals are all characteristics which have been captured in the hybrids, the last mentioned quality being most significant. So far the unique glaucous bloom has proved elusive.

L. brownii F.E. Brown

We do not have to worry from where or from whom Brown got his bulbs. This was 'a trumpet lily of outstanding beauty', but no longer stands as 'the perfection of lily form'. It seems that its era has passed. It was no doubt dazzling in its heyday, but we cannot live on memories, if we are practical gardeners. Even the varieties of the type do not seem real to the vast majority of lily growers, many of whom have never seen either, let alone the type, and yet Wilson was truthfully able to write: 'This is the common trumpet-flowered Lily of China, and probably grows wild in every one of the eighteen provinces from sea-level to 5000 feet (1515 m) altitude according to climate.' This may still be so of var. *viridulum* in which case many would be pleased to make its acquaintance.

The real beauty which has vanished into thin air is called var. *brownii*. It was self-sterile and may have been a hybrid. The two varieties that are in being are var. *australe* occurring in Fukien, Hong Kong, Kwangtung, Kwangsi and Yunnan which may be called the southern form, and var. *viridulum*, despite what Wilson is quoted as saying above, is the form inhabiting central China as far north as Shensi. The latter may be described in the following manner. The seed gives immediate epigeal germination. The creamy white bulb is subglobose being somewhat flattened, 7 cm across, with broad ovate scales turning reddish purple on exposure. The rooting stem is greyish green up to 1.25 m tall clothed with numerous scattered lanceolate 5-7 veined leaves up to 25 cm long and 2 cm wide. The very fragrant flowers, held horizontally, up to 4, open pale yellow inside, quickly becoming white. The tube is green. The outside of the tepals (15 cm long) are variably coloured with rose-purple and, when slightly coloured, rather greenish like the mid rib. The pollen is yellow to red-brown. The pistil is longer than the stamens. The seed capsule is erect oblong-ovoid up to 6.5 cm long and 3 cm across.

The var. *australe* may be distinguished by the taller stem, the narrowly-lanceolate to linear leaves which in the middle are ten times as long as wide, but much shorter at the top, and the flowers being wider open, white inside and white flushed green on the exterior.

Having procured the bulbs, cultivation will become the big problem. The Dutch and Belgians were able to produce the bulbs in large quantity on very light sandy soil enriched with humus and manure, but it seems the purchasers of all these bulbs were less successful and could not keep them going for more than a season or two. If they did it was due to a great deal of time-consuming extra care. Given very good drainage and light soil the bulbs of var. *viridulum* could be planted 20 cm deep and this would make them hardy in many temperate regions. The underground stem bulblets should be lifted out and detached and grown on under glass. Every care should be taken to guard against basal rot and infection from virus diseases. Many will find it easier to grow *L*. 'Black Dragon' and similar trumpet lilies, but then, of course, they are not the same.

L. bulbiferum Linnaeus

The Orange Lily is Europe's upright-flowering species. It is a curious fact that the very few and basically similarly coloured upright or crocus-flowered lilies should span three continents. One might ask which is the closest related to this and it might be presumed to be the Asiatic *L. dauricum*. The area covered by *L. bulbiferum* stretches from the Pyrenees in the west to western Czechoslovakia, Hungary and Poland in the east. From central and southern Germany it reaches southern Italy just below Naples. It strikes one as a little odd that a lily known so well for so long should create problems regarding the status of its varieties and their distribution. We tend to criticise others in distant lands for not knowing enough about their own plants while ignoring at least in specific detail many of our own. We take too much on our own doorstep for granted and copy what has gone before. Because of the wide range of Asiatic hybrids this species and its varieties are not cultivated so much as heretofore. This may be to their benefit and help save them from successive plundering and eventual extinction, but it would be useful for a right-minded person to study them in detail, using, perhaps, successive holidays to investigate the various kinds in the wild.

The var. *typicum*, with its synonym var. *bulbiferum*, has seed exhibiting delayed hypogeal germination. The bulb is almost globose 9 cm across, white, with oblanceolate or ovate-lanceolate scales. The sturdy stem, somewhat woolly towards the top, may be 1 to 1.2 m high, though subject to much variation, and have many scattered lanceolate leaves 10 cm × 2 cm. The flowers usually 1 to 3, appearing in June, may in cultivation be up to 20 and even 50 has been mentioned! They are erect chalice-shaped of a deep orange-red with a central orange patch. The tepals are 8.5 cm long ridged inside towards the base with numerous projections. The filaments are pinkish-orange, the anthers brown and pollen orange. There is no scent. Frequently, but not necessarily, small greenish bulbils are borne in the leaf axils.

The var. *giganteum* found by N. Terracciano comes from the area around Naples. It is generally taller at 1.5 to 1.8 m high, having 12 or so orange-yellow flowers. There are no bulbils. It is possible to find reddish orange flowered plants in this area which are not so tall and this leaves doubts regarding this variety and its constancy. However, it is a flower-growing area and there may have been escapes into the wild too.

The var. *croceum* is strictly the Orange Lily and is the commonest type in cultivation, being plentifully grown in northern England and Scotland as a cottage-garden plant taking the place of the Madonna Lily grown in the south. Its distribution in the wild is said to cover central and southern Germany, Austria, Switzerland, the northern half of Italy, Corsica, the south of France and the Pyrenees.

The main differences to the description given under var. *typicum* apply to the flowers, which are more erect and shallowly cupped. The tepals are light orange, deeper at the base and tip; externally orange with a green keel. The blooms run on well into July and there are no bulbils in the leaf axils on flowering stems.

The var. *chaixii* may be thought of as a dwarf form of the var. *croceum* adapted to the particular conditions of the Maritime Alps which it inhabits. The flower colour is described as saffron or orange-yellow, tipped with reddish orange and spotted towards the base with red-purple projections. On the reverse they are sulphur yellow.

Cultivation is perhaps the easiest of any lily, liking full exposure or some shade and taking kindly to most soils, even the heavier, whether acid or alkaline. It is a stem rooting plant so it should be planted 10 to 15 cm deep and given adequate mulches of humus-rich soil year by year. The hardy bulbs are long-lived, so replanting will be necessary at least every three years to split them and to remove to new beds the stem bulblets which have grown below ground level. If var. *chaixii* is more difficult as has sometimes been suggested this may be due to its holding a more unique ecological niche in nature. This would support justification for maintaining it as a separate variety. Should a choice be available, *croceum* is the variety to grow. Its flowers are more numerous and more brilliant than *typicum* which is criticised at times for not flowering, setting itself the task of producing bulbils instead.

This species has been most important in the history of hybridisation. It was one of the few lilies that in the early days provided the stepping stones and founded the path which allowed great strides to be made in recent years. It is a parent of *L. hollandicum* so commonly, outside the USA perhaps, called *L. umbellatum*. Here it was joined with the Japanese *L. maculatum*, itself a variable lily. Just as important were the crosses made between *croceum* and the Chinese *L. davidii willmottiae* in the 1930s. Much of this work was the basis of the great race of Asiatic lilies that were to follow. It may be doubted whether *L. bulbiferum* will be used again. Its days at stud are most likely over. Back crossing may be an advantage from time to time, but nobody is going to start at the beginning again.

L. callosum Siebold & Zuccarini

Although possessing the widest distribution of any east Asian lily, this small elegant species is seldom seen in cultivation. This is surely a great pity as its easier availability would enhance the growing of the species amongst gardeners. Another factor worth considering is the distribution itself, which Wilson thought remarkable. It stretches over 24° latitude from Taiwan in the south to the Amur River in the north experiencing a great variety of climatic conditions. Taking note that this shows an exceptional adaptability at some stage in its evolution, it seems also that certain forces impeded its path eastward. It reaches Khabarovsk 135°E in the USSR and a similar longitude in Japan. The reasons for this do not seem very obvious and this north-south distribution is difficult to understand.

To be more specific the distribution covers southern Japan, the South West Islands on the Ryukyu Islands, north Taiwan, around Khabarovsk, on the Ussuri north of Vladivostok, both North and South Korea, including Cheju-do, north-east China along the Amur River, Hupeh and possibly southern Anhwei. In the north it grows in meadows, among shrubs, on slopes of hills and often in humus-rich soil. Wilson saw it in Japan at nearly 1000 m growing on grass-clad cliffs and among low shrubs giving it some shade.

Seed gives immediate epigeal germination. The white bulb is small and round but for a slightly flattened top and base with 7-9 waisted oval scales. The rooting stem rises direct from the bulb giving the plant a height up to 1 m. The scattered leaves are linear or linear-lanceolate up to 10 cm long and 5-6 mm wide, often terminating in a rough or callose tip. The racemose inflorescence has up to 9 unscented brick-red or orange-red turkscap flowers up to 2.5 cm diameter, obscurely spotted at the base. The perianth segments carry horny bulges at the tips, or, as Wilson says, they are callosely mucronate at the apex. The stamens are shorter than the tepals with glabrous filaments, the pollen orange to orange-red. The style is shorter than the ovary, stout and straight with capitate stigma. Flowering is not until late, often August, but the source of the bulbs might affect the period. Seed capsule is oblong-ovoid 3-4 cm tall.

There is one named variant, var. *flaviflorum* Makino which is indigenous to Okinawa. Apparently it does not have the calluses of the type and, of course, the flowers are yellow. It is probably not now in cultivation, but it should be worthy of reintroduction as it comes occasionally from seed when from the right source.

Cultivation of this lily should not present great difficulties, but it is not known whether forms from differing latitudes and climes have inbuilt requirements. One can hardly expect a bulb from northern Taiwan reacting in a like manner to one from northern Manchuria. The species is lime-tolerant and well-worked garden soil with a reasonable or high humus content and good drainage should prove adequate. Regrettably the bulbs are not long-lived, but this is a relative term and, if in the past this has referred to imported bulbs, then by raising them from seed and adapting the bulblets early to their permanent home the story may be different. Even so it is wise policy to raise a few new bulbs with each crop of seed.

This species has been little used in hybridising.

L. canadense Linnaeus (Figure 7.2)

The Meadow Lily as it is often called, may be one of the most beautiful of the American species and even of the whole genus. Its grace, poise and fine proportions give it a special character setting it aside from the rest – which are never lagging far behind. Yet as it has no scent to some people this takes it off the summit at once.

This was the first American lily to be seen in Europe being introduced by the French early in the seventeenth century. It was described by Parkinson in 1629 as 'Martagon Canadense maculatum. The spotted Martagon of Canada' and was reasonably well illustrated. Of the flowers he wrote 'from among the uppermost rundle of leaves break forth four or five flowers together, every one standing on a long slender foot stalk, being almost as large as a red Lilly, but a little bending downwards, and of a fair yellow colour, spotted on the inside with divers blackish purple spots or strakes, having a middle pointel, and six chives, with pendents on them.'

It has a wide range of distribution within eastern North America, starting in the north on the Gaspé Peninsula in Quebec (at the mouth of the St Lawrence on the southern side), New Brunswick, Nova Scotia, Ontario, south through New England to Maryland; and south from Pennsylvania through the mountains to Alabama. With one exception, it is a lily of wetlands, meadows, ditches, stream and lakesides, but normally never in the water except of snowmelt or flood. The bulbs are found in reasonably light free-draining acid soil, not in stagnant conditions. It may be fully open to the sun when in the company of coarse grasses partly shielded at the edge of woodland or under a light canopy of trees.

Seed germination is hypogeal with the seedling bulb usually produced in a cool period preceded by a warm period. The first true leaf appears above ground following a cold season. The bulb is ovoid to almost globose, white or yellowish, with short ovate scales, and formed annually at the end of a stout white stolon up to 5 cm long. The roots are like thick white cotton thread. The rooting green stem rises to 1.5 m high and carries whorls of lanceolate or oblanceolate leaves up to 15 cm long by

Figure 7.2
L. canadense

2 cm wide, with a few scattered leaves towards the top. The umbellate or racemose inflorescence has up to 30 pendulous campanulate yellow or orange-yellow flowers, variably spotted deep maroon within, hung on long curving pedicels. The tepals are up to 7.5 cm long flaring out at the tips but do not recurve. The straight style with brown tri-lobed stigma normally protrudes beyond the stamens with brown anthers and orange-brown pollen. The seed capsule is erect oblong, 3 cm tall.

  There is considerable variability in the species even within quite small areas. This affects the flower colour, the type and quantity

97

of spotting, the length of the pistil and the colour of the anthers and pollen which may sometimes be yellow. The red-flowered kinds usually come within var. *coccineum* Pursh, more commonly referred to as var. *rubrum* Moore or forma *rubrum* Britton. The flowers are normally dark or deep brick-red with strong, large spotting. The more significant red variety comes from the Appalachians in Pennsylvania and southwards to northeast Alabama. This is called var. *editorum* Fernald which grows on limestone, producing alkaline soils. The habitat is usually drier, on wooded slopes and open upland meadows. The flowers are red with a narrow tube and narrower tepals up to 1.5 cm wide instead of up to 2.5 cm wide. The leaves are broader and only slightly tapering. Knowing how variable the species may be, it does not seem necessary to continue to advertise the old names. Some are more yellow than others, some are somewhat striped red and yellow, some heavily spotted and a few unspotted. Each has a life and usually, when dug from the wild, a short one. If a distinct clone, and to be propagated vegetatively for distribution, it can be given a fancy name and properly registered.

Three things trouble this species. The first is drought, the second is virus disease, and the third is an alkaline soil. The last may not trouble var. *editorum*. That we are attempting to prove, but the hard limestones of the Appalachians are still not very similar to, say, the chalky soils of southern England. The gardener must, therefore, contrive a way of keeping the soil moist without getting it stagnant. As with so many lilies and particularly those from North America the water must be there, but on the move. Separation will tend to keep virus problems to the minimum. A neutral soil may be made acid, and an alkaline soil less so, but unless something really clever can be done by those who garden with this difficulty, then it is better to leave it to someone else. Propagation is easy from seed and scales, but both lots of bulblets demand the cold season or the use of the refrigerator before commencing growth above ground. Once this stage is past progress is relatively fast.

Many attempts have been made to cross *L. canadense* with other American lilies, both eastern and western species, but little evidence remains except with those made with *L. grayi* and *L. michiganense* both of which are very closely related. In fact the hybrids resulting may look like nothing more than variants already found in the field.

L. candidum Linnaeus

The White Lily, the latter-day Madonna Lily, has virtually, like so many plants which have proved useful to mankind, lost its home after having been cultivated for thousands of years. Even before direct cultivation took place it still might have travelled around the countries bordering the eastern Mediterranean through the agency of man. In the wild state today it can be found in the Balkans, and in particular Greece, usually in more inaccessible sites; likewise on cliff edges in S.W. Anatolia and adjacent islands. Possibly it may be in the Lebanon and in early days found as far south as Israel. *Flora Europaea* modestly suggests it is naturalised in Albania, France, Corsica and Italy including Sicily and Sardinia. If this limited range is correct, it shows that the Madonna Lily has not broken loose from its tie to the Mediterranean and doubtless it would demand similar climatic factors in other parts of the world.

In those forms which are fertile, and indeed most of us know the lily from one or two widespread infertile clones, seed germination is epigeal and immediate in warmth. The bulb is broadly ovoid up to 9 cm high and wide, white or yellowish, with the scales broadly ovate. It is shallowly planted to an extent like no other lily and, in a loose way, has been referred to as evergreen. Like some other Mediterranean plants it puts out fresh growth in the early autumn in expectation of the first rains, and this takes the form of basal leaves which, if conditions allow, last through the whole winter and beyond. The stem arises in spring and is 90-130 cm and may be as much as 180 cm high. The scattered leaves are lanceolate ascending and glabrous with the lower ones long and those as they are higher up the stem shortening and somewhat clasping the stem. The flowers may be about 7 but possibly as many as 15, pure white broadly campanulate with segments about 8 cm long. The stigma is greenish and the filaments white. Pollen is golden-yellow. The sweetly scented flowers are in bloom in early July.

The cultivation of the Madonna Lily must surely be easy. However, there are a number of factors that might be considered, having transplanted the bulbs during that short period in late summer when the plants would seem to be near to dormant and ensured they were planted shallowly with the noses at ground level or just below. Growth seems to be more vigorous in neutral and alkaline soils and looks better more often than not in gardens where it might be little cared for. It is the lily of the cottage garden even more so than *L. martagon*, and rarely, today at least, graces the enthusiast's garden or finds its way to the show bench. This lily in its common sterile variety is shunned for carrying mosaic virus and for being subject to *botrytis*. How disappointing it is to see those beautiful flowers standing above decaying and prematurely dying foliage! Nowadays even in the cottage garden due to the benefits of modern drains the country lily does not get its bowls of soapy water thrown out from the scullery, which kept it clean and disease at bay. The outlook for the Madonna Lily in northern latitudes is not good. Its position has certainly declined. It will not disappear, but its heyday has passed.

Other forms of this lily, especially if fertile and so able to be grown from seed, may give some cause for optimism amongst keen growers, but it would seem the special cultivars known in the last century and the early part of this have died out. It may be, of course, that they still lurk in some forgotten corners of old untended gardens. There was var. *aureo-marginatum* which had a broad gold margin to the foliage said to be especially valuable in the winter garden. Another was var. *purpureum* (also called *striatum*) where the flowers were streaked with purple on the outside. A third was called var. *plenum* (also *spicatum*, *florepleno* and *monstrosum*), a double form described by Dr Wallace in 1879 as 'an abnormal form, the flowers being abortive, and the bracts dilated, white and petaloid'. Yet another has been called var. *variegatum* as the leaves are blotched yellowish white. The variety *cernuum* (syn. *L. peregrinum*) returns us nearer to normality and it is a kind which may be expected to be still in cultivation and more closer to some of the wild forms found in recent years. It is said to be a more slender plant with a purple stem, narrower leaves, and segments of the perianth narrower, longer, more acute and more spatulate. Another vigorous cultivar of French origin is called 'Charles X'. It grows to 180 cm tall and bears 20 or so enormous white flowers. Surely a lily worth searching for.

The first fertile clone to gain notice was named by Stoker in 1935 var. *salonikae* although E.A. Bowles had been growing it and spreading it around in cultivation since 1917. Again the leaves are narrower, more spreading and more undulate. The flowers open more widely and are about a fortnight earlier. The filaments are shorter and the pollen pale yellow. The Cascade Strain originally developed by Professor George Slate and later by the Oregon Bulb Farms would have been based on this fertile clone possibly with the incorporation of later introductions from the Balkans.

Every lily grower is expected to know that this lily together with *L. chalcedonicum* produced in the early nineteenth century the first lily hybrid to be grown in the western world. It is interesting to note the affinity of the two species. More recently (1971) C. Robinson of Ontario, Canada, proved a successful cross between var. *salonikiae* and *L. monadelphum* calling the lily 'June Fragrance'. This too was an important breakthrough and landmark, adding to our knowledge of the evolution of the genus *Lilium* besides giving us another beautiful lily from which might follow many more.

L. carniolicum Bernhardi

Emanating from the Balkans the group of lilies placed under this heading are important and interesting to specialists but have raised little enthusiasm amongst gardeners generally. All are of turkscap form with scattered leaves and include the type species, *L. carniolicum* with red flowers and the varieties, *L. albanicum*, *L. bosniacum* and *L. jankae* with yellow flowers. In *Flora Europaea* it is said that the variation between them is not fully understood, but more information is gradually coming to light and being pieced together. Their closest relatives may not be *L. chalcedonicum* living near by, but *L. pyrenaicum* to the west and *L. ponticum* to the east.*

Seed of *L. carniolicum* is a russety brown with a sheen, firm and heavy. It has epigeal germination which may be delayed, but is better described as erratic. There are obviously inhibitors at work which make a simple quick and even means of germination unobtainable. The stem, arising directly from the white or pale yellow ovoid bulb (7.5 cm high by 6.5 cm wide), may be 90 cm tall fairly stout and green. Foliage is scattered and lanceolate 7.5 cm long by 2 cm wide with three prominent veins. There are hairs along the veins on the undersurface and along the margin of the leaf. The flowers may be up to 6 in an umbel or umbellate raceme, pendulous turkscap with the tepals strongly recurved hiding the base of the flower joining the peduncle. The colour is red spotted or rather streaked with black towards the base. The stigma protrudes forward of the anthers and the pollen is bright red. It is scented but not heavily so. Fairly early in the lily calendar flowers should begin to bloom by mid-June. Seed is easily produced and the dry capsules measure 35 by 20 mm.

The species is a sub-alpine and alpine plant and in its eastern section may be found in western Romania, east Serbia, western Bulgaria and east Macedonia in Yugoslavia. The western section covers north-east Italy, northern Yugoslavia thence south-easterly down to Montenegro.

In cultivation this plant is not difficult and is long-lasting. Its

---

*Matthews has now chosen to place *L. carniolicum* and *L. ponticum* as subspecies under *L. pyrenaicum* which is the earliest name.

101

drawbacks may be the time needed to obtain floriferous bulbs from seed and even then it is not over abundant in bloom. However it comes early in season, has clear bright red flowers which are not overburdened by the foliage as in *L. pyrenaicum*. In producing hybrids it has not proved useful as a parent though Dr North tried in the late 1960s.

L. carniolicum albanicum (Grisebach) Baker

This is a southern counterpart of the type species frequenting mountainous areas in western Macedonia, Albania and north-western Greece, being bounded by the Vardar valley.

Seed and germination is similar to the type species. The bulb is ovoid 5-6 cm high by 4 cm wide white becoming purplish on exposure. The stem is variable in height – there appear to be dwarf alpine forms – up to 80 cm or slightly more. The scattered foliage may be longer (86 mm) and narrower (9 mm) than *L. carniolicum*, 7-veined with the central vein prominent smooth and non-ciliate. Flowers may be up to 5, possibly more, strongly recurved so that the segments turn back on to themselves, of a clear yellow unspotted. They are faintly scented and open from mid-June. If it is the same lily, recently a spotted form has been found in northern Greece.

As with the type, cultivation is not difficult, time and patience being the best ingredients for growing this group of lilies which are generally calciphiles, but still willing to grow on acid soils. As a garden plant it overrides *L. pyrenaicum*, so in the early lily season there is no yellow turkscap available to trounce this one. It would benefit any plantsman's garden.

L. carniolicum bosniacum Beck

This variety is a Yugoslavian plant coming from N. Macedonia, Bosnia and Hercegovina, which has been considered as a separate species and as a form of *L. jankae*, which follows, at different times. Its true status may, therefore, still be in doubt and that it may be a natural hybrid is an interesting supposition.

The stem is up to 80 cm high, is hairless and has scattered leaves glabrous or nearly so, some few hairs being present on veins on the undersurface. Flowers in the wild are usually single, but may be as many as 8, the perianth segments being a yellow-orange with dark spots. Apparently it flowers later in July.

This lily is not known to be in cultivation and its collection would prove most useful so that it may be compared with other Balkan lilies.

L. carniolicum jankae

This variety is the eastern yellow form of the type, as it comes from eastern Yugoslavia and the Rhodope Mountains of

Bulgaria where it inhabits rocky slopes and sub-alpine meadows.

The stem is 80 cm high with the scattered foliage hairy on the veins underneath. Flowers may be up to 12, yellow with dark violet spots mottled darker at the base. It is strongly scented.

This is a larger plant than *L. albanicum* and is said to be more vigorous, but that does not mean it is quicker growing. It is in cultivation and seed is offered from time to time, but it seems to remain in the hands of a few specialist growers, more the pity.

L. catesbaei Walter

Of all the lilies on the American continent this appears to be the most unique. It has an upright flower, its stem leaves scattered and not in whorls, and basal leaves occurring as an extension of the bulb scales. These features may not be common in the other lilies, but are not unknown. They all appear to manifest adaptations to the particular environment of the S.E. United States and show a fairly extreme development in the genus *Lilium*. No other lilies growing closer to the tropics have required to adapt so markedly, so the cause may not only be due to low latitude and year-round warmth, but to its habitat of swamps and pinelands.

The full range of distribution would include the states of Florida, Alabama, Mississippi and Louisiana and to the north Georgia, South and North Carolina and south-east Virginia. The var. *typicum* described immediately below would seem to inhabit Florida, Louisiana and parts of Carolina.

The germination of seed is immediate, said to be epigeal, above ground in 40 days. The bulb is up to 2.5 cm across with slender, erect, loose, narrowly lanceolate, whitish scales, about 2 cm long, apices blunt with scars of fallen basal leaves. The stem rises directly to 30-60 cm high and is clothed with numerous alternate ascending linear-lanceolate leaves up to 10 cm long. The basal leaves are very narrowly oblanceolate about 10 cm long, growing during the winter. The single large flower (rarely 2) appearing from June to October, or even later, is upright, wide-spreading, distinctly clawed at the base. The tepals recurving at the ends are about 10 cm long, deep yellow with scarlet towards the tips, heavily spotted dark maroon towards the base. The erect stamens and style are shorter than the tepals, the pollen orange-brown, stigma dark red.

Var. *asprellum* (Wherry) Stearn grows along the coast of the Gulf of Mexico, and is found in the states of Florida, Alabama and Mississippi sometimes seen with the type. The stem rises to 1.2 m high and is leafless and rough on the lower half with the numerous leaves crowded about the middle in conical formation.

Var. *longii* Fernald is more northerly and comes from south-east Virginia, North Carolina, Georgia and Alabama. This variety is said to be completely hardy. It has no basal leaves which suggests no winter growth. The stem leaves are broader, 6-13 mm as against 2-12 mm in the type. The tepals are not so wide-spreading nor so long in the tip.

Those who have cultivated this lily have not done so for very long; there are many who would try, but have not had the opportunity. Should one difficulty be eased out of the way the other of cultivation seems sure to arise. The adaptation of this species to its particular environment suggests this would be the case, but not necessarily. There could be a greater chance of success using var. *longii* as the problem for many would be how to keep it growing, even if slowly, through the winter. It needs to be planted only about 5 cm deep in peaty sandy soil. Watering should be adequate up to flowering time or early autumn whichever is the later. It would be interesting to know how the lily might grow in south-west Ireland or on the west coast of Scotland to prove whether the hot summers were essential.

Emsweller produced seed from *L. philadelphicum*, *L. grayi* and *L. superbum* when pollinated by this species.

L. cernuum Komarov (Plate 4)

Of the few species of pink-flowered lilies this is the smallest, but even so one of the most desirable to grow. It belongs to the group of Asian species with turkscap flowers and scattered leaves, including *L. callosum* and *L. pumilum*. This lily has been described as a pink form of the latter without being quite so floriferous.

Compared with its related species this lily holds a relatively small distribution, which includes both North and South Korea. In the USSR it is found around Vladivostok in the Premorie province, the most northerly site being south-east of Lake Khanok. In north-east Manchuria, in the areas of Shenyang (Mukden) and Kirin where Komarov discovered this species, he often found it abundant. Wilson said that it grows in grass among low shrubs. At one site it was on alluvial soil, and on another it was on palaezoic slate rocks. Its preference is for stony slopes, on cliffs or high stony meadows amongst oaks with humus over clayey stony soil.

The seed is light to medium brown, 6-7 × 4-4.5 mm, and gives immediate epigeal germination. The white bulb is ovoid 4 cm tall by 2.5 cm wide with firmly imbricated lance-shaped waisted scales. The rooting stem rises directly reaching 70 cm high, but usually less. It is smooth and cylindrical and has scattered linear leaves up to 15 cm long, principally on the lower third. The scented flowers may be up to 6 (or more in cultivation) in a racemose inflorescence, pendent, turkscap, 3.5 cm diameter, lilac-pink, speckled or spotted wine-purple; anthers brownish, pollen lilac. The capitate stigma is slightly lobed. The globose to obovoid seed capsule is 2 cm tall.

There is one variety described by Nakai in 1917 and this is var. *candidum*, which comes from Gwanmobong at about 700 m. The flowers are white faintly spotted purple at the base.

It is only right to say that this lovely lily is not so easy to grow as *L. pumilum*, but all it requires is just a little extra care. Why this should be is not easy to explain, but the same may be said of other pink lilies. For instance, *L. columbianum* is easier to grow than *L. kelloggii*, *L. davidii* is easier than *L. lankongense* or *L. wardii*. Of the group of small turkscap Asiatic lilies, *L. cernuum* has the smallest distribution and from most accounts is the least common. There is some reason behind all this, but to the gardener it means taking a little more trouble. If though his soil is suitable and his climate none too good (!), then this lily will thrive. Even so, like its kind, the bulb is not long-lasting and seed should be sown regularly to keep the stock refreshed.

The use of this species by Dr Patterson at the University of Saskatchewan, producing a seedling 37-538 with *L. davidii*, paved the way for a whole new world of Asiatic hybrids taken up by the Oregon Bulb Farms and others since, and culminating to date in a very broad range of pink, lilac and white lilies in various forms and often scented.

L. chalcedonicum Linnaeus (Figure 7.3)

Including *L. heldreichii* Freyn as a variety or form of this species, this is the highly prized and much sought after red turkscap lily of Greece. It comes from the Peloponnese, Epirus, eastern Albania, Thessaly and Euboea, but apparently not from further east, although it made its way into general cultivation via Istanbul. It grows in a variety of habitats generally on limestone in stony humus where it is well drained and may be in full sun or semi-shade. Particular sites mention growing in chestnut woods, in heavy soil and dry torrent beds in mountainous regions, putting little doubt about its hardiness.

Seed germination is epigeal and often delayed and erratic, but fresh seed, if obtainable, sown in the autumn kept cool and moist germinates readily. Mature bulbs are broadly ovoid about 7.5 cm tall and broad having broadly lanceolate yellowish scales. The stem which arises directly may be up to 1.2 m high, but

Figure 7.3
L. chalcedonicum

often less, is sparsely hairy, having numerous 7-9 veined silver-edged leaves. The lower leaves are lanceolate or oblanceolate spreading or ascending up to 11.5 cm long by 1.6 cm wide. Upper leaves are smaller, almost erect, pressing round the stem. The flowers umbellate may be 4-6 in number but possibly as many as 10, are pendulous, turkscap, 5-6 cm in diameter, orange-red, scarlet or tomato red, and in the type unspotted. The tepals are papillose on the basal half. The bud is 6 cm long and the peduncle 15 cm long. The filaments are yellowish, the anthers 12-14 mm long and reddish; the pollen is orange-red. The style of similar length to the stamens has a tri-lobed stigma. In Britain flowering is usually in the latter half of July carrying on into August. It is faintly scented, agreeably to most people, but not all! The seed capsule is obovoid with the apex depressed about 5 cm high by 2.5 cm diameter. Seed is medium brown and slightly winged.

Although this beautiful and for centuries much admired lily has become scarce it is not a difficult lily in cultivation. It adapts to

106

various soils, as long as they are well drained, whether acid, neutral or alkaline and submits to considerable shade as well as full sun. Even the depth of planting or lack of it should not be much of a restriction. What should concern the grower is the quality of the bulbs, because the species is obviously susceptible to disease. Growing from seed is especially advocated for this reason. The foliage and stem are prone to *botrytis* and similar fungal attacks should damp close conditions apply in the summer when the lily expects a dry air environment.

This lily is famous for being a parent of the first hybrid *L. testaceum*, *L. candidum* being the other. No repeats of this cross have ever been marketed, but Oliver Wyatt, apparently with some difficulty produced a line of hybrids, 'Apollo', 'Ares', 'Artemis', 'Hephaestus' (Plate 9) and 'Zeus' by crossing *L. chalcedonicum maculatum* back on to *L. testaceum*. The result was a race of beautiful hybrids of varying shades but, although a few bulbs of some of those named may linger on in Britain, they are now better known in literature than in gardens. It would be worthwhile cleaning up the remaining clones of the Wyatt hybrids by micro-propagation. A few other keen growers are to be commended for endeavouring to remake similar crosses, so may our summers bless them with seed! May others be encouraged to try their hand.

The variety *maculatum* is similar in most respects to the type, the main difference being the spots or short black lines or flecks on the scarlet segments. This spotted variety is earlier in flowering and usually more vigorous, but seemingly less common.

L. heldreichii has been reported in the past for many of the same sites as *L. chalcedonicum*, so obviously there has been much confusion. If, however, one is to be differentiated from the other, then, *L. heldreichii* may have more star-shaped flowers with less reflexed tepals, a tomato red colour, broader leaves where the silver margins are less marked and a shorter stem. The style is roughly triangular with blunted angles and slightly concave sides. There are no bracteoles on the peduncles. These are not really distinguishing points of great moment, but show with the spotting of var. *maculatum* the variation that is likely to obtain in a species inhabiting a broad area of the mountainous regions of Greece and Albania.

L. ciliatum P.H. Davis

Two lilies from N.E. Turkey, this and *L. ponticum*, may be considered closely related to the *carniolicum* group of the Balkans and *L. pyrenaicum*. They are all turkscap lilies with

107

scattered foliage. The flowers vary from red through shades of orange and yellow to this the palest which may be close to white. This species is the most recent of the group to be named, which was in 1965, following a spate of expeditions to the area in the early 1960s by Furse & Synge, Furse, Apold, Cox & Hutchison, and Stainton & Henderson. Furse had given a good description of the lily in the RHS *Lily Year Book* for 1964, but was blessed by having no good name to give it. It had been known of earlier, since 1933 in fact when collected by Balls, after which it had grown at Quarry Wood, but unfortunately was confused with *L. ponticum.*

The range of this lily overlaps that of *L. ponticum,* but it also occurs west of Trabzon as well as to the east. It is not known to occur anywhere else in the world but in the mountains some 130 km long bordering the Black Sea in the north-west corner of eastern Anatolia. Between 1500 and 2400 m it inhabits margins of forests, clearings, scrub and rich meadows above the tree line on acid soils.

The rich brown seed gives hypogeal germination which is delayed requiring a cold spell before emergence above ground. The bulb is large and oval 5-10 cm across with many slender scales about 10 cm below the surface. The stem, which is rooting late in the season after flowering, may be 60-150 cm tall, having spirally arranged leaves 7-12.5 cm long by 1.25 cm wide. They are glabrous on both surfaces but have long flexuous hairs fringing the margins. These hairs are smooth and unicellular, unlike the short unicellular hairs with a striate cuticle found on the veins on the undersides of leaves of *L. ponticum* and *L. jankae.* The flowers in June and July usually number 5-8 but may be as many as 21. They are turkscap, 5 cm diameter, ivory, cream or pale sulphur with purplish brown centres and finely spotted in the upper part. The external base of the flower is *not* purple. The filaments are 20-28 mm long and the style 15-20 mm long. The pollen is orange. Furse described the scent as half-way between the sweet *szovitsianum* and the pungent *ponticum.*

The lily collected by Balls lived at Quarry Wood at least thirty years. We have no idea how old it might have been when found in 1933, but there can be no doubt they are long-lived. Where the soil is acidic cultivation should present few problems. Some shade, but not too much, would seem to be beneficial, as would excellent drainage. Most concern would arise in the period between seedling stage and maturity and this may be three or more years depending on conditions. There are bound to be losses on the way. Furse reported scales producing bulblets easily.

As with its relatives, Dr North crossed this spieces with *L. pyrenaicum* and brought the hybrids to flowering using embryo culture. The results he considered did not 'have any horticultural qualities which could not be found by selection of *L. pyrenaicum* itself'. A pretty damning appraisal following upon so much hard work.

L. columbianum Hanson

As some plants have only a few meadows or a piece of woodland on the world's surface, some have thousands of square miles and the run of great mountain ranges. This species belongs to the second category as its spread is the largest of the Western American lilies. Due to this spread it enjoys many climates, many soils and many aspects and when it comes into our gardens it is fortunately as easily accommodated. In the past it has been somewhat maligned, not coming up to the high standards of Californian lilies to the south. Purdy described it once as a miniature *L. humboldtii*, damned it with faint praise and said it varied little. In Woodcock & Stearn it says: 'Considerable variation in such a plant is not surprising' and Synge writes: 'so it is not surprising that it is a variable plant.' The present writer will even the score and join with Purdy and say that with his small experience it varies little. Even the one named variety, *ingramii*, would be instantly recognisable as of the species, a factor which cannot be said of all Western American lilies.

The range of distribution is from Humboldt County in California northward through Oregon, Washington and west Idaho to southern British Columbia including Vancouver Island. It frequents mountainous and valley areas, in woodland, meadows among brake ferns, and with low shrubs, so in sun and shade from 1500 m down to sea level.

The seed has hypogeal germination which occurs under cool autumnal conditions and growth above ground comes with the spring. The whitish bulb is ovoid (not rhizomatous), about 4 cm across, with narrow lanceolate unjointed scales. The slender stem may be from 60-150 cm high, exceptionally up to 210 cm, carrying whorls of smooth oblanceolate leaves up to 16 cm long, with a few scattered above the topmost whorl. The racemose inflorescence has usually 6-10 pendulous, turkscap flowers, but there may be as many as 40. They are held on long arching pedicels. The tepals may be orange-yellow, pale orange to reddish orange, spotted purple, finely or coarsely but heavily towards the throat, up to 6 cm long, reflexing from just below the middle. Stamens slightly longer than the style, the pollen is

109

usually yellow but red-anthered flowers occur in British Columbia. Flowering is from early July.

Var. *ingramii* is a more vigorous plant with larger deep orange flowers, sometimes burnt orange or crimson which was collected near Powers in south-west Oregon. *L. bakeri* Purdy, which may be considered a synonym of the species, came from sandy woods along Puget Sound, Washington and southern British Columbia. It was said to be very fragrant.

This is one of the easiest of the West Coast lilies to raise and grow. It requires a not too heavy acid loam ideally with some light shade and the protection given by dwarf rhododendrons. It should have plenty of moisture during the growing season, but it is not a bulb from wet areas.

L. columbianum is very accommodating as a seed and pollen parent and has been crossed with a number of Western American species, some to good effect, as with *L. rubescens*, and others rather nondescript. Being a widespread species, it may be responsible for some of the wild hybrids occurring in N. California and S. Oregon.

L. concolor Salisbury

To the Russians this lily growing in the USSR is known as *L. pulchellum* Fischer, a name published in 1839. Salisbury described *L. concolor* in 1806, although not knowing it at the time, from plants emanating from China, and the Siberian lily has generally been considered a variant of this with the name *L. concolor* var. *pulchellum* (Fischer) Regel (1876). This is but one of the difficulties now attached to this species. More of a problem may be its position in the genus, as it bears little relation to the other erect-flowering lilies. Possibly it is more directly attached to one of the lesser Chinese turkscaps with pendent flowers.

The original type was given a distribution in central China including the provinces of Hupeh, Hunan and northern Yunnan. Wilson often saw it growing around Ichang in Hupeh between 300 and 1200 m 'always a rare plant and with unspotted flowers'. He also refers to it from Shensi and Chekiang. The spotted form is said to come from Shantung where it occurs on rocky hillsides between 300 and 600 m. Further to the north the var. *pulchellum* has an extensive range in north-east China, North Korea, around and to the north of Vladivostok in Premorie, and along the Amur River to the west almost to 110° longitude. Baranova states that it prefers high open slopes on sandy hills, growing among bushes and in drier meadows. In Japan *L. concolor* is sparsely distributed throughout Honshu, Skikoku and Kyushu, sometimes in the same areas as *Ll.*

auratum and *japonicum*. In N. Korea Wilson saw it in similar vegetation, but on stiff loam.

Seed has immediate epigeal germination. The bulb is white, ovoid up to 2 cm across with a few closely overlapping ovate or ovate-lanceolate scales. The slender, rigid stem is 25-60 cm high and often purple-tinged. The scattered leaves are linear or linear-lanceolate, faintly 3-7 veined ciliate beneath, up to 8.5 cm long by 1.5 cm wide. The slightly fragrant 1-10 flowers are erect, star-shaped, unspotted, glossy scarlet with the tepals 3-4 cm long slightly recurved. Filaments, pollen and stigma are similarly coloured to the flower. Flowering is late June and July.

Over such a wide and discontinuous range there are not surprisingly a number of varieties. The var. *stictum* Stearn (f. *sinicum* Wilson) is the type form where the flowers are spotted black, originally coming from Shantung; among the population yellow spotted and unspotted kinds were to be found. The northern variety, var. *pulchellum* (Fischer) Regel is the most important botanically. It has a smooth green stem sometimes wandering underground. Buds are sparsely to strongly hairy. Flower colour is generally bright scarlet, but more variable, and usually unspotted. The style is shorter than the ovary, a distinguishing mark. The var. *coridion* (Siebold & de Vriese) Baker is citron-yellow with small purplish brown spotting and was said to grow wild in Mongolia. It is considered to be a yellow form of var. *pulchellum*. Another yellow form with larger unspotted flowers emanates from Japan and is called 'Okihime'. The last variety to mention and the most curious is var. *partheneion* (Siebold & de Vriese) Baker having spotted red streaked green and yellow flowers. If this strange and surely virus-riddled apparition is lost to cultivation we should not worry much until it turns up again. What does seem odd is that the name has got attached to the Korean *L. concolor*, which as var. *pulchellum* must surely exist in the north, but doubtfully in the south. Professor Lee describes the plant with 1-5 deep pink erect, purple spotted flowers slightly recurved. Anthers are pink and stamens shorter than the tepals. Distribution is shown as in the north and east of South Korea. Dr Lighty did not find the plant in the wild or in the Seoul herbarium. It would be no bad thing to clear up the status of this lily in S. Korea.

Cultivation is not difficult. New bulbs may be raised quickly by seed to keep a stock in hand as bulbs are likely not to live long. An acid sandy compost in full exposure, but amongst other plants of smaller or similar stature seems the ideal, but as the lily is said to be lime-tolerant and in some areas grows on stiff soils it should be adaptable to all reasonably well-drained garden soils.

The status of *L. concolor* as a parent may have been thought most important when it seems it was the parent of *L.* × *maculatum* and so heading the family tree of the Mid-Century Hybrids. Now that has been strongly disputed by Shimizu and this species must bow out. More likely it could play a part with *L. pumilum* (Is it a parent of 'Red Star'?) and *L. cernuum* and get into the hybrid world by another route. Would this be to any great advantage? Its qualities in nature are admirable, but it does not have a unique contribution to make. Its not being a long-lived bulb may be a disadvantage. Perhaps its wild beauty should be allowed to range over the wide hills of eastern Asia unensnared.

L. dauricum Ker-Gawler (Figure 7.4)

Other spellings of this lily are *davuricum* and *dahuricum*, but the spelling given in the heading is the original. The name is taken from an area of south-eastern Siberia once called Dahuria, included in the Sretensk district of the USSR to the east of Lake Baikal. It may be thought of as the centre of the large area covered by this lily in eastern Asia. It is one of the few but important erect-flowering species linked easily to *L. maculatum* from Japan and to *L. bulbiferum* in Europe.

Its main distribution is in the eastern USSR stretching from the Yenisei River in the west to Kamchatka in the east. In the north it reaches, so far as is known, 64°30′ latitude at the Noginsk Mine on the Lower Tungusk River. In the south it is found in north-eastern Mongolia, north-east China, N. Korea, Vladivostok and Hokkaido. It grows in damp meadows, on the edge of forests, in mixed herbaceous vegetation on sandy soil. Wilson wrote of it growing in N. Korea close to swampy places on black volcanic soil amongst coarse grasses and shrubs. On Sakhalin *L. dauricum* often grows with *L. medeoloides* with such other liliaceous plants as *Hemerocallis middendorffii*, *Convallaria keiskei* and *Polygonatum humile*, but generally inhabits the more open, higher and drier positions.

The seed has immediate epigeal germination. The white bulb is globose, 5-6 cm diameter and 4 cm high. The scales are loosely imbricated, lanceolate and jointed on mature bulbs. The stem is somewhat wandering below ground (stoloniform) and rises from a few centimetres to nearly 1 m high, slightly ribbed and usually hairy, according to situation and location. Leaves are scattered narrow oblong-lanceolate 3.5-15 cm long by 0.3-2.5 cm wide, 3-5 veined. Flowers numbering from 1 to 6, exceptionally up to 15 are erect open vase-shaped, orange-red, orange and red, orange, or orange and yellow, spotted purple from the base to in length to the style which has a slightly triangular stigma. The capsule is globose about 2 cm long.

The var. *imberbis* was collected by Farrer in Upper Burma. This had no beard at the base of the tepals, was scentless, of a clear yellow freckled internally towards the base.

The form collected in the Tamnyen Chu valley (L.S. & T. 4967) had purple spots on the outer bulb scales. The flower was greenish yellow, paler within, with black-purple streaks on slightly saccate bases outside. Filaments were greenish yellow, anthers deep purple turning brown. Ovary was green with broad black-purple lines, style green streaked black-purple towards apex, stigma green.

None of these collections regrettably has ever been introduced into cultivation. Many of us might find it as hard to please as *L. nanum*, but the opportunity to learn more about this dainty lily has yet to come.

L. fargesii Franchet

This is the least attractive of the lilies of eastern Asia, said Wilson, and when introduced, which he did not trouble himself to do, will interest the collector only. Somebody has to be at the bottom of the class, but, if you are a lily, you are already among the elite!

This species is distributed in central China including western Hupeh, north-east Szechwan, south-east Shensi and north-east Yunnan. It inhabits open grassy country in the mountains.

The white oblong to narrowly ovoid bulb up to 2.5 cm across has firmly imbricated oblong-lanceolate scales. The rooting stem rises direct to 20-60 cm high and is sparsely clothed except for the centre with scattered, linear leaves up to 15 cm long and usually 2-3 mm wide. Flowers from 1-6 are greenish white, spotted rose-purple of turkscap form. Pollen is yellowish. A photograph of the type specimen collected by Farges appears in Woodcock & Stearn's *Lilies of the World*, Fig. 45.

Despite this lily, which may be related to *L. callosum* and the other small Asiatic turkscaps, being less exciting than most it would still be very interesting to have it available in cultivation.

More recently *L. xanthellum* Wang & Tang has been named, said to be close to this species, but with upright flowers. It comes from Szechwan as does var. *luteum* Liang.

L. formosanum Wallace

This should be an indispensable lily for most, if not all, gardeners, so easily and quickly does it come from seed which it provides in ample quantity. But you can hear the criticism as you

119

write. Voices are saying, it is very short-lived. What if it is? Because some lilies are long-lived, surely we do not despise those that are here for a short bright life. Are we not more fortunate to have so many kinds? The more versatile the genus *Lilium* is found to be surely the better for all of us who enjoy lilies.

This species used to be thought of as a variety of *L. philippinense* to which it is obviously closely related. Its other neighbour across the water though more distinct, *L. longiflorum*, is also a relation.

L. formosanum is only known from Taiwan, where it inhabits open grassy places from sea level to 3700 m. It is said to be inhibited by forest land which it shuns. In some areas it is very abundant. It varies more than a little in size of plant, particularly height of stem and overall vigour, rather than by size of flower, so that in var. *pricei* we have a small or even very small plant, but with the trumpet flower hardly diminished in size.

The seed in warmth speedily gives immediate epigeal germination. The white bulb is tinged purple at the top, subglobose, 3 cm high by 4 cm across. The usually purple-brown stained stem rooting at the base may vary in height from between 10 cm and 2 m, but more usually between 50 cm and 1 m. It is clothed in numerous scattered, 3-5 veined, dark green, linear leaves up to 20 cm long and 1 cm wide. The scented flowers may be solitary on dwarf or young plants, but up to 10 on strong specimens. They are in umbels, horizontally disposed and commonly facing north, at least, when north of the equator. The large narrowly-tubed trumpets are pure white with vinous-pink coloration on the exterior keels of the tepals, which are up to 15 cm long and recurved at their tips. The tepals and pistil are much longer than the stamens with yellow pollen. The style has a large tri-lobed stigma. Flowering season is August-September. Seed capsules are erect cylindric up to 9 cm long by 2 cm wide.

As is to be expected from a species varying in the wild and cultivated so readily a number of forms and varieties have from time to time been named. Knowledge of their names does not add greatly to our knowledge of these lilies however. The most commonly recognised is var. *pricei* Stoker. This refers to an introduction by Price in 1912 of seed collected near Arisan at 2590 m on Tung Shan (then called Mount Morrison). This is referred to as a dwarf form, that is, compared with a tall kind 2 m high. They were 30-60 cm high, 1-2 flowers per stem, flowers smaller with much darker markings, and flowering earlier in July. On his own report though the seed he brought home was from a different batch, which he thought similar. It seems

120

1   *L. japonicum*

2   *L. alexandrae*

3 *L. nanum*

4 *L. cernuum*

5 *L. henrici*

6 *L. taliense*

7 *L. grayi* at Southampton, Mass.

8   Lilies from a cross between Paisley Hybrids and *L. tsingtauense*

9   *L.* 'Hephaestus', raised by Oliver Wyatt

10   *L. sargentiae*

11 *L.* x *dalhansonii* originated in the late nineteenth century

12 *L.* 'Piratenkönig', raised by Fritz Ewald

13   *L.* 'Lady Bowes Lyon', raised by Gerald Darby

14   *L.* 'Coachella', raised by the author

15   *L.* 'Rosewood', a selection from the Bullwood Hybrids

16   *L.* 'Lake Tulare', raised by the author

17   *L.* 'Fairy Atom' — a complex Oriental hybrid

18   A red *parkmannii* hybrid of New Zealand origin

Price did not go or did not find the lily higher up, but he reported Yasheroda talking of single-flowered plants 30 cm high covering the slopes at 2750 to 3350 m in hundreds of thousands. Today it is commonplace, rightly or wrongly, to call any dwarf or very dwarf form var. *pricei*. If hardiness is dependent on the elevation then those growing above 3000 m should be particularly tough. Other names used for differing forms are 'Intermediate Pure White', 'Kenya' and 'Wilson's Pure White'. From these and *pricei* have come further selections and been given names generally for commercial reasons. Whether any can be positively identified is extremely doubtful.

Where lack of hardiness is not a problem cultivation is very easy, but it does mean keeping a new supply of young seedlings at the ready. They are, however, so easy and quick to raise that they do not pose any difficulty. They may be brought to flowering in six months to a year, but this is dependent on light and warmth. The species is susceptible to virus disease and is a noted ready indicator succumbing easily and exhibiting frustrated growth, twisted foliage and badly shaped flowers. Growing in well-drained soil it keeps green into the winter, maturing seed late if the frosts are not too harsh. As it is a stem rooter it can be planted deeply and mulched well to give the bulbs added protection from cold where necessary.

In a restricted sphere *L. formosanum* has been used as a parent with *L. philippinense* and *L. longiflorum*. With the latter species an interesting cross has been made with the tetraploid form 'Tetrabel' producing the sterile triploid 'Formobel'. Der Zwet produced 'White Superior', Tuffery 'Florosanum', Woodriff 'Easter Early' and others have acted similarly, but there has been little breaking away from this little ring.

L. georgei (W.E. Evans) Sealy

This species (which is not to be confused with the Caucasian *L. georgicum* Mandenova a synonym for *L. ponticum*) was named in honour of George Forrest who found it in N.E. Burma in 1924. It is close to *L. souliei* from which it differs in the number of leaves and the colour of the perianth. It grows at an altitude between 3400 and 3700 m. The following year he collected it again in open stony alpine meadows. Seed was sent back to Edinburgh which germinated, but the plants were lost before flowering.

The bulb is broadly ovoid nearly 5 cm high with fleshy lanceolate scales. The stout stem grows from between 15 and 45 cm high with only scale-like leaves at the base, but densely set with blunt, elliptic-lanceolate leaves up to 5 cm long 1.25 cm

121

wide in the upper part; sometimes they are in whorls. The terminal inflorescence is a large solitary, broadly campanulate, soft blue-purple, nodding flower, shortly stalked and barely rising above the topmost leaf. The outer tepals are narrower than the inner, and markedly pouched at the base while the inner are just slightly pouched. The stamens half as long as the tepals, have slender, linear filaments and purple anthers. The ovary over 1.25 cm long is slightly longer than the style with its tri-lobed stigma. The seed capsule is oblong, *c.* 3.8 cm long.

L. *grayi* S. Watson (Plate 7)

This is a very uncommon lily and one closely allied to *L. canadense*. In fact it has been said often that this species might only be a variety of its big brother. The subject will not be contested here, because for gardeners and lily enthusiasts it always looks to be unique and in no way easily confused. It has also been said that this lily is less vigorous than *L. canadense*. What does this mean? Of two plants of the same species one may be more vigorous than the other, but two 'unlikes' are not easily compared. Anyway if anybody doubts the vigour of this species they should see those grown by Ronald Beckwith in Massachusetts over 1000 km to the north-east of their native home.

The range of distribution is generally confined to the Appalachians forming the boundary between North Carolina and Tennessee in the Great Smoky Mountains and the Blue Ridge Mountains in Virginia.

The seed (9 × 7 mm) has delayed hypogeal germination most likely similar to *L. canadense*. The bulb is stoloniferous. Annually a new bulb is composed at the end of a short stolon, comprising short white, fleshy, rounded scales up to 1 cm high. The stem rises to 1.75 m high and is clothed by 4-6 whorls of lanceolate or oblanceolate leaves slightly rough at the margin and on the veins beneath. The inflorescence is umbellate to racemose with up to 12 pendulous, campanulate, deep red unscented flowers heavily spotted purple towards the base inside, held on long bracteolate pedicels some 30° to 40° from the vertical. The tepals are spreading but not recurved, more purple at the base outside sometimes paler in the throat other than the spotting. The stamens are shorter than the pistil and held within the bell. The pollen is dull orange-brown, the style red and the tri-lobed stigma green. The seed capsule is obovate about 4 cm long.

Those who have the opportunity of growing this lovely lily should look upon it as no more difficult or fussy than *L. canadense*. It can be grown happily with open exposure in both Edinburgh and Massachusetts where the summer maximum temperatures are much different. It has been grown well in slight shade, which it should prefer, in southern England. It seems to demand an acid soil and plenty of moisture during the growing season. Propagation may be from seed or scales, with both being given a cool period, and division when the mother bulb is vigorous enough to grow two or more stolons in a season!

This lily has been hybridised with *L. canadense*. One such hybrid was growing at Kew in the mid-sixties; being somewhat intermediate it possessed nothing outstanding and so seemed a poorer version of either species.

L. hansonii Leichtlin

Some species may be distributed over large areas and be little known to horticulture, others, like this species, may come from one small place on the globe and be described by gardeners as common. This lily is a true turkscap lily closely allied to *L. martagon*. It comes from the island of Ullung (previously called Dagelet Island and Takeshima) in the Sea of Japan east of S. Korea and apparently nowhere else, although Ohwi gives it in the *Flora of Japan* saying 'said to be spontaneous in Hokkaido'. Little or nothing has been heard of this lily occurring naturally in Japan, so it may be assumed that the reference to Hokkaido is to introduced stock or an escape from cultivation. The Japanese call it Takeshima-Yuri and the Koreans Soemmalnari. Dr Lighty records it growing above the sea from 300-1000 m in rather heavy woods, the volcanic soil having a high organic content. Usually it was on slopes where the herb layer was otherwise slight. The lily generally in cultivation in the West rarely sets seed and the bulbs may be all from one clone. Dr Lighty has introduced new stock so gradually some true fertile seed will be passed around.

The bulb is ovoid to nearly globose, yellowish white turning pale pinkish purple on exposure with numerous triangular to narrowly ovate scales. The green stem rooting is 1 to 1.5 m tall with 2-3 or more whorls of 6-7 oblanceolate leaves 10-18 cm long, up to 4 cm wide. Shorter scattered leaves are found above the topmost whorl. The nodding fragrant flowers in June through to July are up to 12 per stem, orange-yellow, spotted brown-purple within. The tepals are thick and fleshy, like orange peel, and do not recurve so strongly, as in *L. martagon*, back to the pedicel or base of the segment.

Cultivation must be reckoned as easy, as the species takes to a variety of soils, including those with lime. The bulbs are long-lived and divide frequently when well-grown. Propagation may otherwise be from scales. A watch needs to be kept for *botrytis* or the vigour of the plant can suffer badly, accordingly the lily should not have too much shade. On the other hand full exposure will bleach the flowers.

As recorded under *L. martagon*, this lily readily pollinates that species and has produced many famous hybrids. In recent times its effect, and development through the hybrid, *L. dalhansonii* (Plate 11), with the upright *L. tsingtauense* as the other parent has been interesting but much needs to be done before the results can vie with the best Asiatics.

L. henrici Franchet (Plate 5)

This beautiful species gets its name from Prince Henri d'Orléans who discovered it in Yunnan on the Mekong-Salween Divide towards Loukou (? Lushui) on 11 July 1895. Later Forrest collected it in the same area between latitude 26° 10' and 26° 30'N at about 3150 m altitude. He also found it to the south-west on the Schweli-Salween Divide between 25° 20' and 25° 30'N where the plants agree with the var. *maculatum*. Unless the fragmentary specimen obtained by Kingdon-Ward in Burma was this species, this is the full range of this lily as known, and it may be considered fairly rare.

In the past opinions have been divided as to whether this species should be considered a nomocharis or a lily. The present established criteria as suggested by Sealy easily show it to be a lily. Nevertheless it would seem to be close and, appreciating that it is a man-made division which separates the two genera, it is difficult to see how evolutionary development kept them so close. Would it be heretical to suggest that a lily, such as *L. henrici*, found it beneficial to look like or remain like a nomocharis, in an area where nomocharis lived since before the great divides were great or even divides at all?

The seed gives immediate epigeal germination. The purple bulb is broadly ovoid 4.5 cm wide with about 30 visible lanceolate or elliptic-lanceolate scales. The stem suffused with brown arises directly to a height of between 90 and 120 cm and is clothed with numerous scattered narrowly lanceolate leaves 10-12 cm long and 7-12 mm wide. The racemose inflorescence may have up to 7 slightly pendulous open campanulate flowers with the tepals producing a very short tube at their base and recurving at their apices. The colour is whitish suffused rose-purple, being appreciably darker at the base outside; in the throat dark purple. Tepals are 5.5 cm long by 1.8 cm wide. Stamens are shorter than the style. Filaments are slender, glabrous, green; pollen yellow. The green style thickens to a conical capitate lobed stigma.

The var. *maculatum* which occurs in the more southern site and to some extent with the type, has the tepals white within and especially those of the inner whorl marked at the base with a few scattered but rather large and well-defined crimson-purple spots.

This species has for 50 years been remarkably well cultivated in a few gardens in Scotland. That it is difficult to please is not hard to judge when generously so much seed has been distributed in the past with such apparently little end result. However, anyone with the opportunity to try should grasp the lily, if not the nettle. The seed quickly germinates and the young bulbs grow fairly strongly. It was a joy to flower this lovely lily in Essex over two years, but unfortunately it did not take, cut first by late frost and succumbing to virus. An acid compost with a high humus content would seem essential. Plenty of moisture should be available throughout the spring and light shade should be given.

L. henryi Baker

This Chinese species, the 'Orange Speciosum' was discovered on the limestone cliffs and some of the glens of the Ichang Gorge in the valley of the Yangtsze Kiang in Hupeh by Henry in 1888. According to Wilson the bulbs in this locality were 'virtually exterminated' by 1900. He found the species, though, at other sites. One on conglomerate rocks from 16-48 km south of Ichang at 1060 m altitude growing plentifully in copses and dense thickets among a table of small trees, shrubs and coarse herbs. Another site was 80 km north-west of Ichang where there were a few plants on limestone cliffs. This is a very restricted distribution for a plant in central China. Strangely, Père Bodinier collected a lily in 1898 on the Kien-liu-chan near Kweiyang in Kweichow province and Léveillé called it *L. callosum*, but Wilson, who had later seen the specimen, said it was *L. henryi*. This is an odd outlying station for what must be a rare lily in the wild. The Japanese obtained the lily before 1900 and grew it for export.

The seed is golden-brown 9 × 6 mm and gives immediate epigeal germination. The bulb is white purple-tipped quickly turning mahogany-red on exposure. It is large, subglobose, up to 18 cm across with thick imbricated ovate-lanceolate scales. The tall, rooting purple-brown stem has an arching habit, possibly an adaptation to vertical cliff faces, and may be 2-3 m long. The numerous scattered shiny leaves are lanceolate up to 15 cm long except at the higher portion of the stem where they become short and broad, ovate. The racemose inflorescence on horizontal pedicels, may have 2-40 or exceptionally even more, pendulous, orange, dark-spotted flowers, which are strongly recurved, showing the green nectary furrows and prominent papillae of the 8 cm long tepals. The anthers are orange. The flowering season is late, August in England. The seed capsule is ascending, obovoid to ovoid up to 4 cm long and 2.5 cm across.

This lily is a gift for those gardeners with a limy or chalky soil. With plenty of humus in the deeply-worked loam they can attain very floriferous specimens of great size. The gardener on acid soil who thinks that all lilies should grow given the 'right circumstances' sees his specimens deteriorate and die out. Propagation is simple from seed, scales or just taking the basal stem bulblets from well-mulched plants. Full exposure might be acceptable to the health of the plants, but the flowers bleach easily and should be given dappled shade and, to overcome the arching habit of tall specimens which might look gawky and awkward with adequate staking, the bulbs should be grown amongst suitable shrubs and tall herbaceous plants. This species appears fairly free of disease, and its shiny leaves, useful to a lily living in a high summer rainfall area, are not usually susceptible to *botrytis*.

This lily is famous for being one of the parents of the original *L. × aurelianense*: that goes back to 1928. What proved of greater interest some 30 years later was the cross made by Woodriff with the, to some extent, similar looking *L. speciosum*. The result was 'Black Beauty', a lily of good proportions, good quality flowers, vigour and a sound constitution. Its sterility does suggest the distance the two species have journeyed apart since their evolution.

L. humboldtii Roezl & Leichtlin (Figure 7.5)

Whether we are splitters or lumpers we are bound to recognise that all the lilies that might be included under *L. humboldtii* are not exactly similar. All are agreed that the type var. *humboldtii* inhabits the Sierra Nevada in California. Some way to the south around Los Angeles another lily appears usually called var. *ocellatum* (Kellogg) Elwes, but separated by Lawrence Beane as *L. ocellatum* (Kellogg) Beane subsp. *ocellatum*. Further south again is found around Mount Palomar var. *bloomerianum* Purdy, which has been separated as *L. fairchildii* M.E. Jones (1930) and although not generally accepted was supported by Beane in 1955. Mount Palomar is in the north of San Diego County. Lower down in the centre of the county occur the Cuyamaca Mountains where var. *bloomerianum* occurs again, and this is generally recognised, but as it is thought of as being a smaller form of var. *ocellatum* Beane has recognised it not as a variety of *L. humboldtii* but as a subspecies of his *L. ocellatum*, so that it

Figure 7.5
L. humboldtii *var.*
ocellatum

becomes *L. ocellatum* subsp. *bloomerianum* (Purdy) Beane. In the following paragraphs the conservative and generally accepted view will be taken, allowing for three varieties of *L. humboldtii*.

At the turn of the century Purdy gave the range of the type in the Sierra Nevada as from Fresno County to Tehama County. Beane (1955) suggests that it does not now occur south of Amador County which is south-east of Sacramento. It grows in the yellow pine belt (*Pinus ponderosa*) at an elevation between 600 and 1200 m 'in open woods among low undergrowth in a more or less rocky red clayey or volcanic soil, perfectly drained and not at all rich in mould'.

Var. *ocellatum* has a west to east range, rare for almost any lily in North America. In the west it is found near Santa Barnara in the Santa Ynez Mountains then as you come east in the San Gabriel and San Bernadino Mountains. Besides these mainland locations it also grows on the islands off the Los Angeles coast – Santa Cruz, Santa Rosa and Santa Catalina. Ford gave it a somewhat larger range, including the Santa Ana Mountains below Los Angeles and higher up the coast to San Luis Obispo. It is found in semi-shade in a leaf mould-covered granular soil well above the stream bed in remote canyons. Emsweller wrote of a plant 2.9 m high which had borne 25 flowers. It was growing under the driest conditions (September). The soil was heavy, but sloping and very well drained. There was 7-15 cm of leaf mould covering the soil made use of by the stem roots; the bulbs were 10-25 cm beneath the surface.

Var. *bloomerianum* may be confined to mountainous areas within San Diego County, but some authorities say that it is also in Riverside County and San Bernardino. Beane wrote of his subsp. *bloomerianum*: 'In a cool, damp canyon in the San Bernardino Range, Dr. Vollmer and I found nearly 100 plants which were almost impossible to distinguish from the species' (meaning *L. ocellatum*). No doubt they were! Some would say they *were* var. *ocellatum*.

The seed germinates hypogeally in late autumn under cool conditions. It may be found that the more southern varieties are less seasonally dependent as spring germination is possible without delay. Taking the type the bulb is large ovoid-globose, lopsided and oblique with thick ovate or ovate-lanceolate unjointed white to yellowish scales up to 7 cm long. The stout, non-rooting stem grows to 2 m high exceptionally more, and is clothed in whorls of undulate, oblong-lanceolate leaves up to 12.5 cm long and 2.5 cm wide. The pyramidal inflorescence may hold up to 16 nodding turkscap flowers, 7.5 cm across, but rarely many more, on long curving pedicels. The tepals recurve not excessively and are up to 10 cm long, bright orange conspicuously spotted maroon. The widely spreading slender filaments have long purplish anthers with orange-brown pollen. The curving style is of similar length to the stamens. The seed capsule is obovoid acutely angled 5 cm long. Flowering is in July.

Var. *ocellatum* has a bulb of similar size and shape to the type but the large flat scales are 2-3 jointed. The stem roots at the base. The orange tepals are generously splashed with crimson towards the tips and the spots are aureolated with crimson.

Var. *bloomerianum* has a much smaller bulb with jointed scales. The stem is shorter rarely over 1.2 m high. The smaller flowers are similarly coloured to var. *ocellatum*, but not so richly.

Of the American West Coast dryland bulbs this species and its varieties must be considered the least fastidious and least difficult to manage in cultivation. It has to be appreciated that it wants virtually dry conditions from July to November and that the drainage must be very good. The soil does not require the humus of the wetland bulbs except as a top layer mulch. This last point is particularly valid for var. *ocellatum*. It loves the sun and heat, but high light top shading is acceptable. Propagation from seed and scales is straightforward, but the large bulbs take a few years to mature with four years to first flowering from seed.

This species crossed with *L. paradalinum* was one of those important marriages that have proved so beneficial to lily growers, even more to latter-day explorers into the hybrid world. The joining of the 'dry' bulb genes with those of the 'wet' bulb produced the Bellingham Hybrids and amongst that gathering *L.* 'Shuksan', which is a great lily. It would indeed be a great help if other specifically named varieties of this group could be positively identified. Without dwelling though in the past it does seem that the possibilities to be achieved with the varieties of *L. humboldtii* have by no means been thoroughly worked out, and so the seed of the idea is offered to anyone with the time, space, and the opportunity, to obtain the correct materials with which to work.

L. iridollae M.G. Henry

This is Mrs Henry's pot of gold at the end of the rainbow found in the deep south with the collection of some seed in 1940. The resulting plants flowered five years later. It has similarities with *L. superbum*, but it also has strong differences and has been maintained as a separate species for nearly 40 years.

The range of the species is relatively small from Baldwin

County in Alabama to Walton County in Florida. It grows in sphagnum over black muck, also moist sandy peat, 5-8 cm down, in sun or occasionally in semi-shade along wooded creeks in swamps and the like.

The seed is said to germinate very quickly. The stoloniferous bulb is less than 2 cm diameter with the stolon bearing a few scattered scales. The rooting stem grows from 50 cm to 2 m high and is clothed with verticillate or scattered leaves oblanceolate to obovate, rarely elliptic, up to 9 cm long and 2.3 cm wide, but the uppermost small and sparse. Flowers 1-8 nodding turkscap form, like *L. superbum*, warm buff-yellow to golden-yellow, conspicuously spotted hessian brown, apices stippled pinkish red. Petals up to 10 cm long by 2.5 cm wide, sepals slightly longer and wider, each with a green nectary furrow. The slender filaments widely outspreading, the anthers shrinking to 1.4 cm long, pollen is deep brownish red to brownish yellow. The slender style has a greenish yellow to darkest brown tri-lobed stigma. Flowering season is late July to August. 'In August a cluster of narrowly linear leaves begins its growth on the bulb for the ensuing season' and over-winters, so the plant remains in leaf throughout the year. A similar procedure is found in the typical form of *L. catesbaei*, another southern lily.

Mrs Henry would seem to have raised this lily from seed to flowering state in a frame at Gladwyne, Pennsylvania, during the war years with little attention except for watering. The climate and conditions it enjoys, however, would not make it an easy plant for many gardeners. From the accounts recorded by Mrs Henry it must be assumed that this species is now very rare in the wild and is under great pressure, because of the effects of unregulated grazing.

L. japonicum Thunberg (Plate 1)

Of the pink lilies, and all are especially attractive to gardeners, this one seems to have the quality and ethereal beauty which sets it apart from the rest. What also sets it apart is its independent spirit and unwillingness to be seen frequently in cultivation. The Japanese find it as difficult as most of us. To say that it is lacking in stamina begs the question. It is strong enough to maintain an important position throughout its range of the southern half of Honshu, Shikoku and an outlying spot in Kyushu, withstanding (we hope) the annual cutting of many thousands of stems for flower decoration and festivals. So its place in the wild is strong whichever way we may view it, but for man's depredations. We must, therefore, look into its life a little closer if the answer is to be found. It is not particular about

130

elevation for it is at home close to the sea shore and in regions up to the mountain haunts at 1070 m. Shimizu tells us that as to habitat, in general, locations are sloping to the east or north and fully exposed. However, half the stem of Sasa-yuri, the Japanese name, may be enveloped by *Sasa* sp. (Bamboo grass), *Miscanthus*, *Ilex*, *Rhododendron* and other low shrubs. Further the bulbs are well protected by leaf mould. In this situation drainage and moisture retention reach a state of perfection for this lily. A westerly or southerly aspect would (in Japan) be too dry. Wilson vividly recalls coming upon this lily when he was tired, hungry and drenched to the skin, but he had to linger and drink in the beauty. He concludes that where this lily grows it never suffers for lack of water and the soil is always cool, but the drainage is good.

The seed is 8.5 × 7 mm, light brown and has delayed hypogeal germination. The whitish bulb of 4 cm diameter turns pale pink on exposure and has closely imbricated ovate scales. The rooting stem rises directly to 1 m high and is sparsely clothed with scattered, petiolate, lanceolate 3-5 veined leaves up to 15 cm long by 2.5 cm wide. The fragrant flowers, 1-3 but rarely up to 5, are a glistening pink varying in shade from very pale to deep-coloured. They are horizontally poised short trumpet or broadly funnel-shaped with the tepals up to 15-cm long and recurving towards the tips. The stamens are shorter than the tepals, pollen reddish brown, with the style and capitate lobed stigma slightly protruding. The flowering period in the wild extends from May to August according to altitude. The seed capsule is obovoid, 4 cm long.

There are a number of varieties distinguished, the most well known being var. *album* Wilson. This is the fairly common occurring white form, which presumably would have yellow pollen (mentioned as of rare occurrence by Shimizu) in true albinos. From around Tosa in Shikoku grows var. *albo-marginatum* Makino, which has light rose-coloured flowers and yellowish white margined leaves. Var *abeanum* Kitamura is a dwarf plant up to 30 cm tall with flowers of 5 cm diameter early in the season from the serpentine area in Shikoku. It is said to be easier to grow. In the Kumano mountains in Wakayama Prefecture in southern Honshu grows var. *angustifolium* Makino noted for its specially strong fragrance. Var. *platyfolium* presumably has broader leaves than the type.

Cultivation of this species has never been thought easy, but in places where it has been established it has proved long-lived and performed well. Referring to the heavy summer rains which it receives in nature followed by a dry autumn, most gardeners may have to admit that their natural conditions are usually the exact opposite. What is required seemingly first and foremost is sufficient moisture right up to and including the flowering time. Shade will be needed too to give the moderate temperature. This is no exact science and half-way to meet the best conditions will most likely be satisfactory given clean healthy bulbs. This may be the problem, not helped by a paucity of seed and that this in any case takes some years to give mature bulbs. Nevertheless, there is no better way if one can maintain a careful eye on the youngsters and exercise patience. As the species is self-fertile a pot grown plant brought in under glass for the autumn may be one answer to obtaining a fresh supply of seed.

The fine shape, graceful appearance and delicate shades of pink that this lily can exhibit make it a most important subject for breeding. In fact some of the newer Orientals have a degree of *japonicum* blood in them, together with that of *L. rubellum*. Further work will not go amiss to produce a strain of hybrids with the best characters of this species without the difficulties, which are sometimes too much of a challenge to many of us.

L. kelleyanum Lemmon

Under this name will be considered the turkscap lilies of the Californian Sierra Navada other than *L. pardalinum*. The other names concerned are *L. nevadense* Eastwood, *L. fresnense* (Eastwood) Eastwood, *L. inyoense* Eastwood, *L. nevadense* var. *monense* Eastwood and *L. shastense* (Eastwood) Beane. There are other synonyms beside.

L. kelleyanum was the first name to describe lilies collected 'along the west rivulets of Copper Creek, a few miles north of Camp Colby (30th June 1902) and in marshes along Bubb's Creek, about seven miles from the Grand Canyon of King's River (13th July)' in Fresno County.

The various lilies grow over a great area of mountainous country at elevations between 1200 and 3200 m and besides having similarities, as is only to be expected, they have their differences. In common they have rhizomatous bulbs growing in wet conditions and spotted nodding turkscap flowers of a shade of yellow or orange-yellow. The leaves are scattered or in whorls or a mixture of both.

The most northerly type is *L. shastense* which Beane raised to specific rank. It is restricted to Plumas, Shasta and Siskiyou Counties. At Castle Creek the lilies may be found growing along the stream, many right at the edge of the running water. In September a few were found near dried-up pools and Emsweller concluded the species was under considerable water during parts of the rainy season. The flower colour is basically deep cadmium yellow with the tips of the petals stained a brownish red which diffuses over the entire petal as the flower ages and dies. The brown-purple spotting is generally confined to the lower part of the tepals but when not, and in the reddish area, the spots are ringed with yellow. Pollen is ochre-yellow and dries brownish. Leaves are linear to lanceolate and are erect whether scattered or in whorls. One or more stems arise from the end of the rhizomatous bulb which is unbranching.

At the southern end of the range is found *L. fresnense* which was originally considered a variety of *L. nevadense* but later raised to specific rank by Alice Eastwood. It comes from Fresno and Tulare Counties. When collected near Churchill Creek it was in black, muddy soil usually under running water and the bulbs up to 30 cm deep. Other collections were made by Emsweller and his party in this area close to the Sequoia National Park and all were in very wet conditions. The flowers are relatively small, tepals only 5 mm wide, more yellow than orange and delightfully scented. This lily must be very close to the true *L. kelleyanum* and the differences with *L. nevadense* are not significant.

The latter was said to be found in Sierra, Butte, Lassen, Plumas, Shasta, Trinity and Siskiyou Counties, but this crosses and includes the territory of *L. shastense*, and from this point on it becomes perfectly obvious that there is no demarcation line that can be drawn across country dividing the species, nor another between the lilies themselves. The names may be handy to use from time to time, but have very little scientific purpose.

The variants *L. inyoense* and var. *monense* indicate further minor variants from the east side of the Sierra Nevada. They may well be accepted with the others already mentioned within a general description suitably embracive under the name given above, *L. kelleyanum*.

The seed germinates hypogeally under cool conditions in late autumn. The rhizomatous bulb has numerous fleshy white jointed scales. The stem may be up to 1 m high and have scattered, scattered and whorls, or whorls of narrowly lanceolate, lanceolate or oblanceolate leaves. The inflorescence, if more than solitary, will be umbellate if few, or racemose if many flowered. The flowers will be turkscap form with the tepals usually recurving strongly, of a shade of orange-yellow with maroon spotting with or without more or less superficial red coloration over the tepals towards the tips. The slender filaments will be spreading and have anthers bearing orange or orange-brown pollen, the style with its tri-lobed stigma will be about as long as the stamens.

This group of lilies is not difficult to grow, but may be difficult to grow very well. Like *L. parvum* which inhabits like situations, it wants its bulb kept moist enough while its foliage remains warm and dry. For many gardeners this is not too easy. Perhaps those with the right natural conditions should be more adventuresome and try a few of these lilies by the stream side or even under running water, presuming there is a stony or sandy bedding to plant them in. It could be likened to a form of hydroponics. One of the problems will come with the far greater vigour of many of our other streamside herbaceous plants which can too soon smother an emerging lily like this however happy it might be below soil level. Other than that the lily will take to a reasonably acid loam with plenty of humus. It should be in an open and exposed situation so as to prevent close atmospheric conditions. If this can be achieved, and without too much compromise a little light shade provided, then all should be well. Propagation from seed and scales is best dealt with in the autumn as with most of these American West Coast lilies; the usual practices are adequate.

Whatever name we choose to call it this lily has been and still can be very important as a parent. Wyatt's fair Maids were said to have *L. nevadense* as a seed parent. The bulb used was most likely a hybrid itself to have procreated such a range with a first cross. But if *L. nevadense* was behind that, as well it might have been, rather than *L. parryi*, it proved its worth. And that is only a beginning, for both 'Yellow Maid' and 'Bridesmaid' have been found to be useful parents.

L. kelloggii Purdy

This turkscap-flowered species from the Coast Ranges of north-west California is the nearest approach of any American lily to the true martagon type. The tightly recurved tepals, their colour, the whorled leaves and the concentric type of bulb all tend to suggest this. Its nearest relative, though, is most likely *L. bolanderi*, growing quite close in the same area and yet nobody has suggested this to be a martagon.

The limited range of this lily is within the two counties, Del Norte and Humboldt in the 'fog belt' of the Coast Redwood, *Sequoia sempervirens*. Unlike *L. columbianum* it is not found close to the sea, but on high ridges some kilometres inland. It is a dryland bulb but may be found in locations close to *L. vollmeri* in quite different conditions. On Mount Baldy Emsweller wrote of *L. vollmeri* in spring with stems jutting up out of running water, but then in the fall was in a stagnant bog. He continued 'Near the edge of the bog, but on higher, dry land, we found plants of *L. kelloggii*. At another location they were at the very edge of a cliff gradually crumbling away. On a further occasion it was above the redwoods in open forest consisting mostly of fir, oak and madrone in very dry soil (September).' The elevation would be under 1100 m. Soils may be heavy, yellow, gravelly clay or quite rich brownish red loose loam. Drainage may be considered very good in these dry rocky places and Purdy said there was little humus in the soils it favours.

The hypogeal seed germinates in cool conditions of late autumn and sends the first true leaf above ground in the spring. The white bulb is broadly ovoid up to 5 cm high with lanceolate scales. The slender stem rises directly and grows from 30-125 cm high, exceptionally more, and carries whorls of rather undulate, lanceolate or oblanceolate leaves up to 10 cm long 2 cm wide usually with a few scattered above the topmost whorl. The inflorescence may have from 1-100 flowers, but a good spike would have about 20. When few they are in an umbel, when more racemose, and held on graceful long curving pedicels arched at the top to take the pendulous, fragrant, turkscap flowers. The strongly recurved tepals, 5 cm long, are basically white with a median band of yellow into the throat. The white is overlaid mauve-pink to a varying degree, according to age and light conditions, and the lower half is finely spotted dark maroon. The stamens are slightly shorter than the straight style with its green tri-lobed stigma; pollen is orange. Flowering is in July.

The bulbs should be raised from seed sown in autumn. Kept at c.5-10°C (41-50°F) through the winter by spring the minute bulbs will throw their first leaves. These may be potted as required and grown on. Planting out would be best at two years in well-draining gritty loam about 4 cm below ground level, allowing the young bulbs to move further down as required. Flowering may begin from three years onwards. Some shade is preferable and sufficient moisture available to ensure no drying out until the flowering. This lily is accustomed to fog and dew so should not be too shaded or too exposed in regions of dry atmosphere.

All the pink Pacific Coast hybrids have been dependent on this species for their coloration. It is true that in some of the darker shades *L. bolanderi* might have played some part too. *L. kelloggii* also has the advantage of throwing 'albinos', that is, truly when there is no superficial pink colour at all which is rare. Usually there is a light pink suffusion as in *L.* 'Lake Tahoe'. Occasionally lilies have been reported in the wild with no yellow median stripe, presuming them to be *L. kelloggii*. This is strange

135

indeed for the dominance of this colouring, directing pollinating insects maybe, is indisputable. You can play about with the other colours to your heart's content – but not that one!

L. *kesselringianum* Misczenko

This Caucasian lily is little represented in our gardens, but may be a little more than we realise as those collections around Artvin close to the Soviet border were only recognised as of this species by Davis & Henderson in 1970. Previously they were thought of as *L. szovitsianum*, but in truth they should look distinct in flower with the narrow tepals to the trained eye. This species comes from the southern side of the Caucasus behind Sukhumi on the Black Sea. It therefore occupies an area to the north-west of *L. szovitsianum* in Georgia. It also occurs, as already suggested, in Turkey in the Artvin district at the very east of the Black Sea Region. In the west Transcaucasus it grows in sub-alpine meadows and shrub groves and the Turkish sites are described as wooded slopes and meadows at the edge of spruce forest at altitudes between 1450 and 1800 m.

Seed germination may be expected to be of the delayed hypogeal type. The bulb is broadly ovoid up to 6 cm across with ovate yellowish scales. The stem rises 1.2 to 1.4 m high but may sometimes be in excess of this. The leaves are spirally arranged, narrowly lanceolate 9-13 cm long by 1.1-1.5 cm wide, being shortly setulose on the margins and veins below. The flowers up to 7 are held in a loosely pyramidal inflorescence and individually are *c.* 9-14 cm diameter but at times even 20 cm, of a recurved campanulate shape, pale cream to straw-coloured with small purplish spotting in the throat and purple at the base on the exterior. The tepals are linear-lanceolate tapered at both ends, very acute. The filaments are 4-4.6 cm long, the anthers brown and the pollen orange. The style is 2.7-3.4 cm long. The flowers opening in June and July are strongly scented, stupefying at close range.

Little precise information is available on the cultivation of this desirable lily, but its requirements should be little different from the other Caucasian lilies. It may not be so vigorous or so easily adaptable as *L. szovitsianum* has proved, otherwise it would have a stronger hold in gardens than it has currently. There is nothing to say regarding its use as a parent.

L. *kosa* Orekhov & Eremin

If this lily is to be treated as a distinct species, and there are doubts that it should, then there is difficulty in how the name should be spelt. Eremin used the spelling shown above, but *kosii* and *kossii* have also been seen in print. Even supposing this lily is not distinct it is important to list it. It has not yet exhibited its pink coloration in cultivation, but we have to believe that it did in the wild. We still wonder from which limb of the original lily these Caucasian lilies came and any clues are worth investigating.

This lily was found in Kabardino-Balkaria on the northern side of the Caucasus in fairly inaccessible mountainous country not far from Nalchik. This is central to the area from which *L. monadelphum* comes and it may be that this is a variant of the latter.

The bulb is enormous weighing up to 2 kg and being broadly ovoid 18 cm long by 14 cm wide. Young bulbs have pinkish yellow outer scales which in old bulbs are pale yellow. The stem, strongly rooting in the summer, rises to 1.5-1.8 m high. The numerous light green leaves are scattered, elongated lanceolate, the lower being 12 cm long by 3 cm wide and higher up 8-10 cm long by *c.* 1 cm wide. The 2-5, occasionally up to 7, flowers open in the second half of June and are tubular campanulate. Under natural conditions the colour is pale yellow slightly pinkish with cinnamon-red spotting. The outer tepals are 10 cm long by up to 2 cm wide and the inner tepals are slightly wider. The anthers are bright yellow and the pollen rusty yellow. The flowers are pleasantly scented of night violet, *Hesperis matronalis*.

Growing conditions and cultivation may be expected to be similar to *L. monadelphum*.

Apparently pollen of this lily readily fertilises Michurin's *L.* 'Fialkovaya' which is normally sterile. 'Fialkovaya' is given as *L. szovitsianum* × *L. maculatum*. It has been suggested that it was this lily that Michurin obtained as the maternal parent, and not in fact *L. szovitsianum*.

L. langkongense Franchet

This handsome pink lily, one of the group of large turkscap-flowered species of China, has been known for nearly 100 years, for Delavay collected it in 1886 at Langkung now named Erhyuan which is 32 km north of Lake Tali (Erh Hai). Later it was found by a number of collectors to the north and west of Likiang and Kingdon-Ward found it further west again in the Kong Tö valley of Zayul. To sum up this is sub-alpine and alpine N.W. Yunnan, S.E. Tibet and possibly a corner of W. Szechwan at altitudes to above 3000 m. This is a relatively small distribution and not uncommon in this remarkable terrain of the Salween-Mekong-Yangtze Divides. No doubt the species could be growing in parts yet unseen by collectors. It was originally confused with *L. duchartrei* which Delavay had also collected the same day. Because of this, interest was put back many years which was a great pity, as it is a lovely species like its neighbour, *L. wardii*. Not being too easy to please it plays a small part and has only a fragile existence in our gardens in southern England, but seed is offered from time to time and it should be tried.

The seed gives immediate epigeal germination. The white bulb turning pinkish on exposure is ovoid up to 4 cm across with firmly imbricated, ovate-lanceolate scales. The stoloniform stem runs below ground and rises erect and rigid to 1.2 m, being slightly ribbed, and carrying numerous scattered, oblong-lanceolate leaves, more crowded at the base, up to 10 cm long and 1 cm wide. The racemose inflorescence may carry up to 15 scented, pendent, turkscap flowers (on long ascending pedicels) of a pale pink or rose sometimes tinged with mauve, spotted crimson-purple, nectary conspicuously green. The tepals are up to 7 cm long, 2 cm wide with the stamens shorter; anthers yellow-purple, pollen bright orange. The curving style projects beyond the anthers and has a small slightly lobed greenish purple stigma. Flowering is in July.

Cultivation has proved a problem to many of us while a few lucky ones, mainly in the north of Britain, have found it fairly easy. A cause of the problem is often virus disease to which it is most susceptible, though not being killed outright, but from which it degenerates. Clean stock and isolation from possible carriers is therefore essential. It is lime-tolerant, but a loose friable soil with much humus is obviously to the liking of a plant that sends its stem about giving a bonus of bulblets. An open exposure would be best except where conditions are too hot when continuous light shade is preferable.

Following embryo culture of the resulting seeds from crosses with *L. davidii*, Dr North has been able to introduce many excellent hybrids, in which the contribution of *L. langkongense* has been outstanding, bringing scent, a unique colour range, but no seeming susceptibility to virus disease. May it be that with some the sterility problems will be overcome and others may continue this handsome race.

L. ledebourii (Baker) Boissier

This lily was recognised as far back as 1831 by Meyer after collecting it in the woods of Talysh. In 1875 Baker separated it as a variety of *L. monadelphum* and Boissier as an independent species in 1889. In recent years it has achieved new fame as the only lily growing in Iran. In 1969 at the Lily Conference Furse, with more than a glint in his eye, on the subject of Caucasian lilies, said 'the story may not be finished; perhaps there will still be lilies found in the Iranian forests around the Caspian!' He was right, for in 1972 Mrs Ann Ala, having been shown a photograph of a lily found growing in the Elburz Mountains, visited the area with a small party and found a few lilies growing like hedgerow weeds. The following year in company with Tom and Richard Hewer many more lilies were found, but still in a very restricted area. The possibility which had dwelt in a number of minds for many years had come true.

In the Talysh Mountains in Azerbaijan this species grows at altitudes between 1000 and 1500 m in oak and hornbeam forests and clearings. In Iran some 320 km to the south-east it grows on the northern slopes of the Elburz Mountains at 1600 m amongst blackberry, berberis, hawthorn and other shrubby scrub and bracken where grazing is difficult.

The seed set is good when self-pollinated. Germination is hypogeal and delayed through a cold period before the first true leaf shows above ground. The bulb is broadly ovoid 11 cm tall by 7-9 cm wide, the outer scales white turning yellowish on exposure. There are stem roots and the stem is 1 to 1.2 m high glabrous, slightly rough. Leaves are fairly dense scattered or spirally arranged. The lowest are broadly linear 11-12 cm long by 2 cm wide 5-veined, the other leaves are narrow linear with the smallest at the top. Eremin stated the inflorescence contained 1-3 flowers. More are seen in cultivation and Mrs Ala saw 15 on a wild Iranian plant. The colour is pale yellowish white with dark purple dots in the middle of the tepals, which are 6.5-7 cm long, 1.3 cm wide rapidly narrowing towards the base. The segments are recurved to a greater extent (?) than *L. monadelphum* from about the middle of their length. The pollen is bright orange-red. The flowers, which are sweetly and pleasantly scented, open in May and June from the Talysh area, but the Iranian lilies are still flowering in July. Seed capsules are 4 cm long, 2 cm wide containing 250 seeds. Bulbs mature in 4 to 5 years from sowing under Russian conditions.

Cultivation follows that for the other Caucasian lilies. The bulbs are long-lived and may be expected to succeed in a variety of soils given some light shade. Eremin considered this lily one of the most beautiful so it is deserving of the best treatment we can give it. Unfortunately, the political climate for spreading this species further afield is now very cloudy.

Zalivsky produced hybrid seed with *L. candidum* but due to war the seedlings were lost. It would be wise and beneficial to repeat this cross using Iranian stock.

L. leichtlinii Hooker

This species from eastern Asia is closely related to *L. tigrinum*. The type is the yellow or albino form of *L. leichtlinii maximowiczii* (Regel) Baker which is red-flowered. The story behind this strange situation is that the yellow lily came to light (in front of European eyes) with a consignment of *L. auratum* imported by Veitch from Japan in 1867. It was obviously an exciting find and Hooker named it in honour of Leichtlin. About the same time the red-flowered form came to Europe and was named by Carrière *L. pseudo-tigrinum* and by Regel *L. maximowiczii*. Carrière's name was published the same day as Hooker's, 1 November 1867, but Regel's antedated both by a year if the early date cited is correct. However, when Baker united these names in the *Gardener's Chronicle* in 1871 he chose *L. leichtlinii*. Not surprisingly this situation is not accepted worldwide as is plain to see in the RHS *LYB* 1969 where both Baranova and Shimizu use *L. maximowiczii* Regel.

In Japan this lily is the most common in the country extending from Amami O Shima in the south to Hokkaido in the north. Distribution is from sea level to 2000 m altitude. In Korea it extends along the west side and across the central area of the peninsula. In Soviet territory it is found in Premorie and in Khasan district near Lebeda. It is also reported to grow in north-east China. Wilson reported it growing in Korea between 300 and 600 m among coarse herbs and bushes in black mould alongside streams and ponds, in swampy places and on slopes. Baranova says it grows in river valleys, on hills among grass and bushes, often on humus-rich soil. It should be appreciated that the yellow-flowered type, which emanated from Japan, is rarely if ever seen in the wild and exists in a fragile way in cultivation. Shimizu marks four sites, two in northern and central Honshu, one in Shikoku and the fourth in Hirado Shima in the south-west.

The following is a description fitting var. *maximowiczii*. Seed has immediate epigeal germination. The whitish bulb is broadly ovoid and compact, 4 cm diameter. The stem grows horizontally from the bulb underground 15 cm or more according to conditions, rooting as it bends to break the soil and then rising to 1.5 to 2 m high. The scattered leaves are lanceolate, sharp at the tips, 10-12 cm long by 1.5-2 cm wide. Flowers, commencing in April in the south-western islands of Japan and extending to August in northern mountainous areas, may be 12-15 orange-red, dark maroon spotted, 7-9 cm in diameter. The tepals are strongly recurved. Anthers and pollen reddish brown. Capsule rounded cylindrical 3-4 cm long.

The type var. *leichtlinii*, is very similar though not so strong or tall in build and the tepals are yellow with dark spotting.

Whereas var. *maximowiczii* is reckoned by all to be an easy plant to grow – a rather indistinguished Tiger Lily – *leichtlinii* is commonly said to be one of the most difficult of lilies. This may or may not be true. It has grown well here in the past, if poorly now, but has not died out as others have done. A light humus-rich acid soil with plenty of late spring moisture should suit it well. Also it should be kept healthy. Raising from seed is best, but it seems to be rarely available. It is well worth the trouble.

L. leichtlinii, i.e. the yellow variety, makes a good parent and does not pass on its weaknesses or difficulties, so with its use hybridisers may easily raise strong yellow and pale orange lilies of varying form, depending on the other parent.

L. leucanthum (Baker) Baker

To save a long rigmarole Henry discovered the type of this species in the glens of the Ichang Gorge in Hupeh and sent bulbs to Kew in 1889. The var. *centifolium* (Stapf) Stearn was introduced by Farrer as F 316 from two cottage gardens outside Siku in southern Kansu, where he found two plants in 1914. The type would appear to have been long out of cultivation, but the var. *centifolium* has figured large in lily growers' gardens both as itself and as a parent of many, perhaps most, of the trumpet hybrids we grow and take for granted. Where Farrer's plants emanated from we shall never know, but Dr Griffiths later showed that from a single pod of seed can come plants similar to both the type and the variety. If this is so then *centifolium* may be more truly only a form. But consideration would need to be given to the seedlings raised in the early days of Farrer 316, because there should have been signs of variation and reversion (?) producing shorter stemmed and less highly coloured flowers in some plants. However, with the chance of new introductions we may be able, in the course of time, to solve 'this little problem.

Wilson gave a distribution far wider than the Ichang Gorge of the Yangtze Kiang, stating mountains of western Hupeh, eastern and central Szechwan to the western limits of the Red Basin. If this holds then *L. centifolium* may be found close to the boundary of *L. sargentiae*. Wilson maintained these two were closely allied. The species grows in rocky places among grasses and shrubs being especially partial to cliffs. 'On red-sandstone cliffs in the Red Basin I have often seen it thrust at right angles from niches in the vertical walls of rock.'

The type grew to little over 1 m high with a smooth green stem, having numerous 3-veined leaves 10 cm long. The 3-5 large trumpet flowers were milky white, tinged pale yellow inside on the lower half and having a narrow greenish band down the outside of each segment. The var. *chloraster* (Baker) Wilson from Hupeh may be considered as within this description but that the trumpet is more open and the green on the keel is also on the inside of the tepal.

The var. *centifolium* may be described as follows. The seed, up to 1 cm long, gives immediate epigeal germination. The yellow-brown to reddish brown bulb is globose to 7 cm across with thick, imbricated ovate scales. The rooting, somewhat glaucous stem rises directly to 2 m or even exceptionally 3 m high clothed with numerous, scattered, glabrous, dark green, 3-veined, linear leaves up to 25 cm long by 1.8 cm wide. The racemose inflorescence in cultivation may have 15 or so fragrant trumpet-shaped flowers slightly pendulous white inside with a pale yellow throat. Outside there is a suffusion of green and purple with a rose-purple keel. The tepals recurve at the tips and are 17 cm long. Anthers and pollen are red-brown. Filaments and style are densely pubescent in their lower half. Stigma is purplish. Seed capsule is oblong 6 cm long by 2.5 cm across. Non- and weakly-flowering plants sometimes have bulbils in the axils of the upper leaves.

Cultivation of this lily is not as easy as one may first imagine. It depends, of course, on where you live. One essential is very sharp drainage, but the big question is, is it likely to prove hardy in colder areas than southern England? This may depend on the state of the ground during the winter – a dryish soil seeming preferable – and the thickness and permanence of snow cover. It certainly has lime-tolerance and comes readily from seeds. Full exposure may be given, so long as the lower stem and roots are shaded.

Reference has already been made to the part played by this lily in creating our modern-day trumpet hybrids; the de Graaff Green Magic, 'Black Dragon', Olympic Hybrids and Pink Perfection all have var. *centifolium* in their blood. In England Darby produced a differing range, including such as 'Air Drop', with similar mixed parentage.

L. longiflorum Thunberg

Commercially this has been the most important lily and possibly it still is. Its many names testify to this, such as Easter Lily, Bermuda Lily, 'Harrisii', etc. At the height of its fashion it was the lily for every wedding bouquet, and as most florists treat all occasions alike, most funeral wreaths! If the majority of people do not confuse lilies with Arum Lily, *Zantedeschia æthiopica*, they think of this one, and when they do they go on record as not liking lilies as they remind them too much of funerals! Nevertheless this lily is big business and this species is a beautiful example of the genus.

The ease with which this lily may be forced for flowering suggests its latitude, if not quite its native home. This is the Ryukyu Islands between southern Japan and Taiwan. Okinawa, the main island, lies just between 26° and 27°N. Unlike the related species in Taiwan and Philippines, which mainly, but not exclusively, live in the mountains, this one grows at sea level and has an existence where it is never dormant. It is, of course, a tender plant and few gardeners who grow lilies would think of growing it without some protection. Shimizu says the species is widely distributed in the islands between Kyushu and Okinawa, and suggests its original native home might have been one small island, as in the case of *Ll. alexandrae* and *nobilissimum*. The reason being that it was the custom from olden times for the inhabitants in these areas to plant lilies around graves. There are a number of localities where these lilies seem to be escapes. One may pose the question why the other two species were not moved about in a similar manner, or were they less amenable? Anyway Shimizu has made a reasonable point.

The seed gives immediate epigeal germination. The yellowish bulb is globose or subglobose up to 6 cm across. The rooting stem grows up to 1 m tall and is clothed in numerous, scattered, lanceolate to oblong-lanceolate leaves, 3-5 veined, up to 18 cm long and 1.5 cm wide. The inflorescence may be solitary or more when disposed in an umbel. The fragrant, pure white funnel-shaped flowers are horizontal or slightly ascending. The tepals join into a tube in the basal half, their tips recurve and are up to 18 cm long. The anthers have yellow pollen and the protruding style carries a large greenish tri-lobed stigma. The seed capsule is erect, oblong, up to 7 cm long.

To describe the many varieties in order to define their various differences would be a thankless and no doubt impossible task. In the *International Lily Register* they take up six pages and everyone a white trumpet lily! What may be beneficial would be to mention some of the characteristics of the species and relate them to the varietal names.

Forms have arisen with variegated foliage, one of which is named *albo-marginatum* T. Moore, and, although it describes itself, the bluish green foliage is as distinctive as the white margin. Another is var. *vittatum* in which the leaves are edged with reddish brown and margined with a silvery line. It would be interesting to know whether the latter is still cultivated or has died out. The fashion for seeking out curiosities disappeared for a time, but now seems to be coming back into favour. The true Bermuda Lily has a narrower cylindrical tube to the trumpet with the tips of the tepals more recurved. It is strictly called var. *eximium* (Courtois) Baker but everybody in the trade in Britain has always called it 'Harrisii'. The var. *takeshima* is often known as var. *giganteum* because of its tall stature and floriferousness. From this 'Hollands Glory' was developed with the aid of 'Erabu' and in New Zealand this was further developed and selected, the strain being called 'Dutch Glory'. All this group produce much good seed and may be recommended to amateurs who wish to raise clean healthy stock. Famous names from America include 'Creole', 'Croft', 'Estate', 'Georgia' or 'Georgia Belle', 'Howard', 'Oregon Glory', 'Slocum's Ace' and many more. Selection has been made on the basis of a number of factors, height, number of flowers, their position, quality and ability to withstand bruising, their season and their ease of forcing. Two others which may be mentioned, are var. *insulare* from Japan which, with greater hardiness to recommend it, has flowers more horizontal, and the vigorous var. *nobile* having many large flowers, being more greenish than pure white, and dark green foliage. Lastly, in a class by itself for its size and vigour, while still retaining all the beauty of the species, is the tetraploid 'Tetrabel' developed by the John Innes Horticultural Institute with a bulb from Emsweller at the US Department of Agriculture – a truly international lily venture!

There is an extensive literature on the commercial cultivation and production of this lily and those requiring this information will seek it out. For the amateur an understanding of its more or less continuous life cycle, its tenderness and its susceptibility to disease is what matters. The latter point can be overcome by raising a good variety from seed which takes only one season and keeping this process going as required. Being tempted into taking bulbs of unknown provenance and health is foolhardy and unnecessary. Unlike some of the more tender bulbs this one is very suitable for pot culture. For a variety of purposes, we may over-winter the plants under glass bringing them out for display when frosts have passed. If the conditions are varied then a succession of flowers could be aimed for. As this lily is lime-tolerant special composts of an acid reaction are not required.

Although it has been crossed with *L. formosanum* and *L. philippinense*, the resultant hybrids do not appear to have taken on as important a role as some of the varieties mentioned above.

144

L. lophophorum Franchet

First described as a fritillaria, then as a lily, next as a nomocharis, it is now back as a lily again. Wilson, with a little more courage, would have placed it in a separate genus of its own, but with more wisdom left it to others to play with. It was collected first by Prince Henri d'Orléans in 1890 in W. Szechwan near Kangting, better known in horticultural circles as Tatsien-lu. The elevation was between 2750 and 4000 m. It has also been found in Kansu, N.W. Yunnan and S.E. Tibet where it is a high alpine plant between 4000 and 4600 m. It is said to be close to *L. oxypetalum* from the central Himalayas.

The bulb is from 4-5 cm tall with oblong fleshy scales. The stem measures from 10 to 45 cm high and is clothed in scale-like leaves on the lower part, but in the upper, 5-10 are clustered together and measure up to 10-13 cm long by 2 cm wide. They are ovate to oblong-lanceolate with long points. The terminal flower, rarely 2, is bright yellow, creamy yellow or greenish yellow sometimes red spotted, and would be 10 cm across if properly opened, but is often somewhat lantern-shaped as the tips of the long slender pointed tepals often adhere together. The inner tepals are bearded at the base. The stamens are half the length of the tepals with slender white filaments flattened at the base. The tri-lobed stigma protrudes beyond the anthers. The seed capsule is about 2.5 cm long.

The var. *wardii* from S.E. Tibet has very narrow leaves and narrower tepals.

At one time this species was growing at Edinburgh, but is now not thought to be in cultivation.

L. mackliniae Sealy (Figure 7.6)

The 'Manipur Lily' KW 16008 was discovered by Kingdon-Ward on Sirhoi peak near Ukrhul in Manipur in January 1946, and later named in honour of his wife, formerly Miss Macklin. The altitude is 2550 m, and the soil 'light and full of stones, the kind of soil which scores of meadow herbs find suitable', on this treeless slope, burnt over annually. In summer the climate is 'a perpetual mist bath, warm temperate saturated atmosphere, and 100 inches (254 cm) of rain or thereabouts'. 'In winter soil and air are rather dry – there is little dew; frosts occur every night, but only the surface is frozen, and that quickly thaws by day'. On the windward side of the slope there were single-flowered specimens less than 30 cm high, but on the leeward they were taller with 3 flowers. In really sheltered spots they could be 1.5 m tall bearing 6-7 flowers per stem.

Figure 7.6
L. mackliniae

The seed is darkish or orange-brown, 8 × 7 mm, giving immediate epigeal germination. The bulb is broadly ovoid or obloid up to 6 cm across; the outer yellowish to dull reddish brown scales ovate-lanceolate. The rooting stem rises directly to a height of 20-100 cm, exceptionally to 1.5 m, and is clothed with scattered or towards the apex subverticillate lanceolate-linear or narrowly elliptic-lanceolate leaves up to 6 cm long and 1 cm wide. The racemose inflorescence carries up to 9, exceptionally more, semi-pendulous, campanulate flowers up to 7 cm diameter. The tepals up to 5 cm long are very pale purple inside and purple-rose outside. The stamens are within the bell and the pollen pale yellow. The green style with tri-lobed stigma projects beyond the anthers. The seed capsule is 3 cm tall by 2 cm across.

In the colder temperate regions this lily is most likely not hardy and it would be wise to give some form of protection. Otherwise

146

cultivation must be considered relatively easy in a neutral or acid soil which is well-drained and not going to be over-wet in winter. Although it has full exposure in Manipur full sunlight is masked by cloud or excessive humidity, so it is good for it to have light shade, but this will depend on the garden's climate and latitude. Hailed as an easy plant following its introduction, as with so many others enthusiasm waned when it showed its susceptibility to virus diseases. It was hardly to be expected that a lily species isolated on one mountain in Manipur should be tolerant of such diseases. However, it does not die immediately, but tries to carry on. If not disposed of, it is likely to infect others in this state. Seed is easily produced and is a ready means of healthy propagation, but it would seem to be partially self-sterile, so cross-pollination is recommended for good germination.

No hybrids are recorded. It is said that *L. henrici* may be the most closely allied species; *L. bakerianum* may also have an affinity, so little opportunity has presented itself as yet to the hybridist. Who is going to say that they can improve upon this beautiful lily, a beauty even among its kind?

L. maculatum Thunberg

It has been customary in the West to consider this name as appropriate to a hybrid between *L. dauricum* and *L. concolor* following a paper by Berckmüller in 1927, although the name had been extant since 1794. Stearn revived the name in *Lilies of the World*. Berckmüller fertilised *L. concolor*, a form with vermillion-red flowers sparsely spotted black, tomentose buds and a green stem, with pollen of *L. dauricum*, a red-flowering kind with a creeping stem. He obtained viable seed whereas the reverse cross failed. The results varied in growth, and in form and colour of flower within the limits of what was known as *L. thunbergianum*. One seedling was like var. *bicolor* only densely spotted, two were very near to *biligulatum*, one fairly spotted, the other nearly spotless. Others were dwarf and of an impure red. On these results the conclusion of hybridity was reached. Now it might be said that the variation obtained from this one cross in the experiment supposedly between two species, is too great and suggests the likely hybridity (unlikely in the *L. concolor* used) of the red *L. dauricum*. What was its origin? Could it not have been *L. dauricum* × *L. maculatum*, a garden form or a garden form naturalised? It seems very likely.

In 1960 Shimizu in the NALS *Year Book* showed that by chromosome morphology certain varieties of *L.* × *elegans* could be linked to *L. dauricum* and *L. maculatum*, but there was no evidence of *L. concolor*. He maintained that *L. maculatum* was a distinct species, albeit variable, and that is accepted here. The distribution is limited to Honshu and some small neighbouring islands. (*L. dauricum* is limited to Hokkaido.) There are three types. The first may be distinguished as the Pacific Coast type where it is adapted to shore life with its habitat restricted to sand, rocky cliff or meadow within 50 m of the coast. On the Izu Archipelago, however, it can be found up to 500 m altitude and 2-3 km from the coast. Flowering is late from mid-July into August. *L. wilsonii* is synonymous with this type. The second occupies the west coast and may be called the Japan Sea type. Here the habitat is not so extremely maritime, as the lilies extend further inland and reach up to 1000 m altitude. Flowering is early, starting in late May, and continuing into June. The third type may be referred to as var. *bukozanense* (Honda) Hara which is a rare cliff dweller only found on Mount Buko, north-west of Tokyo, at 600-700 m above sea level.

Seed has immediate epigeal germination. The bulb is white, oblate and has a delicious taste! The stem may be stoloniform for 10 cm or so in sand or on rocks and reaches 20-30 cm, but in meadowland may be 1 m high. The scattered leaves are lanceolate, dark green and lustrous, each having a basal lobe with tiny nipple-shaped protruberances. The upper part of the stem and the buds have a slight hairiness, disappearing before flowering. Flowers 2-3 on rocks or sand, up to 12 in meadows, are erect open-vase shaped usually orange-red covered with dark spots. Occasionally red and yellow variants occur and very rarely unspotted flowers.

The var. *bukozanense* already referred to has orange flowers with more slender and delicate tepals and leaves. As a cliff hanger it has a horizontal to pendent stem, but it turns its flower bud to the vertical to open erect. This characteristic of stem and flower is said to be retained under cultivation.

With the wealth of Asiatic hybrids little interest is shown today in growing this rather easy-going species. On the other hand little authentic material is available in the West and the specialist is wary of treating himself to a mixed bag of old-fashioned hybrid material. Nevertheless var. *bukozanense* is out of the ordinary and var. *flavum* always excites attention for its beauty. Coming after the main season the Pacific Coast types can keep the lily garden colourful without too much difficulty.

Something has already been said about this lily's place as a parent, but the historical conundrums mainly involved the early flowering Japan Sea type with the similarly early flowering *L. dauricum*. It is the later flowerers that are such an advantage, and the writer has been pleased to introduce *Ll.* 'Yoma',

'Rangoon' and 'Martaban', whilst hoping to do more, as even these can be improved. Perhaps others will try and do similar.

L. maritimum Kellogg

The Coast Lily as it may be called is found along the Pacific coast in California from Mendocino County south to San Francisco. Little is known or seen of this lily in or around San Francisco today, but apparently it was once common. This species may be thought of as taking over a position left vacant by *L. occidentale* in the north, or vice versa. Yet the make up of the plant is so different. If you grow the inland species *L. parvum* you cannot help relating these two instead. Purdy wrote 80 years ago that this part of the Californian coast was 'a region of abundant winter rains, brisk winds, and frequent summer fogs'. He thought the lily seldom grew more than 5 km inland.

It is to be found in a dwarf form in the dry sandy barrens, growing finely among the ferns on the forest border in a soil rich with mould, and still better in peat bogs on tussocks and hummocks, the water under rather than around the bulb. Alice Eastwood wrote of it growing at the White Plains of Mendocino. Here are *Pinus contorta*, *Pinus muricata* and *Cupressus pygmaea* (which never become large trees), rhododendrons, squaw-grass (*Xerophyllum tenax*), manzanita (*Arctostaphylos setosissima* and *Schizococcus nummularius*) and Labrador tea (*Ledum columbianum*). Wayne Roderick spoke of the plants at Havens Neck, where on the ridge among trees they were 1.5 m high producing up to 20 short-trumpeted red flowers. Just beyond the belt of twisted *Pinus muricata*, *L. maritimum* is less than 30 cm high with flowers 'just above the short grasses in low wet areas'. 'At the far end of the headland among one group of sand-blasted and wind-sculptured rocks is the gem of all: some tiny *L. maritimum* not over 10 cm high. The plants are so dwarf one has to look closely to see them.'

Seed germinates hypogeally in late autumn in cool conditions and grows away immediately thereafter producing its first true leaf. The shortly rhizomatous white bulb is not branching and so not clump-forming and has tightly massed lanceolate scales some single jointed. The stem arises directly growing from 10 cm to 2 m high according to habitat and carries, if a dwarf or young plant, scattered narrow oblanceolate to linear leaves mainly from the base. If a taller, more vigorous, mature plant some of the leaves may be carried in whorls and be up to 13 cm long, 1.5 cm wide. Dwarf and semi-dwarf plants may carry 1-3, tall vigorous plants 12-20 slightly nodding campanulate flowers, red to reddish orange spotted within deep maroon on long upright pedicels. The tepals are 4 cm long recurving towards the tips paler on the outside and greenish at the base. The stamens are shorter than the tepals and slightly shorter than the style. The pollen is orange-brown.

Seed should be sown before the end of the year and the young seedlings grown on in pots for one or two years, when it is safer to plant them outside in a sandy humus-rich loam with some protection provided by dwarf shrubs and light shade. Too much shade and they will not flower. Young bulbs should be placed about 6-8 cm below the surface and mulched with peaty leaf soil as they get older. Adequate water rather than feeding should be the rule, but their demand for water is not so high, as their natural habitat suggests. Care should be taken against frosts damaging the young growth as the plants grow up early in the spring.

It is surprising but true that the dwarf and dwarfer forms come true to type from seed even though they are cosseted in cultivation and separated only from their taller partners by yards rather than miles.

L. martagon Linnaeus (Figure 7.7)

If any species in the genus is more important than any other, then *L. martagon* may for several reasons be considered the most important. Its range over two continents is greater than any other lily; its spread by naturalising is extensive; its time under cultivation spans hundreds maybe thousands of years; it is the dominant parent in its own category of hybrids running through numerous clones and strains; and its adaptability in the wild has allowed it to exploit and to survive in many and varied circumstances and so achieve this unique position. Synge has written that 'its capability of growing in quite dense shade may have been one of the main factors enabling it to survive and spread over such a large area'. Many monocotyledons have the ability to survive under trees for years using bulb, rhizome, stolon or some device for keeping a reserve food store. Other plants may achieve the same ends, by doing it in a detached manner using seed that remains viable for many many years. Their growth each year is small – not enough to flower, but to keep them going or ticking over – waiting for the day after maybe tens of years when a tree falls or by some means a clearing is made, and the lower plants can reassert themselves and flower again. This situation suits *L. martagon* admirably, having secured the whorled leaves which gives it the ability to secure most efficiently most of the light available.

Flora Europaea gives the following countries where this lily may

Figure 7.7 *L.
martagon*

be found: Portugal, Spain, France and Corsica, Switzerland, Germany, Austria, Italy, Czechoslovakia, Hungary, Yugoslavia, Albania, Greece, Poland, Romania, Bulgaria, Turkey and the USSR in the Baltic, Central, South-western and South-eastern regions. Without looking in more detail this shows a relatively southern distribution as Britain, the low countries and Scandinavia are absent from the list. In the Baltic countries its most northerly site is in Latvia, on a latitude with Moscow and Edinburgh. It is naturalised in Britain, Belgium, Holland, Denmark, Norway, Sweden and Finland. East of the Urals in Asia the lily stretches to 124°E on the River Vilyui and the River Lena. Its most northerly station in Siberia is 68°40′ N on the lower reaches of the River Yenisei. To the south it is found in northern parts of Mongolia, in the Caucasus (known to the Russians as a separate species, *L. caucasicum* Miscz (Grossheim) but not generally accepted elsewhere) and the western area of northern Turkey in Asia.

Over all this vast range it is never far from woodland. Baranova

151

says the lily is met with in forest glades, on the edge of forest among bushes and on herb-covered meadows. Eremin tells of its growing in the Caucasus under the canopy of oak-beech forest, in fern pastures on mountain slopes in the long grass zone, and in dense pure chestnut forests with a 'dead' undergrowth. In western Europe it grows up to 2000 m and a little above, but man has not pushed it to these heights, because it can still be found in modest country not far from towns, villages, cultivation, close to roads and streams. Soils may be acid or alkaline, but rarely extremes of either.

L. martagon varies much throughout its range as might be expected and so it may be better, first, to give a general description of the plant and then to give brief descriptions of subspecies, varieties and forms that the keen gardener may come across or hear about, in order to point out where the differences may occur.

The seed germination is hypogeal and delayed during a cold season before the first true leaves appear above ground level. The bulb is slow to mature taking five years even in cultivation, but is long-lived; it is ovoid 2.5 to 8 cm across with numerous yellow narrowly oblong or lanceolate pointed scales. The stem rises directly rooting at the base, being usually dark or purplish and 1-2 m high. It carries a number of whorls of leaves with sometimes a few scattered; the leaves in whorls of 8-14, oblanceolate up to 16 cm long by 6.5 cm wide usually glabrous rather than hairy. The flowers appearing from June onwards according to situation and season are scented, usually quite strongly, and the scent is thought by many to be unpleasant. They are pendulous turkscap in a tall raceme up to 50 in number on relatively short pedicels making in consequence a tall narrow plant. The colour varies but is often a dingy pink spotted dark purple, but good colour forms do exist and should be allowed to perpetuate. Seed is readily produced and has a high percentage of viability. Many forms would appear to be self-fertile.

The most commonly grown distinct form is var. *album* with creamy white flowers unspotted. Not a hairy plant it has green stems and paler green leaves. It is particularly beautiful in the evening when the scent does not seem objectionable. Another white unspotted form is 'Album Superbum' being presumably an albino of var. *cattaniae*. It is larger-flowered than *album*, hairy in the bud and a very fine plant. The third well-known white form is var. *albiflorum* where the stem is purplish but the flower white spotted pink, and it is what one would expect should one chance upon an albino in a normal European population. One of the most desirable kinds to grow is var. *cattaniae* Visiani (also known as *dalmaticum*). This variety is taller than most having a dark rich vinous-red colour completely unspotted. This was found in Dalmatia by Maria de' Cattani. The other dark-flowered form coming from Yugoslavia and the Balkans and having spots, like the normal *martagon*, is called var. *sanguineo-purpureum* Beck. It has been thought that *cattaniae* was sufficiently distinct to be accorded specific rank on the grounds of colour, broader tepals and being a Mediterranean plant (which is very doubtful), but this has never found favour. To Russian botanists, however, they see their southern turkscap lily as a separate species and call it *L. caucasicum* (Miscz) Grossheim. Cut off from the main stream of *L. martagon* way back in past aeons they see *L. caucasicum* as having developed as a separate entity. This then might be true of *L. martagon* in Asiatic Turkey and in the Balkans, yet there is insufficient morphological evidence to substantiate this theory. *L. caucasicum* comes from around Sukhumi in Abkhazia and the Cis-Caucasian region to the north-west. The leaves are rough-edged otherwise glabrous, elongated obovate sharply narrowing to the base. The stem is 80-150 cm tall rooting at the base. The buds are densely pubescent, the 5-10 flowers opening to lilac-rose with somewhat fused dark red spotting, recurved almost from the base. The anthers are dark purple and the pollen bright brick-red.

Another *L. martagon* variant is found on the forested banks of the western Dwina between Koknese and Plavinas in Latvia and is called var. *daugava* (or *koknese*). The bulb is golden-yellow and the stem anything from 30 cm to over 2 m high, the upper part covered with short sharp hairs and green or reddish speckles. Leaves are up to 5 cm wide covered with short hairs and the undersides having 7-11 veins. Flowers are 3-10 light purple-red with darker spotting. The tepals are up to 4 cm long much recurved with red hairs at the ends and a fringed nectary. The most distinctive point about this lily is that the seeds germinate immediately after sowing and are not delayed as in the type. Another factor is that the lily inhabits limy soil 45-60 cm thick with a dolomitic layer below.

To the east from the Volga to the eastern limits of the species in Siberia the var. *pilosiusculum* Freyn occurs. The stem is shorter, only 30-60 cm high, round, rugged with short hairs, chartreuse, with red speckles. The whorled leaves are elliptical-lanceolate, above which are a few scattered shorter leaves. There are 5-10 pendulous flowers of a wine-coloured purple with darker spotting and covered with web-like hairs. The seed pod has six sharp ribs. It smells of sweat. It inhabits thin coniferous forests and mixed woods, birch groves, stony hillocks and slopes in sub-alpine meadows. In cultivation this lily has grown much taller and had as many as 40 flowers. Baranova has mentioned that many minor variants have been brought to the fore from time to time as might be expected from a lily extending over such a vast area. She mentions var. *orientale* with greyish flowers and dark red spots and one whorl with scattered leaves above and below. A form has been collected with yellow flowers (as was one in Bavaria) covered with hairs and, as might be expected, white-flowered specimens have been found.

Hairiness attracts attention and the var. *hirsutum* has been distinguished since the time of Linnaeus and no doubt earlier. The form is widespread with the stem and undersides of the leaves being hairy. The lily found in the Maritime Alps and named var. *villosum* would probably be best placed here, but of a better substance than many as it has slightly larger richer-coloured flowers.

Others that might be considered include var. *plenum* with double flowers first mentioned in 1676. A flesh-coloured unspotted form, var. *carneum*, came from Austria and was mentioned by Clusius in 1601. A form, var. *alternifolium*, was described in 1916 following the collection in Gehrental in Switzerland of a non-whorled specimen. Another, presumably somewhat similar, was called var. *bucegicum* having been found in the Bucegi Mountains in Romania. This is no doubt a fairly common occurrence.

It should be stated that over the years many martagon lilies have been named either from collected bulbs or raised from seed and selected for their various qualities. Few of these have been offered commercially, but many may have been handed around to other gardeners as their owners thought fit.

L. martagon has been described as an easy-going lily so little needs to be said about its cultivation. A few points, however, may be worthwhile. Most things give of their best when treated well and this species is no exception. Because this species may, if all circumstances are put together, be said to grow anywhere, it does not mean that any one clone will be suited to all gardens. It should be appreciated that some will grow better on some soils and others on another. It will be a question of mineral content, acidity or alkalinity rather than anything else, but season and duration may have a good or bad effect. A specimen from a high altitude may not adapt easily to a climate where winter never comes. Similarly one from a high latitude will be accustomed to a short season of long day-length rather than a long season of moderate day-length and shorter.

L. martagon, though as a long-lived bulb is moderately tolerant, does suffer from disease. It is prone to *botrytis* and should be treated accordingly. It is also, in the writer's knowledge, the only lily together with a hybrid, to show broken colour in the flower reminiscent of some tulips. This is caused by mosaic virus and besides being a hazard to all neighbouring lilies causes the gradual demise of the lilies infected. If such as this is found eradication is the only answer. The easy-going lilies must be kept healthy just like any thought more difficult.

Many good hybrids have been blessed with *L. martagon* as a parent. Division II of the accepted horticultural classification is entirely devoted to them. This is not because this species will hybridise with most or many lilies. It will not; in fact, with only very few of its own kind like *L. hansonii*, *L. tsingtauense* and *L. medeoloides* all in their manner distinct martagons, but separate species. The most important crosses in truth remain the original ones: with *L. hansonii* producing the Backhouse Hybrids raised by Mr and Mrs R.O. Backhouse, and the Paisley Strain as it was produced by the Oregon Bulb Farms. Whether the clones as originally named or the seedlings, they are all good lilies. *L.* 'Marhan' is *L.m. album* crossed with *L. hansonii* and will shortly be celebrating its centenary, but are all the lilies possessing this name the same or even seedlings of the original? It is very doubtful as the name seems to be in quite common usage for all these crosses. The *International Lily Register* says the correct name to call all *martagon* × *hansonii* hybrids is *L. dalhansonii*. The name belonged originally to one lily which first flowered in 1890, made with *L.m. dalmaticum* (or should we say *cattaniae*) as the female parent. Over the years the name has been used for any repeat of the cross and for all the hybrids with deep reddish maroon, orange-spotted flowers. In more recent years, especially following the work of E. Robinson in Manitoba, more use has been made of these hybrids, by introducing them to the red upright-flowering *L. tsingtauense*.

L. medeoloides A. Gray

This martagon lily is Kuruma-yuri, the Wheel Lily of Japan. Moto'o Shimizu says there is no alpine plant more sacred. Legend tells it is the most favourite flower of Konohana-Sakuya-Hime, Goddess of Mount Fuji who has a fancy for its pretty flowers as ornamental hairpins. It is also called Kome-yuri, the Rice Lily, and it also has several other vernacular names.

Its distribution in Japan takes in Hokkaido and Honshu south to Mount Odaigahara in Nara Prefecture, but its range is far wider. It is found in Sakhalin on the Kurile island of Kunashiri. Further to the north it grows on Kamchatka reaching 56°N. To the west it is found in an area east from the Bureya River including the middle and lower courses of the Amur River. Apparently it is not in Korea as once reported and this makes its position much further south in Chekiang doubtful. In the USSR it is said to flourish in river valleys along damp slopes in forests, among scrub, in meadows, on damp rich humus soils, less so on rocky ground. In Japan it is seen from 1200-2500 m but further north in Honshu and Hokkaido it comes lower down to 200 m where it inhabits half shady places under trees, otherwise it lives with the other alpines.

Seed has hypogeal germination with delay of a cold period. The bulb is small (2.5 cm) almost round with white narrow-pointed jointed scales – the top of the scale like a grain of polished rice. Many lily bulbs seem fragile but this one does more than most. The rooting stem may be up to 80 cm smooth and cylindrical. The leaves are lanceolate, glabrous 8-10 cm long by 1-2 cm wide usually in one whorl at about midway up the stem, rarely with a second whorl and occasional scattered leaves higher up the stem. The scentless flowers, pendulous and recurved like a turkscap, are cinnabar-red spotted with black only 3.5 cm across. The anthers are purplish, the pollen red. There may be 2-10 umbellately-arranged flowers starting to open in early July, but according to provenance and situation this may be delayed even until mid-August.

The Japanese have described the following variants. From Mount Shirouma comes var. *ascendens* Nakai where the pedicel curves like a bow. There is a spotless Wheel Lily from Mount Fuji and that is called forma *immaculatum* Takeda. In Hokkaido, Sakhalin and the Kurile Islands a narrow-leaved variety is to be found (the leaves being 1 cm or less in width) and it is named var. *kurilens* Nakai. There is also a broad-leaved variety from Sakhalin with the leaves 3 cm or more in width and this is var. *obovatum* Fr. et Sav.

Although this lily is very common in parts of its range, the bulb being used as a food source as it is so rich in starch, this must remain the most difficult of the martagon lilies in cultivation. It is by no means impossible, but it does require greater care and careful positioning and even so it does not seem to be long-lived. Propagation would be by seed or scaling. Planting under dappled shade should be in humus-rich acid soil with the nose of the bulb 10 cm or so below ground level. This lily is for those who like to take a little more trouble.

A hybrid called *L. Marmed* was raised by Grove using *L. martagon album*. Given the opportunity this and similar crosses should be made by enthusiasts. The results might easily be seen as broadening the variety of present martagons, while giving gardeners a better and easier Wheel Lily to grow.

L. michauxii Poiret

This is the Carolina Lily, sometimes in the past and rarely even today called by the invalid name of *L. carolinianum* Michaux. Unusual among the eastern American lilies in that it is scented and then only at 21°C (70°F) and over. When at 27°C (80°F) Showalter has described it as having an intense fragrance of delightful quality.

The range of distribution of this interesting species is more southern than the main species of the eastern States. It is found in Florida, Georgia, Alabama, Mississippi, South Carolina, North Carolina and southern Virginia, its most northerly state. It may be seen in many places along the southern half of the Blue Ridge Parkway. It is said to grow from sea level to an elevation of 760 m in the Appalachians. Although it gained the name of Southern Swamp Lily this is a misnomer, as it has a relatively dry habitat, usually a woodland plant, often on hillside slopes where it is well drained, in ravines, in sandy peat, and always well above the waters of small streams.

The seed has hypogeal germination and considering the southern distribution and the evidence of Showalter a well-defined cold period before growth recommences may not be necessary. 'Seed freshly harvested begins to germinate in three weeks at 70°F.' The bulb is stoloniferous somewhat like that of *L. superbum* with short whitish ovate scales. The rooting stem rises to 1 m high and has a number of whorls (3-4) of wavy oblanceolate to obovate rather fleshy leaves up to 12 cm long by 4 cm wide. There are often a few scattered leaves below and above the main whorls. The inflorescence of 1-5 pendulous scented flowers each 10 cm across are held on pedicels at about 45° from the vertical. The orange-red or pale crimson, sometimes orange-yellow tepals, purple spotted yellowish in the throat, are strongly recurved up to 10 cm long, the inner broader than the outer which have sharp ridges along the keel outside. The long spreading slender filaments almost as long as the pistil carry long thin purplish brown anthers with orange-red pollen. The style has a prominent tri-lobed stigma. The seed capsule is oblong, 4 cm long. Flowering time is in late July and August.

The colour of the flowers varies in the wild and Mrs Henry found pink and cream flowers where normally they were red and yellow. She also reported flowers of pure orange, i.e. no red, and one so heavily dark spotted the throat appeared black. *L. fortunofulgidum* is a variant that has recently been named.

157

This species has rarely been seen in cultivation, but that has been mainly due to lack of opportunity rather than difficulty in growing the plants. It might well be thought that it could be far less temperamental than other eastern lilies which inhabit wet areas. Drier, lightly wooded hillsides may be easier to copy in the garden than prairie marshes. An acid sandy loam would seem preferable with sufficient moisture while growth is active. Hardiness would only become a problem where really severe conditions apply. Mrs Henry had no problem at Gladwyne, Pennsylvania, and she referred to the winter temperatures dropping frequently to below 0°F in their native haunts. This would most likely refer to material from the northern part of the range.

It is not difficult to imagine that *L. michauxii* is closely related to *L. superbum*. Some have referred to it as a shorter-stemmed, fewer-flowered kind, but with those flowers larger than in *L. superbum*. Showalter found that *L. michauxii* hybridised not only with *L. superbum* but *L. canadense* and *L. michiganense* as well. He went on to make further crosses with West Coast species. Details of this work is related in the NALS *Year Books*. Others may wish to take up this work, but whether anything is truly to be gained by crossing the Eastern American species amongst themselves is very doubtful.

L. michiganense Farwell

This species, like *L. grayi*, is very closely allied to *L. canadense* and may be thought of as its mid-western counterpart. Because the petals are wholly reflexed, so looking like a turkscap flower it is also likened to *L. superbum*, but here the differences cytologically as well as morphologically are greater.

It has a considerable range from southern Manitoba (doubtfully) and S. Ontario in the north slightly south-easterly through Minnesota, Michigan, Iowa, Wisconsin, Illinois, Indiana, Kansas, Missouri, Kentucky, Oklahoma, Arkansas and Tennessee. In Illinois it is widely distributed across the whole state occurring in the majority of counties where it is said to inhabit moist woodlands and prairies. The type of soil has been described as 'black muck' when growing in marshy areas and alongside ditches, but 'black loam' in somewhat drier conditions.

The seed has hypogeal germination growth above ground being delayed until following a cold season. The bulb is annual formed at the end of a stolon grown out from the mother bulb. It is globose 3 × 3 cm with about 15 thick yellowish white scales. There are long thin white spaghetti-like roots. The stolon may be 6 cm long and 8 mm diameter with a few sparse scales. The

reduced to varietal status as var. *neilgherrense* (Wight) Hara.

The amount of yellow colouring in the trumpet varies much, some being almost entirely yellow. These have been named var. *flavum*.

With a lack of hardiness and an exaggerated wandering stem there are bound to be cultivation difficulties for most of us should we have the opportunity to grow this most beautiful of lilies. A house is required which gives the moderate temperature, and also the summer humidity of an Indian hill-station. It would be best in open beds with an acid peaty soil very freely mixed with stony material to ensure adequate aeration and perfect drainage. Otherwise boxes or tubs with extra good drainage would be far better than pots, which are really the wrong shape.

L. nepalense D. Don (Figure 7.8)

As Nepal was a closed country for many years little was truly known about this species for some long time following its discovery by Wallich early in the nineteenth century. It was not then introduced and, unfortunately, became confused with *L. primulinum burmanicum* a matter which took much unravelling. It was as late as 1927 when it was at last introduced to flower in 1929. It has been collected many times in recent years and become a well-known lily at least by name, if not from growing in our gardens.

Its range of distribution begins in the central Himalayas around Naini Tal and Almora in Uttar Pradesh, goes through the whole of Nepal, misses out Sikkim and the Chumbi valley of Tibet but is found again throughout most of Bhutan and infrequently in Assam. As for habitat and altitude in the Langtang valley in Nepal it is found between 2100 and 2750 m. Polunin saw it on 'dryish grassy slopes in the vicinity of bushes but not in deep shade'. In western Nepal Williams gave it a preference for east-facing slopes and extended the altitude to 3050 m. Templer on the Milke Danda in east Nepal saw it on steep grassy slopes facing east. If anything in Bhutan it can be seen at lower altitudes even down to 1830 m, but again it is growing on very steep slopes, and it is the same in Assam at about 2100 m.

The narrowly-winged pale brown seed gives immediate epigeal germination. The white bulb, normally marked with purplish red, is globose, becoming oblate up to 9 cm across with ovate-lanceolate scales. The stem is normally stoloniform wandering underground for up to 50 cm, rooting as it goes and producing stem bulblets before it emerges to rise up to 90 cm high. The scattered or alternate leaves clothe the whole stem, but are short and sparse at the base increasing in length and in number in the

Figure 7.8 *L.
nepalense*

upper part; the largest being 14 cm long by 3 cm wide, 5-veined, lanceolate to oblong-lanceolate. The large, slightly pendulous, funnel-shaped, 1-3 flowers are very striking, being greenish yellow, though somewhat variable in hue, with a large mass of claret-purple within the funnel. The tepals, recurving slightly at the tips, are strongly ribbed and transversely corrugated, some 15 cm long. The stigma and filaments are green, the purplish anthers having orange-brown pollen. Flowering is in May to July, according to conditions, with a slight unpleasant scent at night.

The var. *concolor* Cotton has no claret-purple colouring in the throat and it has been suggested that this occurs more frequently in the eastern part of the range, but the evidence does not prove this. It is complicated by there being many intermediate forms where the central dark colouring is faint.

The altitude betokens a lack of hardiness. It has, however, survived winters outside in southern England, western Scotland and rarely elsewhere. The bulbs should in any event be planted well down in stony, gritty, humus-filled acid compost, which might be further mulched and covered thickly with leaf litter in winter for added protection. If indoor cultivation is essential, then adequate room must be allowed for the wandering stems. Large wooden boxes with extra good drainage should be suitable. Here breadth rather than depth of compost should be aimed for. While it is easy to raise small bulbs from seeds it is not so easy to grow them on. Adequate moisture is required with sharp drainage; less water and a less open compost will usually induce basal rot of the mother bulb. But do not despair as further attempts can be made by using the current year's bulblet further along the stem.

The large richly-coloured trumpet flowers have seduced many a pollen-bearing lily grower to try crosses with recognised trumpet lilies. These are, however, genetically distant in the genus and it is not believed any true hybrids have resulted.

L. nobilissimum (Makino) Makino

Most of the trumpet lilies hold their flowers horizontally and, although the sticky stigma may be protruding slightly, the pollen-bearing anthers are held inside. This is partly for weather protection as well as for ensuring pollen distribution upon nectar-seeking insects. It all seems very sensible, so why does this lily act differently and point its trumpets to the sky when it lives in a summer rainfall area? Other upright lilies often show clawed bases or at least show some opening at the base, but, although this species does not make a tight tube, it has shown little desire to compromise. Whatever all this means *L. nobilissimum* has still shown it has power to survive if only on one little island to the south of Japan. It lives on Kuchi-no-shima in the Tokara Gunto at 30° 0'N 129° 55'E at the northern end of the Ryukyu archipelago. With such a small distribution this species must be considered a rare lily, but it is even restricted to the cliffs facing Tamoto Bay at the south-western end of the island. Perhaps this cliff-dwelling habitat gives a clue to solving the earlier question, but still at this distance the answer is evasive.

Being rare and similarly so in cultivation is one of the reasons this lily has been confused in the past with *L. alexandrae* another island dweller further south in the archipelago. The main obvious points of difference are the upright flowers and the yellow pollen not reddish brown. There are, of course, others.

The seed 10 × 7 mm semi-round medium brown gives hypogeal germination and, according to Shimizu, in 30-40 days. The creamy-coloured bulb is globose up to 15 cm across. The rooting stem is purplish green (in the wild) or green with bluish 'bloom' (in cultivation), very strong normally up to 60 cm, but to 1.5 m exceptionally. The scattered leaves are 5-7 veined, short-petioled, dark green, lustrous, leathery, up to 12 cm long and 5 cm wide. Bulbils appear in the leaf axils. The very fragrant, vertically disposed flowers are white, funnel-shaped, 15 cm across and 13 cm deep. The stamens are slightly shorter than the pistil and the green anthers yield yellow pollen. The stigma is greenish white. Flowering in the wild is late July-early August.

Any lily grower who had climbed down the sheer cliff on a wistaria vine in order to collect a few bulbils or a seed pod might be excused if he thereafter paid special attention to the drainage of his precious bulbs. What we do pay little regard to in this and other like instances is the constant supply of fresh water and its superlative cleansing effect, doubtless because it is hard to simulate. Instead we water too infrequently and at some time our compost gets too dry for the plant which is thereby weakened. Then some fungoid organisms start the attack, leading to the breakdown of the bulb. This situation applies particularly to the slightly tender subjects kept in pots.

A few have tried crosses with *L. longiflorum* and species of the Oriental group, but there is little success recorded. The best plan might be to use *L. nobilissimum* as a pollen parent on *L. speciosum*, to which it might be more closely related than first thoughts may suggest, and its fertile hybrids.

L. occidentale Purdy

This species is so named as it is the most western of all lilies in America. In fact it may be beaten by a minute by that more ubiquitous Californian lily, *L. pardalinum* at a site near Punta Gorda to the south. It grows in marshy areas in coastal sites from south of Eureka, Humboldt County for a few kilometres northwards and then reappears near the California-Oregon border and may be found northward again along the coast to the Rogue River where it is seen a few kilometres inland along the valley.

Emsweller described how this lily and *L. columbianum* at an Oregon location grew on opposite sides of the road within a hundred yards of one another. The latter was growing in dry ground (September) that could have been boggy in season, but *L. occidentale* was in a low dry bog where the gullies indicated the bulbs were under water during wet months. The bulbs were 8-12 cm down amidst bracken and *Rhododendron occidentale*. Synge saw the species earlier in the flowering season when the marsh was still wet and saw stems rising from the tussocks and not the dampest areas. Lee Harris said in California it was never more than 5 km from salt water. The type locality at Humboldt Bay is in cattle-grazed fields close to the lighthouse.

Having been described at one time as the rarest lily in the world, others may now be under-privileged enough to take this title, but it must be assumed to be very rare. Like all Pacific Coast lilies, it must be considered under very great threat from man's activities and whether this lily and some others will last the century out is very debatable. They cannot be saved by closeting in botanic gardens, because they demand their own wild stations. To the south along the coast *L. maritimum* takes the place of this species. It is another wetlands bulb and thought to be closely related.

The seed gives hypogeal germination in late autumn. The bulb is rhizomatous, not branching nor clump-forming with scales once or twice jointed. The stem rises directly to a height of between 60 cm to 2 m and is clothed in several whorls of linear-lanceolate or lanceolate leaves up to 13 cm long by 1.5 cm wide and a few scattered below the lowest whorl. The racemose inflorescence may have up to 20 pendulous unscented turkscap flowers held on long pedicels and usually rather small for the size of plant, but at times up to 7 cm across. The tepals are crimson with orange towards the base spotted deep maroon, externally green or purplish at the base. The filaments, hardly spreading and slightly shorter than the straight style with small tri-lobed stigma, have purple anthers with orange-red pollen. It is July flowering.

This species enjoys a mild soft climate with plentiful rain, fog and mists and lives in bog conditions except for the dry period of late summer and autumn. Despite what we say of our microclimate, few of us contend with this type of extreme and as gardeners, we know that rarely are they sought by the plants themselves. This species can live happily without this abundant moisture. It should be given a deeply worked site with plenty of rough humus in the acid loam and not be allowed to dry out until late in the season. Hardiness may be a problem. It does grow close to *L. columbianum* but this is a species with a far wider range. Considering its rarity and that it could well produce cultivation problems, this lily is not such a beauty which cannot be far excelled by others. Only the real enthusiast will have to flower this one.

L. oxypetalum (D. Don) Baker

This is a choice Himalayan species that is at times confused with
L. nanum, perhaps because they are both dwarf lilies and in the
western and central Himalayas cover the same area of distribution. They always maintain themselves as separate entities and
there is no report by any collector or gardener of hybrids natural
or otherwise.

Sealy linked var. *insigne* with this species, though it appears to
have the characteristics of a vigorous form of *L. nanum*. Smythe
collected it in batches of seed that he said might be a mixture of
L. oxypetalum and *L. nanum*. Lowndes thought it might be a
new species, and Sealy after seeing material confirmed a new
variety. Mrs Renton said it came absolutely true from seed and
that *L. oxypetalum* took longer to germinate and longer to
mature. These are further points besides the obvious morphological characteristics.

The range of distribution of *L. oxypetalum* is from Himachal
Pradesh, slightly south of east along the Himalayas into western
Nepal at an elevation varying between 3000 and 4000 m. Its
habitat is similar to that of *L. nanum* except that Williams in
western Nepal found it liked more open ground rather than the
cover of dwarf shrubs. This differing habit may be difficult to
assess where there is much grazing. Presumably there would be
no *L. oxypetalum*!

Wilkie recognised that this lily has a near ally in *L.
lophophorum* further to the east. This species has fewer leaves
and long tapering perianth segments which at times stay united
at the tips.

The seed is pale brown, winged, 9×7 mm and gives
immediate epigeal germination. The bulb is up to 5 cm tall and
loosely set with lance-shaped scales up to 1 cm wide. The stem
arises directly to between 20 and 30 cm high and is clothed with
15-25 narrowly elliptic leaves from 3.8 to 7.5 cm long and
1.25 cm wide with topmost tending to form a whorl below the
terminal flower. This solitary flower (very rarely two) is held
almost at right angles to the stem and is a shade of yellow with
purple markings at the base, the tepals being narrowly ovate and
narrowing quickly to a point. The filaments are slender about
2.5 cm long with versatile anthers. The curving style with tri-
lobed stigma projects beyond the stamens. The seed capsule is
oblong about 3 cm long.

The var. *insigne* has already been mentioned and under *L.
nanum*, but with its linear leaves overtopping the flower which is
pinky-purple and pendulous, it is obviously quite distinct from
this species.

This lily has been superbly cultivated in Scotland over many years. It is justly appreciated, fitting happily into the northern environment, as it does into the sub-alpine Himalayas. In hotter and drier atmospheres it will require some shade and a little more attention. It is easily raised from seed, but the young bulbs only grow slowly to maturity, taking four, five or even more years, according to circumstances, so a quiet corner for them to take their own time while needing little attention is what is required.

L. papilliferum Franchet

But for the enthusiasm and energy of Dr Rock, who organised the collection of a wide variety of western Chinese lilies and their complex shipment from Likiang in 1948 under the most trying circumstances, this species would certainly not be in cultivation today. Not that it is at all plentiful, far from it, it has the most tenuous hold and it says much for the few gardeners who have kept it going. It is another species originally collected by Delavay in 1888; this at Tapin-tze in north-west Yunnan. It would appear to have a limited distribution and to be uncommon in its own area. Forrest collected it only three times in the Mekong-Yangtze and Mekong-Salween Divides. He said it grew in dry situations on the ledges of cliffs and in open stony pastures between latitudes 27° 40'N and 28° 10'N at about 3000 m. Rock's collection was on the west side of the Likiang snow range on (? magnesium) limestone cliffs at nearly 3900 m.

The seed gives immediate epigeal germination. The white bulb is small (2.5 cm across) with ovate and ovate-lanceolate scales. The rooting and stoloniform stem rises to 90 cm, green, heavily mottled and suffused with rose-purple, more or less densely papillose, except at the base. The scattered leaves are fairly numerous linear or linear-oblong 10 cm long and 8 mm wide, the lower being the broadest; occasionally papillose on the veins on the lower surface and papillosely scabrid on the margins. The pleasingly fragrant turkscap flowers, when sufficient in number, are held in a racemose inflorescence with curving pedicels and bracteoles. Their colour is deep purple or crimson-maroon with a central crest of lighter-coloured papillae. The exterior is shaded green. The filaments are flattened, the anthers brown and the pollen yellowish. The style protrudes slightly with a lobed capitate stigma. Seed capsule is obovoid 4 cm long by 2 cm across, furrowed.

This lily is obviously not for all soils and situations otherwise it should have become a little more plentiful rather than remaining extremely rare. It would require the usual very good drainage but plentiful moisture in late rather than early spring. It is a late riser missing the frosts, and should be hardy or sufficiently so with a little extra protection in colder areas. Its growing on limestone in Yunnan does not mean it will prove lime-tolerant on chalky soils.

Dr North apparently had no success with this lily as a parent, but this should not stop others from trying as one or two are doing. May they have good results because *L. papilliferum* has much to add even to a group so diverse as the Asiatic hybrids.

L. paradoxum Stearn

This species from south-eastern Tibet so aptly named, was collected by Tsongpen, on a fruitful but frustrated section of the 1947 Ludlow Sherriff & Elliot expedition. It was the 9th June at 3600 m near Showa Dzong, Pome, lat. 29° 55′N, long. 95° 25′E. (This is very close to the main southerly turn of the Tsangpo when it makes its way through the gorges before emerging in N.E. India to become the Brahmaputra). Stearn said this species connected *Lilium* and *Nomocharis* as redefined by Sealy in 1950 and could with almost equal propriety be placed in either. The operative word is 'almost'. One interesting feature about this lily and there are many, is the whorled and relatively broad leaves. This characteristic is not seen in any Himalayan or western Chinese species and belongs only to the true martagons and most of the American species. It might show that the lily in its early evolvement had the ability to adapt in this manner under certain environmental conditions and these would be those of the woodland or forest. Is this lily a remnant of an early martagon that stayed at home? Or did it gradually make a positive adaptation to its own external surroundings? There is little information to go on.

The small bulb is about 2.5 cm across and has ovate scales. The rooting stem grows to 45 cm high, is naked at the base with above a few scattered sparse leaflets and smaller leaves. In the middle and upper part there are 2-4 whorls bearing up to 8 leaves, elliptic up to 3.5 cm long by 1.5 cm wide on the middle whorls, and oblanceolate up to 3 cm long, 9 mm wide on the upper whorl. There is a solitary terminal flower possibly erect, purple, darker in the centre, unspotted, if naturally outspread, up to 7 cm across. The tepals apparently spreading from the base, are normally narrowly elliptic up to 3.5 cm long, 1.4 cm wide. The 1.6 cm long filaments from a broad base are drawn out to a fine tip. The stamens are shorter than the gynœcium. The style is 1.7 cm long and the capitate stigma 6 mm wide.

This lily awaits introduction.

L. pardalinum Kellogg

This is presumably the best-known American species among gardeners. Its adaptability to many differing conditions has made it so, besides its stately appearance, brilliant and sometimes gaudy flowers. To press the matter further one might say that behind every American hybrid – well, many of them – stands a smug *L. pardalinum* immodestly declaring it is all her own work.

It is a wetland species and belongs mainly to the Coast Ranges, perhaps, having the longest and narrowest distribution of any stretching from the very south of California in San Diego County close to the northern border with Oregon. Some say it is found further north, but then we have to discuss what is *L. pardalinum*? Are they relics of plants distributed by man? More curious would it be to find the species a little further south in Mexico and a yellow-flowered form too. To the east, it is found across the Sacramento Valley particularly on the western side of the Tahoe National Park at elevations up to 1200 m.

Frank Ford talked of this species 'always growing in moisture', but was more precise when he said 'in moist soil along springs or streams'. This referred particularly to those in the south, var. *fragrans*, in the Cuyamaca Mountains. In the Santa Cruz Mountains the habitat is similar. Near Fort Ross it is found 'with its roots in muddy soil at the edge of a small running stream' surrounded by a mass of vegetation, including *Carex*, ferns, skunk cabbage and *Ledum*. Further to the north by the Mattole River many of the plants are but a few inches from the water line, and Emsweller said 'since this was near the end of the dry season, it seems certain that many of the bulbs were under water during the winter and even after growth started in the spring'. Bulbs were found up to 15 cm below the surface in saturated soil. And again south of Snow Camp beside a running stream the bulb was in muddy soil and there was no question it was under considerable water during the winter months. Across country in Bear Valley on a steep slope the bulbs were either under running water or in muddy, marshy soils between 5 and 10 cm below the surface. The var. *giganteum* is found along the Van Duzen river which, according to Beane, can become a raging torrent in the rainy season washing out entire colonies of lilies along its banks. From the same cause bulbs may be buried under 60-90 cm of sand. Giving Purdy the last word, he said: 'It glories in air and sunshine, and where the stream banks are shaded never equals its stature in more exposed places.'

The seed germinates hypogeally in late autumn in cool conditions. The rhizomatous bulb is branching annually and so forming large clumps. The numerous scales are single or double jointed, white, tinged red on exposure. The strong non-rooting stem grows from 1.5 to 2 m high sometimes more, and is clothed with many whorls of linear or lanceolate 3-veined leaves, up to 18 cm long, with a few leaves scattered below and above the whorls. The inflorescence usually racemose, may contain up to 10 normally unscented pendulous turkscap flowers held on long arching pedicels. The strongly recurved tepals up to 9 cm long, are rich crimson towards the tips, and orange-red to orange towards the base with much deep maroon spotting the outermost haloed with orange. The spreading stamens are about equal or slightly shorter than the style with its purple-brown tri-lobed stigma. The reddish brown anthers have orange-brown pollen. Flowering is in July.

There have been a number of varieties named some of which may have vanished over the years. Var. *angustifolium* Kellogg was stated by Kellogg to be common about San Francisco which it is not today. It is said to have had very slender grass-like foliage. Var. *fragrans* Purdy comes from San Diego County and strictly belongs to the red not yellow substitute for *L. warei* found by Purdy's collectors. The fragrant form may still be found in the Cuyamaca Mountains. Var. *giganteum* Woodcock & Coutts is well distributed and well known by various names, such as Sunset Lily, Red Giant and Chinook Lily. It was also named as a separate species, *L. harrisianum* by Beane & Vollmer, but this has not generally found acceptance. It comes from the Van Duzen River. By its extra vigour and growing close to the old stagecoach route it got taken 'home' to many parts of the land particularly into Oregon, Washington and British Columbia. The plants may be 3 m high and carry up to 50 flowers in cultivation more garishly spotted. Var. *luteum* Ware was a yellow form with brownish pollen which has disappeared. This was yellow unspotted and very fragrant. It is strange that this, with *L. warei*, has not reoccurred over the years, or does it tell us that the vast numbers of this species have deteriorated so greatly that the chance of its happening, always rare, has reduced dramatically. Other varieties mentioned by Vollmer included *pallidifolium*, *robinsoni* (another strong grower like *giganteum*), *californicum* and *pulilum*. Purdy introduced a number of named forms from various parts of California. Few of those named and those unnamed have been well enough described to allow for reasonably sure identification. He did describe the form prevalent in the Sierra Nevada as having a pale red outer section and more orange and at a little distance might be thought to be all orange.

Little need be said about cultivation. It has proved itself a much admired and long-lasting lily in many gardens even on alkaline soils. Propagation is the simplest, especially when well suited, for the multiple new growths may be broken away from the old and replanted. If extra numbers are required more often than not the loose scales that break away by accident will produce new little bulblets and grow on to maturity in their pockets of soil. This lily does not demand a great deal, but, of course, if a great deal is demanded of it then it must like any other garden plant be treated well. A light loam full of rich humus and plenty of moisture during the growing season, which, in truth should be as long as we can make it, should help to produce the sturdy 3 m stems crowned with 40-50 flowers. Such tall stems are remarkably sturdy considering that they carry and will suffer, but protection from strong winds should be a priority when siting the plants. Nothing is worse than having to manage these lilies only with the help of stakes. There is nothing wrong with deep planting if the soil and sub-soil is suitable. Other than that lilies of shorter stature should be chosen.

This is the most important parent of the American species and after comes *L. humboldtii* with which were produced the Bellingham Hybrids. 'Shuksan' the greatest of these is now a good 50 years old and still going strong. *L. pardalinum* will with its var. *giganteum* maintain its unique position, not to produce the fancy frilly pieces of the hybrid world, but to provide the stamina so that we can grow and enjoy them.

L. parryi S. Watson (Figure 7.9)

To many lily growers this species is the most beautiful on the American West Coast. The yellow colour is pure and untarnished, the thin trumpet shape held on tall pedicels is very graceful and the exquisite scent is seduction itself were that necessary. It is also one of the most southerly lilies although not alone in this area of southern California as it is also the home of *L. humboldtii* and *L. pardalinum*.

The actual range of distribution is best defined by the mountains it inhabits. It is no lover of the scorched plains, growing as it does from 1800-3000 m altitude. The most northerly site is of the var. *kessleri* Davidson growing just north of Los Angeles in the San Gabriel Mountains. A little to the south and east in the San Bernardino Mountains it was first discovered growing in a potato patch, by Parry, near the San Giorgio Pass. A little further to the south near Palm Springs it is found in the San Jacinto Mountains. South again there are further sites in the Cuyamaca Mountains in San Diego County. Over to the east but

Figure 7.9
L. parryi

still south again in Arizona it is growing in the Santa Rita Mountains and Huachuca Mountains south and south-east of Tucson respectively.

174

In these detached high mountains there is quite a winter snowfall at higher levels. The species inhabits the small streams and, where circumstances still allow, the open meadows. The soil is sandy loam fairly rich in humus. Emsweller, in the San Jacinto Mountains, found them growing along running water, with some in hummocks of grass and other plants on large rocks in the middle of the creek. In the San Bernardino Mountains, Margaret Cruse told how they were 'shaded by enormous pines and with their feet in deep, deep detritus which is always damp from the springs bubbling up in the area'. Native irises grew by the lilies.

The seed germinates hypogeally and is not restricted to the late autumn winter period like many other American West Coast species. This may be due to the lower latitude. The rhizomatous bulb has numerous jointed scales, white turning yellowish with age. The stem rises directly from between 50-180 cm, rarely something more, high, and is clothed in scattered, or with the lower whorled and the higher scattered, narrowly oblanceolate leaves up to 15 cm long. The inflorescence may be solitary or up to 15, but exceptionally many more, scented, funnel-shaped flowers, borne on long ascending pedicels turned sharply at their apices to give a horizontal stance. The tepals up to 10 cm long are lemon or aureolin-yellow usually with slight maroon spotting in the throat, recurving quite strongly towards the tips, the upper more so usually than the lower. The slender filaments carrying versatile anthers with orange or orange-brown pollen are exserted, with the pale green style and brown tri-lobed stigma. Flowering is in July. The seed capsule is narrowly oblong to 5 cm long.

The var. *kessleri* has broader ovate-lanceolate leaves up to 15 cm long, a less narrow trumpet, smaller anthers and more protruding pistil. It may be more vigorous. The difference in the flower is difficult to see!

This lily may not be easy but it is no more difficult than many others. It is one of the wetland bulbs, which are generally less fussy than the dry from this part of the world. It is troublesome in a humid atmosphere, as the foliage is suited to a dry climate, and can readily collapse. Likewise can the buds, flowers or even stems be hit and crippled by resulting fungal attacks. An open situation with a free flowing air supply should be aimed for, allowing for light shade, preferably from well above. Culture under glass may be the answer in some gardens especially in very cold ones. Ron Beckwith has been very successful in this way with the species in Massachusetts. Propagation from seed is very easy as it will germinate in the spring and grow away without any intervening cold period. Plant out in humus-rich acid sandy loam – the wetland bulbs favour humus, the dryland bulbs tend to dislike it – devising if possible an easy means of watering the bulbs or, better, the roots of the bulbs until flowering is over.

It almost goes without saying that this lovely lily with its fine scent is one of the most important in creating Pacific Coast hybrids. It introduces a clear yellow unmarred by deeper orange pigments, is not too strongly spotted and sometimes spotless and has a distinctive flower shape, large and horizontal. On the debit side very few of the hybrids that have been created have lasted long after their beauty has been extolled. The reason may well be susceptibility to virus disease. They may lose vigour and go into demise. What therefore is required is the quality of *L. parryi* with the constitution of *L. pardalinum giganteum* and we must therefore keep working for that. In the meantime we may obtain much enjoyment and excitement with what does come our way.

L. parvum Kellogg (Figure 7.10)

This Californian lily from the Sierra Nevada bears an uncanny resemblance to *L. maritimum*, which rightly lives by the sea. Whatever way botanists may look at them and compare them with other species up and down the land of the West Coast the answer must come out the same, that there is a close relationship between them. As some of *L. parvum* did not decide off their own bat to go down to the sea, across the Sacramento Valley and the Coast Ranges, and as *L. maritimum* obviously did not do the opposite, and as *L. maritimum* would hardly develop by the sea to look like *L. parvum* living in the mountains and vice versa, we may begin to assume that these species, which may have been one species millions of years ago, had their country split by violent upheavals which moved them asunder. This being so natural selection has done very little to or for these lilies in the ensuing years. We must appreciate that with plants like this, that did most of their development so long ago, and have done so little since, many are today unadaptable relics gradually wasting out their time until some other vegetation overrides them, or, before that can happen, man bulldozes them into history. This is a pessimistic view but realistic.

The precise range of distribution is not too easy to define in its northern limits at least. It is as far south as Fresno County and is found along the Sierra Nevada on both sides of the range to Lassen County. Some literature states that it is also found in the Cascades in southern Oregon, but Purdy said 'it is found only in the Sierra Nevada'. It inhabits the regions between 1200 and

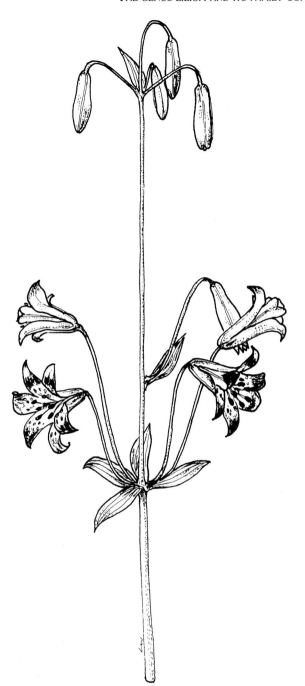

Figure 7.10
L. parvum

3000 m where there are great areas of bare granitic rocks varied by sections of woodland composed of hardy pines and firs of large size. Here and there are moist meadows and alpine lakes.

The finest lilies up to 1.8 m high are in silty loam in thickets of low alders. They are dwarfer at the higher altitudes. 'In tiny meadows about the lakes or in depressions in the granite filled with a deposit of soil looking like a brown peat, but really a leaf mould mingled with granitic sand' they grow in large colonies. Snow lies until June or July and there is plentiful moisture but by the end of the dry season the soil is bone dry. At lower levels the var. *crocatum* Stearn appears; the snowfall is lighter, the soil more loamy with less humus and the plants are tall. Vollmer described how the colour of the lily varied with altitude as follows: 'beginning at an elevation of about 4500 ft (1370 m), it is pure yellow, but as one ascends the mountains it becomes orange, and at the higher elevations it is dark red, and all are spotted maroon.'

The seed germinates hypogeally in late autumn in cool conditions. The small bulb is shortly rhizomatous with white thick, broadly lanceolate, single-jointed scales. The stem grows up to *c*. 1.8 m, but at the highest levels may only be 30 cm. The leaves are single-veined, lanceolate, up to 12.5 cm long, scattered or in whorls or a combination of both. The inflorescence may have a few or up to as many as 25 small companulate flowers generally outward-facing some ascending, others slightly pendulous. The tepals are up to 4 cm long yellow, orange, orange-red or red variably spotted maroon in the sometimes paler throat, recurving only towards the tips. The stamens are shorter than the tepals with pale or deeper orange-brown pollen. The straight style with pale tri-lobed stigma becomes more prominent with the age of the flower. The seed capsule is oblong, about 1.5 cm long. The var. *crocatum* superseding the ambiguous var. *luteum* hort., has clear orange-yellow flowers finely dotted with crimson in the throat.

There is another very fine and distinct lily which may be included here called var. *hallidayi* which is a tall plant with whorled leaves. The flowers are very similar in form to the type, but are basically white in the throat with the apical half or third coloured a rich pink. The throat is strongly spotted and may be seen on the pale exterior and unopened bud, the base of the flower is green. The anthers are deep brown and the stigma is dark. Some may suggest this is a hybrid, in which case with what other parent? The look of such first crosses and their characteristics must be within certain limits and predictable. No, this is normal *L. parvum* of orange-red flower colour, but minus the carotene pigment. It set seed and produced its progeny true to its type, so it would seem to be an isolated community worthy of varietal status.

The cultivation of *L. parvum* does not produce any special problems. It is a wetland bulb inhabiting the wet areas of a 'dry zone' living off snowmelt. Fortunately it does not appear over fastidious about the soil condition as long as it has enough water when required, but plenty of humus or leaf soil may be incorporated. It is less tolerant of damp atmospheric conditions and if such prevail even in good growing days plants may suffer from stem, bud and flower rots, so an open exposed site is preferable to a close one. Having regard to this some light shade would doubtless be beneficial. Propagation from seed and bulb scales is straightforward and may take three years or a little longer.

L. philadelphicum Linnaeus

Under this name will be included *L. umbellatum* Pursh and *L. montanum* A. Nelson to cover the western forms of this lovely lily, which extends over a wider range in North America than any other, and may indeed cover a greater area than any other lily, except *L. martagon*. The question is then asked why should it prove so difficult to maintain in cultivation? It is true only a few growers have kept it going for any time. Most introductions have most likely come from the New England states and some plants from this area are notoriously difficult in cultivation. This cannot be the whole answer, but it is worthwhile attempting kinds from further afield.

Starting in the north-east the distribution ranges from Nova Scotia, southern Quebec and Ontario southward through New England and the states east of the Appalachians as far as North Carolina. To the west it will be found across southern Canada into British Columbia as far as Golden, and then, apparently not crossing the Rockies, southward again to New Mexico. Across the mid-west it does not go below a line drawn from Nebraska through southern Illinois to Kentucky.

This species favours drier situations than all its other eastern counterparts. Often it may grow quite close to, say, *L. canadense* but they will each be in their own habitat. Called the Wood Lily, besides many other vernacular names, it will be found under deciduous trees typically on acid sandy loams, and where the forest is mixed with conifers. If the shade becomes too thick it will not flower and presumably like other woodlanders will go into a kind of hibernation or semi-dormancy until the situation improves sufficiently to permit flowering.

The seed, 8 × 7 mm medium brown, gives immediate epigeal germination in warmth. The globular bulb is stoloniferous with the stolon so short it is not immediately obvious, forming annually with white, ovate scales. The erect stem grows to 1 m high and carries a number of whorls of horizontal narrowly elliptic to lanceolate leaves up to 10 cm long by 1.5 cm wide. The fairly wide-spreading erect flowers are solitary or up to 5 when held in an umbel. The tepals are up to 6 cm long, clawed at the base and recurving towards the tips varying from deep yellow to orange-scarlet, usually yellow spotted dark maroon towards the base. The stigma is longer than the slightly spreading stamens carrying anthers with deep red pollen. The seed capsule is oblong, erect, about 2.5 cm high.

Var. *andinum*, the western variety, or *L. umbellatum* Pursh, covering such a large range may itself be quite variable. The type-locality was Mandan, North Dakota. The leaves are scattered up the stem, except for the uppermost group being in a whorl. They are also narrower, linear 2-5 mm wide, but in other areas of the west broader-leaved forms do exist. Plants in the Rockies may be up to 60 cm high and have 3 flowers up to 8 cm across.

The American upright lilies are, perhaps, the most distinguished and beautiful of the group encompassing the northern hemisphere and it would amply repay the gift of learning to cultivate these bulbs consistently in our gardens. Of course, it is far less troublesome to ignore them and just grow a selection of the current 'pops' of the Asiatic hybrids. But that does not get us anywhere and it is less than satifying. First, unlike many other American species, this one is easily and quickly raised from seed. Granted it may sit still a bit after that, but undoubtedly it likes hot summers to grow well. It should have an acid sandy peaty soil for preference and despite its liking for drier situations plenty of moisture in the growing season. Maintaining the mature bulbs once they have flowered initially is undoubtedly the tricky problem. Presumably in nature they are put to sleep fairly rapidly in the fall, and at some stage frozen in reasonably dry soil. Where it is moister and less cold in winter a few gardeners have been successful just by covering the patch with glass or substitute. This may be useful if done early enough. It might be better to lift the bulbs with a little soil, place them in plastic bags and freeze them until spring!

What was an undoubted cross between an American and an Asiatic species was Skinner's *L. × phildauricum* of the early 1930s, which, as the name implies, was a hybrid with *L. dauricum*. There was a range of cultivars varying in colour and if they were not quite so distinguished as the American parent they certainly grew a lot better and easier. Little is heard of them now, because they have obviously fallen by the wayside through one cause or another. It would be good to resuscitate them, might they be found still in health in some quiet corner of a secluded garden. In any case a fresh start should be made and the cross tried again.

L. philippinense Baker

One of the more southerly of lilies, it inhabits mountainous regions of northern Luzon in the Philippines. This is close to the 16th parallel and the elevation is between 1500 and 2150 m. It is a beautiful trumpet lily which is closely allied to the well-known *L. formosanum*. The plants grow on steep slopes or cliffs among grasses and sedges on burned-over ground, and also among pines on gentler slopes. Dr MacDaniels thought the restriction to steep cliffs was the result of destruction of accessible plants by men and animals. In the wild the lilies flower from early July to September during very rainy weather, when 800 mm may fall in a month. In the winter dry season a few frosts may occur at this altitude.

The main differences between this species and *L. formosanum* are that the latter has a shorter flower with more coloration on the outside, slightly broader leaves often with more veins, and a longer ovary and seed capsule.

The seed gives immediate epigeal germination. The white bulb tinged with rose-purple is subglobose about 4 cm across with lanceolate scales. The rooting stem grows to 1 m high but is usually less, especially in the wild. The numerous scattered grass-like linear 3-veined leaves are up to 15 cm long and 4 mm wide. The 1-3, exceptionally up to 6, flowers are very long and a bud may be 25 cm long by 3.8 cm across. They are fragrant, horizontally poised, pure white slightly green tinted and often reddish towards the base, the long tube flaring characteristically to a wide trumpet bell. The tepals are 18-25 cm long and recurve at the tips. The nectary furrow is papillose. The stamens are shorter than the protruding pistil and the pollen is yellow. The slender style terminates with a large lobed stigma.

Cultivation is not for those who demand hardiness. Its proximity to the equator is in no sense matched by high altitude and at 2100 m it must be considered tender. Propagation is simple as it comes readily and quickly from seed and no other means should be necessary. Planting at 12-15 cm depth in well-worked, well-drained, acid soil containing much humus at least near the surface for the stem roots, should produce good stems with adequate moisture available. As the species lives in the clouds at least during much of its growing season, full exposure is most likely detrimental in dry atmospheres, and so light or dappled shade is recommended.

It has been crossed with *L. formosanum* and possibly *L. longiflorum*. But for the hybrid vigour it does not seem that the results produce anything better than these species which are beautiful in themselves and so difficult to improve.

L. pitkinense Beane & Vollmer

This species from California was one of the most recent to be recognised and is one of the rarest lilies in the world. Although it does not appear to be a difficult lily to cultivate, its chance of survival for any long number of years ahead seems remote. Unless some other marshy areas have been overlooked, which seems unlikely now, it comes only from Pitkin marsh, Sonoma County, nearly 100 km north of San Francisco. It is a very small site only 45 × 14 m banked by high thickets of *Rhododendron occidentale*. As Mayell tells us: 'The Russian river enters the Pacific ocean a few miles to the west, frequently floods in early spring and there are some permanent marshes, gradually shrinking as drainage and irrigation take away the waters that formerly fed them.'

Many have judged this lily to be nothing more than a variety of *L. pardalinum* and this may well be found to be correct, but meantime, despite the hullabaloo of finding a new species, we who are a little way from its native haunt must presume that this Pitkin group is unique from the other of *L. pardalinum* growing fairly locally in the same county.

The seed has hypogeal germination occurring in the late autumn in cool conditions. The bulb is rhizomatous unbranching, composed of non-jointed scales and at times throwing out a stolon on which grows a daughter bulb. The slender glabrous stem grows from 1-2 m high and carries 3-veined, linear to narrowly lanceolate leaves either scattered or scattered with 2-3 whorls of 3-6 leaves centrally placed. In the wild the pendulous, unscented flowers, 1-3, are usually umbellate, up to 9 in cultivation are racemose, carried on long arching pedicels, and are scarlet-vermillion from the tips to the middle, becoming yellow in the throat, with small dark purple spots extending for two-thirds from the base. Stamens spreading as long or longer than the style. The anthers are versatile, brown-purple, pollen rust-brown. Flowering is in July.

One variety has been named var. *fiski* said to have salmon-pink flowers. Presumably it is non-existent today, but it shows the species can be variable even amongst so few specimens. There is also a dwarf form which has maintained this condition in cultivation.

Although the opportunity to grow this lily will not present itself to us all due to its rarity, there are no great problems should the occasion arise. The fact that it is a wet land plant growing in bog or marsh need not deter anyone who can give it good garden conditions on acid soil and try to ensure that it does not dry out at least until flowering has commenced. Some light shade is acceptable and the protection afforded by adjacent plants. Propagation is straightforward from seed or scales and if the stoloniferous aspect asserted itself then this is another, though not prolific, means of adding to the stock.

Although nothing shows itself in the *Register* this lily is known to accept pollen from West Coast hybrids and produce fertile seed. More than that it has come forth with at least one particularly good hybrid. This species may not be the most staggering horticulturally, but it could have some good points in a breeding programme, especially if it produced its pink variant again.

L. poilanei Gagnepain

This species has been found in two mountainous areas, one in north-west N. Vietnam (Tonkin) near Chapa and the other in north-west Laos between Muong-het and Muong-seng. Both would be at about 2000 m altitude. This is a southerly distribution in south-east Asia with only *L. primulinum*, to which it is said to be closely allied, being in a lower latitude when it is found in Thailand. It was not described until 1934 and so far as is known, it has not been introduced, though seeds and further information were requested at the time.

The reddish stem grows from 1-1.5 m high and carries scattered lanceolate leaves 10 cm long by up to 15 mm wide. The funnel-shaped flowers with the upper third of the tepals recurved may number 5-6 and be coloured creamy white or pale yellow slightly deeper towards the apex, unspotted, but having a median stripe of turkey red. The anthers are green and the pollen yellow with the style and tri-lobed capitate stigma projecting.

L. polyphyllum D. Don

This species has the most westerly distribution of all lilies from the Indian sub-continent. Its distribution may be said to comprise those lands in the central and western Himalayas between 1800 and 3500 m from close to the western Nepalese border through Uttar Pradesh, Himachal Pradesh, Kashmir, northern Pakistan and eastern Afghanistan to west of longitude 70°E. From such a range it may quite rightly be assumed that at one time there were frequent opportunities to endeavour to establish this fine lily in British gardens. Unfortunately the few successes have not lasted long, though the reasons are difficult to find other than the poor condition of most imported bulbs. In nature these are very deep even 60 cm below ground level at times. It is a woodland lily scorning the sun with a north-west aspect. Lowndes wrote of it in Kulu where it grows in profusion in moist, or wet stony soil in light woodland on hillsides between 2150 and 3050 m. The more northerly and westerly range means that this lily grows in much drier conditions, the rains (which must vary considerably over this long range) occurring mainly after flowering. The depth of the bulb and the long-lived active basal roots ensure sufficient moisture.

The seed is round in area, unwinged, fairly dark, about 7 mm across and gives hypogeal germination in warmth and is then delayed through a cold season. The white-tinged pink bulb is tall and thin up to 7.5 cm high and 2.5 cm wide, with few sharply-pointed scales. The stem in the wild may be over 2 m high and carry 30 or more flowers, but usually would be up to 1.25 m with up to 12 flowers. The leaves are scattered linear to oblong-lanceolate up to 12 cm long by 2 cm wide. The racemose inflorescence has a number of sweetly-scented tubular turkscap flowers with the amount of the recurving of the tepals being variable in different forms as is the colouring and spotting. They may be creamy or ivory white, rarely pink, with many, few or no spots. The spotting being lilac-red or dark red; the tube is usually yellowish green and sometimes there is green streaking on the back. The yellowish anthers have orange pollen and the curving style protrudes with a capitate stigma. The seed capsule is erect, obovoid, up to 4 cm long.

The problem of cultivation is not solved as recent experience has proved! We may read of the experiences of those who have had some success in the various *Year Books* and may when the opportunity arises try to emulate them. One thing not to worry about is hardiness unless your conditions are colder than those reported by Ruth Clas in Albany, New York. The problem then is summer heat, and so shade and a north aspect should be provided. Lowndes reported *botrytis* in a wet season, which sounds logical, so an airy rather than sultry site is wanted. Otherwise one can only recommend really deep planting, where drainage allows this to be feasible, and in soils which are not contaminated with surface fungal diseases. It is suggested these may be the initial cause of tissue infection in bulbs which have little or no inherent defence.

L. pomponium Linnaeus

This is the red turkscap lily from the European Maritime Alps of France and Italy. It inhabits dry limestone crags looking south to the Mediterranean Sea. Having been much collected in the past it is now found only in the more inaccessible sites up to *c.* 1600 m.

Seed has epigeal germination and finely adapted to its environment germinates during cool conditions following autumnal rains. It is self-fertile. The bulb is ovoid, whitish (yellowish on exposure) under 6.5 cm high and wide with scales ovate or ovate-lanceolate. The stem is up to 80 cm high clothed with numerous narrow linear silver-ciliate margined 1-3 veined leaves which are up to 13 cm long and 10 mm wide. The flowers appearing in June may be up to 10, but a good stem would have 6 or 7 pendulous sealing-wax red turkscaps, purple-green at the base and with minute speckled raised purple dots and lines. They are 5 cm diameter with the outer ovate-lanceolate sepals being a little broader than the inner. The style and stamens are of about equal length with anthers 6-9 mm long and orange-red pollen. The seed pod is up to 3 cm long by 2.3 cm diameter when dry.

Cultivation is not difficult. Although seemingly confined to limestone areas in the wild, it accepts acid soils under garden conditions. The main requirement is an open, preferably hot, situation close to its natural habitat where it is seen amongst boxwood, brooms and lavender species. Some authors suggest it may be grown rapidly from seed, maturing in under two years, but this seems doubtful, although alkaline conditions would more likely promote better and quicker growth than acid composts. Despite the Mediterranean aspect of this lily it is considered reasonably hardy especially where snow cover may be assured.

Little use has been made in hybridising this lily with others to which it is closely allied, such attempts that have been made giving unexciting results. If, however, this lily is more akin to *L. chalcedonicum* than *L. carniolicum*, and certain features suggest this is possible, then a cross with *L. candidum* might yield something of great interest.

L. ponticum K. Koch

Its name and that of its synonym *L. georgicum* Mandenova tell us where this species may be found. To be more precise it comes from the Trabzon and Rize districts in N.E. Turkey and the Kasbek district of Georgia. The var. *artvinense* comes from the Artvin district in Turkey a little further east from Rize. The type may be found between 1800 and 2400 m in rich sub-alpine meadows usually above the tree line but often in shady situations. *Artvinense* on the other hand is always in shade in spruce forest or dense rhododendron scrub between 1500 and 1800 m. Both are on igneous rock.

Although described originally in 1849 this species is little known, seemingly forgotten until the 1930s when Balls confused it, or more correctly himself, with *LL. monadelphum* and *szovitsianum*. In 1941 Mandenova ignored Koch and named *L. georgicum*. Following the Furse and Synge expeditions in the early 1960s the position of this lily was cleared up together with that of the related species *L. ciliatum*. It mostly resembles lilies in the *carniolicum* group and particularly *L. pyrenaicum*.

Seed gives epigeal germination in spring but is usually delayed. The small bulb is conical 3-5 cm across with relatively few scales; it lies about 10 cm below ground. The rooting stem grows 30-75 cm high and has spirally arranged acutely elliptic to narrowly lanceolate leaves 33-82 mm long by 8-20 mm wide shortly setulose on the margins and the veins below. The flowers normally 1-5 but possibly 12 are turkscap, butter-yellow or deep orange, with reddish brown to chocolate spotting in the centre. The tepals are 34-45 mm long and 7-9 mm wide with the apex papillose and the base, hidden by the recoiling, purplish. The filaments are 20-26 mm long, the style 11-16 mm long and the pollen is orange to reddish orange. The scent is strong reminiscent of *L. pyrenaicum*. Flowering June-July.

In var. *artvinense* (Miscz) Davis & Henderson the flowers are fewer, only 1-3, usually tawny orange with the tepals 5-6.5 mm wide. The median leaves are lanceolate to narrowly lanceolate with a length:breadth ratio of 5:7.5 (in the type it is 3:5.5). The plant is more slender and more sparsely leaved. Flowering starts earlier in May carrying on to July.

To a limited extent cultivation has been possible since the introductions of Furse and Synge, but although it has not proved particularly difficult, at least on acid soils, this lily has not raised the enthusiasm of growers and so little material in the way of bulbs or fresh seeds is available. Enthusiasts should try to reverse this situation because it deserves better than being ignored and forgotten. Furse said that scales produce bulblets very easily.

Dr North produced hybrids both with *L. pyrenaicum* and *L. szovitsianum* using embryo culture. An interesting illustration of a fasciated stem of the cross with *L. pyrenaicum* was published in 'Lilies 1974 and other *Liliaceae*', but the overall results will not send pollen dabbers dabbing.

L. primulinum Baker

Fortunately today we do not have to trouble ourselves with the nomenclatural problems that beset this species for many years. Much of it was due to an insufficient knowledge at the time of *L. nepalense*. It is clearly set out in Woodcock & Stearn's *Lilies of the World*. Many gardeners will think this species as nowhere near hardy for them, but it will suit others, and the range of the varieties is so great as to provide many forms. It also covers an area of greatly varying climate and were it possible, we could all choose types according to our needs. Alas, this is not so! Pre-1939 many bulbs came in via Burma, but that happens no longer. A few come into cultivation, and usually from the warmer areas, collected by travellers and explorer-holiday makers!

The range of distribution in the north extends along the Burmese frontiers with India and Tibet and into N.W. Yunnan where moving south and east it is found again in the Likiang and Tali ranges and then across Yunnan easterly and into Kweichow. In the south of Yunnan it is found around Mengtsz and then far to the south-west around Chiang Mai in Thailand from which point a line may be drawn to the north to include the Shan State, the Tengchung section of Yunnan and the Shan Hills.

The type of the species is really a form of the var. *burmanicum* in which the purple throat markings are absent. The flowers are of primrose yellow and the filaments are green. This form was found in Upper Burma.

The var. *burmanicum* has large winged seeds which give immediate epigeal germination. The large bulb is broadly ovoid, 9 cm across, cream turning purplish on exposure. The stem is slightly stoloniform and rooting before emerging to a height of 1.5-2.5 m. The alternate glabrous leaves are sessile or sub-sessile, tri-veined, lanceolate up to 15 cm long by 4 cm wide. The inflorescence of 2-7 fragrant pendulous flowers are yellow conspicuously purple blotched in the throat. The tepals are strongly recurved up to 14 cm long and 4.5 cm wide. The filaments are purplish, anthers dark purple and pollen rusty brown. The large tri-lobed stigma is purple or green spotted purple. This is the westerly and southerly lush growing variety with the larger flowers on tall stems that must be most spectacular both in the wild and in cultivation. The Farrer & Kingdon-Ward collections in northern Burma came from elevations between 1800 and 2400 m.

The var. *ochraceum* has smaller plants and those collected by Delavay on the Tali range in Yunnan provide the basis for the description, but it covers those collected by Forrest in N.W.

Yunnan, the plants from Kweichow and those in the south around Mengtsz. The bulb is up to 3.5 cm across. The stem is more stoloniform, rises to 1.2 m and is usually brown. The alternate leaves may be oblong-lanceolate, 1-3 veined, up to 10 cm long by 1.3 cm wide. The 2-8 or possibly up to 18 flowers are pendulous, yellow or greenish yellow with a dark vinous throat. The tepals (6.5 cm long) recurve strongly on to themselves, leaving the base visible. Filaments are up to 5 cm long, anthers purplish and pollen orange-brown. *L. tenii* Levéillé collected near Tong-chouan in Yunnan may belong here.

How to discuss cultivation, when in Britain this lily has died out, is a puzzle. At the last Conference fifteen years ago there was not even a passing reference to this species in any form. Its lack of hardiness is a great difficulty should one get over the problem of lack of availability. Obviously var. *ochraceum* is the hardier and some may be as frost-resistant as necessary for the United Kingdom. Var. *burmanicum* would be best on the west coast and in fact did survive many years on the Isle of Arran. New Zealand and Australia should in places be able to grow them well. Good acid loam with plenty of humus, excellent drainage and light shade, in fact, basic lily culture should suit them well. They come easily from seed, but cannot stand up to virus disease.

There is no knowledge of any hybrids extant.

L. pumilum De Candolle

This is a very attractive and well-known species which is commonly called *L. tenuifolium* Fischer. It is called short-lived and this is reasonably true, but death of the bulb does not usually occur unless the plant has produced much seed that season. Closely related are the other small Asiatic turkscaps, *Ll. cernuum, callosum* and *fargesii*.

The distribution is widely spread in eastern Asia. In the USSR it is found from the banks of the Yenisei River in the west to the coastal regions of south-east Premorie on the Sea of Japan. It is in North Korea and Wilson collected it near the Yalu River. It is also in central South Korea. To the north-west it is found in north-east China and Mongolia. Coming south it is in the hills around Peking and in the province of Shansi, Shensi and Kansu. As Baronova says it grows exclusively in mountainous country and their foothills. It prefers the dry, open, stony southern slopes, even screes and precipices. It may sometimes be found in forest or rarely meadows.

The seed gives immediate epigeal germination. The white bulb with 5-8 firmly imbricated broad scales is conical 4 cm tall by

2.5 cm across. The rooting stem rises direct and may be 80 cm high, but usually less. Normally green, sometimes purplish it carries numerous, especially towards the centre of the stem, linear leaves up to 8 cm long and 5 mm wide. The racemose inflorescence holds up to 7, or exceptionally to over 20, slightly scented, bright scarlet, unspotted, turkscap flowers of 5 cm diameter. Anthers and pollen are scarlet. The capitate stigma is often lobed. The seed capsule is oblong ovoid up to 3 cm long.

Wilson mentions var. *flore-albo* hort. a white-flowered form said to have been in cultivation in Germany. He thought it a doubtful plant, but Baranova has referred to yellow- and white-flowered specimens found in the southern regions of the Krasnoyarsk area. She also mentions the collection of particularly dwarf plants (7-20 cm high) with narrow, almost hair-like leaves and one or two quite large flowers in the Transbaikal district. Another form is 'Golden Gleam' which originally was said to be a cross with *L. martagon album*. This is most unlikely and is now discounted. At nearly 1 m tall it has pure golden-yellow flowers. How was it propagated? By scales, perhaps, originally, or was it a pure breeding form coming true from seed? More recently it has been criticised for not being the real thing, so might it not now be an intermediate with the type and not 'Golden Gleam' at all. Here *L. chrysanthum* Nakai & Maekawa should be mentioned. This yellow-flowered lily (found by Saito in the north-east of the Korean peninsula), is considered only a form of *L. pumilum*. 'Golden Gleam' may have originated in the same area, as the two are certainly very close.

The cultivation of this bright and charming lily is easy. It comes readily and quickly from seed, when as a small bulb it may be transferred to an open site. The soil should be open and light with much grit and sand added as required. Lots of moisture is needed in the growing season, but otherwise the soil texture should be of the dry kind. Companion plants may be of smaller stature and not too vigorous. To maintain a supply of new bulbs, sowing some seed every spring is a good policy.

Having discounted one possible hybrid, there are doubts about another. This is 'Red Star' which is given as a cross with *L. concolor*, a most likely possibility. This has scarlet outward-facing flowers but apparently breeds true generation after generation, not splitting up into *pumilum* kinds and *concolor* kinds. One could understand it being a *pumilum* or *concolor* freak, but it does not fit as being either of these.

This species should be used more as a parent, as has been the related *L. cernuum*.

L. pyi Léveillé

This is another Chinese lily which has not been introduced. What is known about it may be doubtfully authentic as, according to Wilson, no herbarium specimen can be traced. Jean Py collected the plant in August 1906, at 'Nicou-ko-chan près Pin-tchouan' in Yunnan.

The stem possibly stoloniform rises up to 60 cm. The linear leaves are crowded, except at the base, up to 7 cm long and 0.5 cm wide. The flower is solitary and nodding, concolorous with dark brown spots about the margins. The tepals are recurved gradually narrowing at the base. Stamens and pistil are of equal length almost equalling the tepals.

Léveillé thought this lily was related to *L. concolor* var. *pulchellum* – and that may be as doubtful as the species itself.

L. pyrenaicum Gouan

In many years this lily may be the first to flower in our gardens, being sometimes pushed into second or third place by *L. dauricum* and *L. rubellum*. In southern England it will often flower in late May, so, although not the most handsome lily it extends the season forward. As its name suggests this species inhabits the Pyrenees bordering France and Spain more precisely the eastern section between Eaux-Bonnes and Mont Louis. In addition to the north it is found in woodland in the Department of Tarn. To the west it is found in the Cantabrian Mountains and to the south in Catalonia. The red-flowered form comes from the province of Burgos.

Seed has epigeal germination and is delayed. The bulb is ovoid to almost globose 7 cm tall and broad, with oblong-lanceolate yellowish white scales turning pinkish on exposure. The stem may be 1.3 m tall, but is usually less, clothed with numerous spreading linear-lanceolate 5-7 veined leaves up to 13 cm long by 16 mm wide which are minutely ciliated at the margin. The flowers may be as many as 12, but are often much fewer even on strong-looking stems, and are tightly recurved pendulous turkscaps of a greenish yellow colour, black spotted and streaked towards the base. The tepal segments are 5 cm long. The anthers are brownish but the pollen which is a most distinguishing feature of this lily is described as 'Indian orange'. The scent is strong and is generally considered unpleasant and disagreeable. This is certainly so in a confined garden. It is not uncommon to see flowers without style and stigma and the cause of this is difficult to judge unless it is adverse weather conditions or virus disease; otherwise seed is set readily.

It is said this lily is the easiest in cultivation and few will deny this.

In western Britain it has become naturalised in many hedgerows from south to north and to some it seems a native. This is not to suggest it is common in the wild. Unfortunately it can be the least attractive of our lilies, having a mass of foliage with few small flowers borne on top on rather short pedicels. The scent does not help either. Nevertheless it has its part to play for early flowering and having a welcome place in the wild garden. The variety *rubrum* with orange-red flowers is often in its best or true form a more acceptable plant. The red and yellow varieties crossed together give intermediates that generally produce poor orange tones. Patrick Synge said that var. *rubrum* was rare in English gardens but was seen more often in Scotland. It is in fact well known in East Anglia. Perhaps it performs too early for most lily enthusiasts to be abroad at the time!

As a subject for hybridising this species has proved of little value. Placed as it seems on the edge of the lily world it has almost forgotten its closest relations, which would not necessarily be *L. pomponium*, a species it has earlier been confused with, but *L. carniolicum* in the Balkans and *LL. ponticum* and *ciliatum* in the Caucasus. In the late 1960s and in 1970 Dr Chris North did a lot of work using *L. pyrenaicum* as a female parent. Little fertile seed was produced and the embryos had to be cultured on nutrient mediums. True hybrids were produced in a number of cases with Euro-caucasian species but only crosses with *LL. pomponium*, *szovitsianum* and *chalcedonicum* showed results that might be of interest.

L. regale Wilson (Figure 7.11)

No other lily, except perhaps *L. auratum*, has created so much enthusiasm in the gardening world and beyond as the introduction of this species. It gave a great boost to lily growing which was a little out of favour since it had been found that practically no one could keep *L. auratum* growing for more than a year or two before it fell to the dreaded virus disease. Here at last was a beautiful lily and one for every garden. That still rings true today, but gardening man and woman wanted trumpet lilies of every shade and hue, so *L. regale* has been left behind in the race for more colour; some of these colours are certainly different but not necessarily more beautiful.

In Szechwan in August 1903 Wilson discovered this lily along 'fifty miles of the semi-arid valley of the Min River' between 760 and 1820 m. It appears to grow nowhere else. Many of us in the years since must have considered how and why a lily species isolated in this remote part of Asia may retain the adaptability to be able to grow and prosper in many differing unnatural

Figure 7.11
L. regale

habitats. Not without the gardener's help, however, as it is not becoming naturalised. By our standards it seems to live in a harsh environment 'where the summers are hot and the winters severely cold and where strong winds prevail at all seasons of the year'. In the valley bounded by the steep mountain slopes it grows 'among grasses and low shrubs and in niches on the bare cliffs'. The flowering season is from the last week in May to the first in July.

Seed semi-orbiculate up to 7 mm long gives rapid epigeal germination. The wine-red bulb is broadly ovoid up to 15 cm across, firmly imbricated with ovate-lanceolate scales. The rooting stem arises directly to 1-1.5 m high and is well clothed with scattered single-veined linear leaves up to 12 cm long. The fragrant outward-facing funnel-shaped flowers are yellow in the throat, white in the mouth and a shade of rose-purple without. In the wild there may be 2-6 flowers, but under cultivation this may increase to as many as 30, not necessarily adding to the beauty of the plant. The tepals are up to 15 cm long, recurving at the apex. The filaments are papillose towards the base, bear yellow anthers with golden-yellow pollen. The style and lobed stigma are green. The seed capsule is only slightly ascending, purplish green, cylindric up to 7 cm long and hexagonal 2.5 cm across.

There are a number of varieties, but all have come from selection in one way or another of cultivated stock. The most noticeable difference from the norm is where the outside flower coloration is almost absent. This is called 'Album' and further selections have naturally been made of this form. But it is a point that although *L. regale* is usually very obviously *regale* rarely do two seedlings look and grow exactly alike. On this score selection of seedlings with good characteristics is no bad thing.

Under *L. sargentiae* reference is made to the dominance of this species as a female parent most likely due to apomixis, however, its use as a pollen parent with other Chinese trumpet lilies is undisputed. Nevertheless the premier role in promoting hybrids that might have been envisaged for this species some years ago has never been achieved.

L. rhodopeum Delipavlov

That so late as 1951 such a spectacular plant could still be discovered in Europe seems quite remarkable, but such was the case when Dimiter Delipavlov found this exciting lily in the Rhodope Mountains. Exciting because the flowers are large and beautiful and different to other western European lilies, but also because it has such similarity to the Caucasian lilies like *L. monadelphum*. This species has like many other lilies but a small distribution in the wild and so must of necessity be considered and treated as rare. However, it would be beneficial to the lily world and horticulture in general, even to the species itself, if some fresh seed could be made available. It has grown and flourished in the Munich Botanic Garden and at Schachen above Garmisch and may it still do so.

This lily may be found in meadows suggesting a dryish rather than wet situation at *c.* 1300 m above Sivino, Smoljan district, in the Cepelare region of the eastern Rhodope Mountains, Bulgaria.

The bulb is ovate or rounded-ovate 3.5-4.5 cm long by 2.8-4 cm broad. Scales are linear-lanceolate, white or pale yellow. The smooth stem has a height of 80-100 cm, which is densely clothed in ascending leaves, in overlapping alternate positions, linear to oblong-linear, pointed, with silver hairs on the veins on the lower surfaces and the margins. The flowers 1-2 up to 5 are pendulous, lemon yellow, unspotted, funnel campanulate, the tepals being only partially recurved, 8-14 cm diameter. The stamens are equal in length to the gynœcium or a little longer. The filaments are triangular, the anthers large and scarlet-red and the pollen scarlet. The flowers opening in mid-June are strongly scented and Schacht said it was 'unpleasant as with *L. martagon*'.

Little is known about the cultivation of this rare lily but certain factors might be surmised. Schacht said they grew well both at Munich and Schachen which is at 1875 m altitude. In the wild the grasses included *Cynosurus cristatus*, *Anthoxanthum odoratum*, *Agrostis vulgaris* and *Festuca ovina*, and other flowering plants included *Chamaenerium angustifolium*, *Chrysanthemum leucanthemum*, *Stachys officinalis* and *Geranium sanguineum*.

There is no record of this species being used to create hybrids.

L. rosthornii Diels

Not a great deal is known about this Chinese species. It has been collected only once in August 1891 near Nanchwan in Szechwan and not been introduced to cultivation. Doubts exist as to which other lilies it most resembles, but Franchet's suggestion of *L. papilliferum* seems most reasonable.

The stem rises to 45 cm being stoloniform at the base. The scattered leaves are petiolate linear-oblong up to 10 cm long by 0.8 cm wide prominently single-veined. The racemose inflorescence has showy yellow purple spotted flowers carried on ascending pedicels. The tepals are strongly reflexed, clawed at the base, with numerous raised fleshy papillae on the inner lower third. The nectary furrow is glabrous. The stamens are 6 cm long and the pistil slightly exceeds these.

It would be a very interesting lily if someone can find it again.

L. rubellum Baker

This small trumpet lily, which must be closely related to *L. japonicum* growing further to the south in Japan, occupies a fairly small area in the mountains between Niigata and Sendai in central northern Honshu. Its elevation ranges between 750 and 1850 m and in this region there are heavy winter snows which last from late November until the end of April. This accords with the lily which rises late, then grows and flowers fast. It grows among grass and low shrubs, but at the higher levels will be under conifers and birch and amongst acid-loving ericaceous

194

shrubs of rhododendron and vaccinium. It obviously enjoys a great deal of moisture and in the wild may not seem so fussy about excellent drainage. From winter snowmelt the growing plant moves into warm summer rains. Only in the autumn is the weather dry. Within this same area three other lilies are found: *L. auratum*, *L. leichtlinii maximowiczii* and *L. medeoloides* and the last of these may be seen growing amongst *L. rubellum*.

The seed germination is hypogeal delayed with the initial bulb produced in warm conditions. The white bulb is globose to subglobose about 3 cm across, with lanceolate scales. The rooting stem rises directly to grow to a height between 30 and 80 cm. The rather sparse scattered leaves are petiolate, ovate-lanceolate to oblong-elliptic up to 10 cm long by 3.5 cm wide, 5-7 veined. The very early fragrant flowers up to 6, exceptionally 10, are rose-pink funnel-shaped with a horizontal poise. The tepals are about 7.5 cm long, slightly recurved at the tips and sometimes spotted maroon at the base. The pistil protrudes beyond the stamens, the anthers have orange-yellow pollen. The green style has a large green capitate tri-lobed stigma. The seed capsule is oblong-elipsoid 2.5 cm long.

A white form var. *album* hort. has been known, and thinking of *L. japonicum*, may occur regularly, but it must be very rare as well as beautiful.

This lily should not be difficult to establish especially if it can be given a moist acid soil throughout the summer. A higher water table and more clayey heavier soil conditions may be acceptable. It will take to woodland conditions with half shade. Arising from the ground late it should avoid most late frosts and may accordingly be placed where other early risers could be knocked back. It produces seed well and may be self-fertile, but germination is slow. Growth thereafter is reasonably fast. It is a beauty and distinctive and should be in every suitable lily garden.

The first obvious hybrid cross was with *L. japonicum* and then with the *L. parkmannii* group. To these it gives its particular colour, shape and fragrance, but also the useful attributes of late emergence and particularly dwarfness and early flowering whereby the dimensional range is increased and the flower season extended. Altogether a useful species to know and grow!

L. rubescens S. Watson

This is a beautiful pink Western American species that deserves every benefit that may be bestowed upon it. It has always proved difficult in cultivation, but a few attempts have been well worthwhile, showing that it can be done. It is a lily that has been confused with the type of *L. washingtonianum*, but that should not be a problem for the future. The latter comes from the Sierra Nevada while this species keeps to the Coast Range. Watson gave the area of distribution as Marin County, i.e. immediately north of San Francisco, in the south to Humboldt County in the north. More recent records do not show the plant growing further south than Lake Mendocino and then it stops short at highway 299 between Redding and Eureka. To the north it is then country for *L. washingtonianum purpurascens* and *L. kelloggii*, besides other lilies. It would seem that *L. washingtonianum purpurascens* has been mistaken for *L. rubescens* in the past. Vollmer and his colleagues only found *L. washingtonianum purpurascens* in Josephine County in S. Oregon. Purdy speaks of it as only from the Californian Coast Range.

According to Purdy, it chooses the top of ridges in open timber towards the ocean side. In the hotter interior it is on the northerly slope a little, and grows amongst low shrubbery. It may be in various types of soil, none very rich in humus, in broken down rocks, in sticky clay, in rich loam and in deep alluvial soil wherever it is well drained. Brush fires greatly improve it, cleaning the plants of mildew and pests while giving them more air and light. Emsweller reported that most of the plants were found along the edge of the highway, usually on the high bank side. The bulbs were only covered by *c.* 5 cm of powdery dry soil. Often the other vegetation was sparse. Drainage was considered excellent. A plant 2 m high had 11 flowers.

The seed gives hypogeal germination in cool conditions. The bulb is inclined to be rhizomatous or subrhizomatous, the older scales being retained to one side, so broadly ovoid, 5.5 cm across, with whitish lanceolate scales suffused purple. The stem rises directly up to 2 m high, exceptionally more to 3 m and over and carries whorls of leaves, with a few scattered lower down the stem, lanceolate or oblanceolate up to 12 cm long and 3.5 cm wide. The umbellate, racemose or sub-racemose inflorescence may have up to 30, usually much less, rarely many more, ascending very fragrant flowers, each 10 cm across opening white finely spotted purple, turning rose-purple to purple as they age. The tepals, up to 5 cm long, form a tube along the basal half and then flare widely at the mouth, the tips recurving especially with age. The stamens, slightly shorter than the style with tri-lobed yellow stigma, have yellow pollen. Flowering is in July.

The cultivation of this species remains a problem, like that of the other dryland bulbs just farther to the north *LL. kelloggii, bolanderi* and *washingtonianum purpurascens*. It is the strange mixture of high rainfall, giving way to a very dry period from flowering time through to late autumn, combined with the subtle and somewhat intangible effect of fog and mists, that defeats us. It is possible to keep the bulbs in too dry conditions, but then they fail to increase in growth. If they get too cold in winter then what may be an important slow growing period below ground is halted. This is a most beautiful lily worthy of all the care it demands and it requires someone with a garden providing reasonably suitable conditions to have the patience and an adequate supply of material to expend while working out the details of its culture. Meanwhile the rest of us will just keep trying, hoping for a lucky break.

L. sargentiae Wilson (Plate 10)

This superb trumpet lily is closely allied to the best known of all trumpet lilies, *L. regale*, but it may be found less hardy. Both come from Szechwan in western China. Wilson found the type of the species around the village of Luting-chiao in the valley of the Tung River. It also grows in the valley of the River Ya, a tributary, and in that of the Min River and tributaries further north near Kwanhsien. The elevation varies between 600 and 1650 m. Around Kwanghsien and Mount Omei, Wilson says, heavy summer rains are the rule and winters mild. 'To the west in the valleys the climate is much drier, in some quite arid, and the winters long and cold, and it is there that this lily is seen at its best. It grows amongst rank grasses and scrubby wood growth on granite, slate and mud-shales, where it enjoys good drainage and blossoms in late June and July.'

Seed gives immediate epigeal germination. The broadly ovoid bulb is up to 15 cm across with thick firmly imbricated ovate-lanceolate scales, whitish at the base, old gold on the sides and wine red at the tips. The stout, purplish, rooting stem arises directly and is between 1 and 2 m high. Except for the base, it is clothed with numerous, scattered 3-7 veined, linear-oblong to lanceolate leaves bearing bulbils in the axils. The 2-15 fragrant, funnel-shaped flowers are white within, yellow in the throat and varying shades of rose-purple with green without, up to 18 cm wide. The tepals are up to 15 cm long, slightly recurved. The filaments, papillose towards the base, have purple anthers and brown pollen. The style and stigma are purple. The seed capsule is 5-6 cm long cylindric and furrowed. Flowering is in July, following *L. regale*.

General cultivation does not present any problems but to grow it well certain points should be considered. Unlike *L. regale* it does not like lime and if the summer is wet it is likely to be attacked by *botrytis* and so timely spraying should be carried out. If hardiness is in doubt, and Wilson himself mentioned the unsuitability of the New England climate, then added protection must be sought or the plants grown under glass. When outdoors full exposure with adequate companion planting to shade the roots should be given. Propagation is simple either by seed or bulbils. The former is by far the more preferable, as long as the plants are true and the flowers have not been cross-pollinated by any other lily, because this species is susceptible to mosaic disease. The best way to spread this virus is by distributing the infected bulbils!

This lily is well known as being one of the parents, *L. henryi* being the other, of Debras' famous *L. × aureliense*. This trumpet species has proved more useful than *L. regale* in being behind generations of trumpet hybrids, as, unlike its relation, it is not so fixed in reproducing its own kind.

L. sempervivoideum Léveillé

Père Maire collected this species at Siao-ou-long in Yunnan in 1911 and again in 1912, but it seems it has never been introduced. It grows among rocks and in rocky meadows at about 2550 m. Wilson confused it with *L. amoenum*, thinking the two identical, which they are not. There are useful illustrations of both species in *Lilies of the World*. All writers are together in criticising the ridiculous name given to this lily by Léveillé. It could be a little beauty with its campanulate flower.

The bulb with flattened pointed scales is 3.5 cm long. The rooting stem rises to 15 cm and has numerous narrow, linear single-veined leaves 3.5 cm long by 1-3 mm wide. There may be up to 3 semi-pendulous, bell-shaped white flowers spotted towards the base with reddish purple. The pointed tepals are up to 4 cm long, the filaments 1.6 cm long and the style 2 cm.

L. sherriffiae Stearn

Mrs Sherriff first discovered this species on 23 May 1949, near Lao 80 km to the east of Bumthang in Bhutan. She was very fortunate for she and her companions found the solitary plant which was in flower. Two months later on 22 July Sherriff and Ludlow were at Gortsam 16 km north from Bumthang when they found hundreds of plants in fruit but only one in flower. They were growing at 3600 m where the hillsides were rocky and grassy. In the field note for L.S. & H. 19490 it says, 'Found only in one place, in a very small area, either on open steep grassy hillside in a clearing in Fir and Rhododendron forest, or under trees on very steep banks. Growing among *Fritillaria*,

Polygonatum and *Cotoneaster* sp. Bulbs taken and some last year's seed germinating in the capsule.' Sherriff found it by stopping to put flowers in the press. He did not then know his wife had already discovered it. The species is not known from any other site than these two.

Seed has immediate epigeal germination. Sherriff said the bulbs were white, but Margaret Stones' painting for the Elwes' Supplement shows them, except for the tips, pale gold with reddish brown tinting. The shape is ovoid or narrowly so 2.5 cm high by 2 cm diameter with about a dozen lanceolate or ovate-lanceolate scales. The rooting stem rises directly to a height of 35-90 cm and carries 1 or rarely 2 flowers. The scattered leaves short and sparse in the lower half are narrowly lanceolate-linear and linear towards the top, 3-13 cm long and 3-6 mm wide. The pendent narrowly campanulate flower is dark brown-purple tesselated yellow-gold on the inside. The tepals 5.5 cm long are slightly recurved at the tips, have nectary furrows at the base, the inner ones with cristated margins. The stamens are shorter than the gynoecium, the filaments being slender, pollen golden. The style is narrowly clavate and the stigma tri-lobed.

This lily is unique in being the only one known to have tesselated flowers commonly found in colchicums and fritillarias, and indeed the one growing locally with this species. At first glance it looks like a fritillaria, but its discoverers were not taken in by this mimicry.

This is another plant from the eastern Himalayas which has turned out to be more at home in Scotland. Yet it has been grown in southern England and its fairly swift demise may be due to the greater incidence of diseases and their vectors rather than a dislike of the warmer usually drier conditions. Propagation is relatively easy from seed and a further collection of seed (not bulbs) would be greatly welcomed.

L. souliei Franchet

This little lily has been called a fritillaria and a nomocharis since it was discovered in 1898 by Soulié near Tzeku on the Mekong in N.W. Yunnan. It is also found in S.E. Tibet and N. Assam at elevations between 3000 and 4300 m. Ludlow & Sherriff twice collected it in S.E. Tibet when growing in company with *L. nanum*. It grows amongst grass on open rocky hillsides, open stony and moist meadows and the margins of pine forests and thickets.

The bulb is whitish about 2.5 cm high with loose, narrowly lanceolate scales often tinged purple at the base. The stem is up to 45 cm high but usually less. The scattered leaves are up to

199

6.3 cm long by 1.6 cm wide, lanceolate at the top but broader in the middle of the stem, tapering to a short stalk. The terminal solitary, strongly fragrant pendulous lantern-shaped flower is deep wine-purple. It has also been recorded as deep madder-pink with green patch at base, dark maroon, greenish at extreme base, dark dull brownish red and deep dried blood-red, which amongst these allows for a little variation. The outer tepals are hooded and glossy on the outside, while the inner ones are broader and blunter paler towards the yellowish or greenish base. Stamens are half as long as the perianth with filaments pale green and anthers brownish purple. The style thickens towards the tri-lobed stigma. Seed capsule is globose about 2.5 cm long.

The numerous collections of this curious but attractive dwarf species both before and since the last war (L. & S. 13275 was collected in 1947) have not assured it a place in our gardens. These alpine species from the Himalayas and further east are by no means amenable to cultivation. They seem to hold an independence which endears them to the hearts of mountain trekkers and those who can dream of the vastnesses of the high alpine meadows.

L. speciosum Thunberg

Wilson called this species the most satisfactory of Japanese lilies. That could be thought very dull praise indeed, but some might agree and say we should be thankful that such a beauteous thing should not at the same time be one of the more difficult bulbs in the genus.

But what possessed it to cast its petals back like a turkscap lily? It is not alone in this, because *L. henryi* living in the middle of China does the same thing. If, as one might easily surmise, they originated from trumpet lilies by doing this, they presumably adapted to pollination by large flying insects; some butterfly or large moth, for instance, which would feed on nectar after the summer rains had passed. In no other lilies are the stamens and pistil so flamboyantly exposed. Strange this is that the trumpet species left to us today are so careful about this important matter of protecting their sexual parts. Anyhow, it works for both types.

It has been known to Europeans since the end of the seventeenth century, as Kaempfer had sketched it so well at that time. Thunberg described it in 1794 and von Siebold was able to introduce it in 1830. The Dutch saw good business and wisely propagated it. With all this it seems a little strange that it is not so strongly esteemed in Japan. Indeed it may not be anything like so well known as it only occurs in Japan on the western side of

Kyushu including Koshiki Retto and in southern Shikoku. It is also found in northern Taiwan and in the Chinese province of Kiangsi, where it breaks away from its maritime connection. With this somewhat discontinuous distribution in low northern latitudes it must be doubtfully hardy to many gardeners. Furthermore the very late flowering of some varieties may be a disadvantage to some, but a boon to others wishing to extend their lily season to the extreme limits. It is an excellent florists' flower.

The seed 9 × 6 mm is heavy, thick, dull dark brown and gives delayed hypogeal germination. The yellowish to purple-brown bulb is globose about 10 cm across with thick imbricated lanceolate scales. The strong rooting stem rises directly to 90-150 cm high and is clothed in scattered (obviously alternate in juvenile plants) petioled, 7-9 veined, leathery, broadly lanceolate leaves up to 18 cm long and 6 cm wide. The racemose inflorescence may have a few to 10 fragrant flowers (exceptionally many more up to about 40), up to 15 cm across, usually somewhat pendulous, with the strongly recurved tepals, white, flushed carmine to a varying degree of density and surface area. The frequently wavy-edged tepals are further enhanced by numerous raised papillae spotted crimson and green nectary furrows. The thin outspreading filaments carry narrow versatile anthers with chocolate-red pollen. The protruding slender curving style is capped with a relatively small stigma. The seed capsule is oblong-obovoid 5 cm long.

There are numerous varieties, most of which are concerned with the colour or lack of it in the flowers. The most important are as follows:

Var. *punctatum* Marnock. This has white flowers delicately suffused pink, pink papillae and orange pollen. This may be the kind growing in Shikoku.

Var. *magnificum* hort. Wallace. This comes from Koshiki-jima and is rose-coloured with crimson spots. The pollen is red, the stem purple. Altogether a very good variety.

Var. *gloriosoides* Baker. This represents the species as coming from Kiangsi province in China and Taiwan. We would expect to find some variation between plants from the two areas, but today it is unlikely any authentic material could be found unless re-collected. Wilson's description of one locality in Taiwan is 'on sandstone cliffs round village of Sekitei, Taihoku province'. The other is Dandangai and both according to Price are 'in the rough and rocky foothills of the extreme north!' In the former place they were growing 'in some quantity on a vertical rock face'. The bulb is said to be pure white touched with pink. The tepals wavy, crimson about the middle, spotted scarlet, greenish yellow nectary furrow margined with red, and the numerous papillae scarlet. Plants from the 'Lushan' mountains in Kiangsi were up to 90 cm high with rather narrow leaves and the flowers with much reflexed crisped tepals. This was thought to be one of the most beautiful lilies.

Var. *album* Masters,

Var. 'Album Novum',

Var. *kraetzeri* Grove. These are all lovely white-flowered kinds. The first has a purplish brown stem and retains the normal chocolate-red pollen. The second is superior in quality and substance and has yellow pollen. The third has orange pollen, with the back of the tepals strongly tinged green. A fourth white-flowered kind is var. *tametomo* Siebold & Zuccarini.

The varieties *roseum* Masters and *rubrum* Masters virtually decribed themselves, but the epithets are used too generally and too loosely today for any particular lily to be ascribed to these names, or some of the others which help to fill the pages of the *International Lily Register*. Most of the descriptions available are usually without sufficient detail so the names cannot easily be fitted to lilies either.

As long as hardiness is not a problem or early frosts for late flowering kinds, then the general conditions for cultivating lilies should suffice. Good drainage with much water during the long growing season will give good results. Lighter sandy loam seems to be better than heavier, and a rich mulch of leaf soil will produce good stem bulblets for growing on. This species can be easily managed under glass where this is necessary, or it is desired to produce the flowers over a long season. Seed can be more easily produced by pot grown plants, at least, in England, where otherwise even in the south it is very much hit or miss and usually the latter.

In the world of hybrids what is written about *L. auratum* counts for *L. speciosum* as well, but there is one significant difference, because of the cross achieved by Woodriff in producing 'Black Beauty' using *L. henryi* as the other parent. This hybrid has proved sterile so every opportunity should be taken to make the cross again. It makes a bridge between the Orientals and the trumpet lilies of China, or in other words between the *parkmannii* hybrids and the Aurelians. With a strong bridge ways will be found to a completely new hybrid race.

L. stewartianum Balfour fil. & W.W. Smith

On one occasion only has this lily flowered in cultivation and that was in 1952. The solitary bloom carried no stigma so there was no chance of its producing seed. It is well illustrated in the RHS *Lily Year Book* of 1967. Forrest collected it some four times and the species was described from his herbarium material. Later Rock collected it and it was one of his bulbs that flowered.

It has been found in a very limited area north of Likiang; north-east of the Yangtze Bend, on the Chungtien plateau and north-west of the Likiang range. The plants inhabit stony pastures and limestone cliffs and Rock mentions a pine flat in clayey soil among low oak shrub. The altitude is between 3500 and 4000 m.

The white bulb is ovoid up to 5 cm tall and 4 cm across with the ovate scales firmly imbricated. The slender stem rises up to 60 cm and is clothed in scattered ascending narrow and long grassy leaves, those at the base being shorter and broader. There is a solitary, pendent, fragrant flower 3 cm across of turkscap form but with a longer tube, so that the recurved tepals leave the base of the flower clear. The colour is deep olive-yellow with deep crimson markings.

Wilson considered this species related to *L. fargesii* which has a more eastern distribution. Balfour and Smith thought it related to *L. taliense* and Synge saw it clearly related in form to *L. primulinum*. This makes it so very tantalising.

L. sulphureum Baker

This is truly one of the most magnificent of lilies, but to many it is not an outdoor plant, not being reliably hardy even if bulbs from its higher stations were available. The finest forms come from Burma and may be grown to 3 m high bedecked with huge yellow trumpets, but this is exceptional and not many of us are likely to see such as these except in our dreams.

The first collection of Yunnan plants was by Delavay at Mosoyin near Erhyuan (Lankiung) north of Tali. That was in 1888. As the first Burmese plants were exhibited in flower before the RHS in June 1889 to gain an FCC they must have been collected by Boxall at about the same time. This may háve been around Kalaw in the Shan State, where later on they were collected and grown on for export. Further to the east the species grows around Mengtsz in S.E. Yunnan and here Henry showed Wilson where they grew in 'red-clayey loam very rocky and covered with grasses and low shrubs'. This was between 1200 and 1500 m where in latitude 23°N plants may be expected to grow throughout the year. Otherwise the lily is known from both sides of the Burma-Yunnan frontier in the north-west and within this whole range the species may be expected to be widespread at suitable altitudes far more than the collections suggest.

Of the least confusing synonyms mention should be given to *L. myriophyllum* Franchet.

Seed is golden-brown rather small, narrowly winged and has immediate epigeal germination. The dark purple bulb is almost globose 10 cm across with lanceolate-ovate scales. The rooting stem grows from 1.5-3 m high with numerous scattered linear-lanceolate dark green leaves bearing bulbils in the axils. The racemose inflorescence may have up to 15 fragrant trumpet flowers 18-23 cm long. Woodcock & Stearn mention three colour forms: (1) the Burmese *superbum* deep yellow in the throat becoming creamy white towards the tips, outside more or less pink-flushed; (2) Henry's pale Chinese form with yellow throat but the upper parts of the tepals pure white, the outside mostly greenish; (3) yellow to the tips without any pink flush outside. Filaments are up to 15 cm long, anthers purplish yellow, pollen orange-brown. The style is up to 15 cm long, stigma tri-lobed purple and green. Seed capsule is cylindrical, 10 cm by 2.5 cm across. Flowering August onwards.

Cultivation of this beautiful lily can only be considered where it might be hardy or the facilities exist to grow the large plants under glass. On the Pacific coast of North America, Australia and New Zealand, and southern Japan, should prove successful areas compared with most of Europe, especially where a deep acid loam is available and sufficient moisture to keep the plants growing through a long season. Although it has been reported as lime-tolerant it seems most likely that a chalky soil would be the least beneficial. Even the magnesium limestones of Yunnan are not comparable and at the altitude of this species the soils may be expected to be sharply acid. This species is possibly the most in demand by those who read the literature and it is fortunate that by recent hard endeavours a new but very small supply of the bulbils is being distributed. Unless the bulbs mature in a site where they may set good seed, enthusiasts will be dependent on the plants being kept free of virus to produce healthy bulbils. This is not an easy task.

Many of the early hybrids have disappeared or are lurking behind corners of greenhouses in ill health. Those, however, which have taken on the hardiness and disease tolerance of other parents, but still retain the golden qualities of this lovely species, are those we should grow and improve further if we can.

L. superbum Linnaeus

This species, so aptly named by Linnaeus, was introduced to Europe in the first half of the eighteenth century and at that time, August 1738, Ehret made a beautiful painting showing everybody then and since what a stunning lily it is to behold. It is grown far and wide from its native haunts in the eastern United States, but not as much as its beauty and ease of cultivation should demand. There is a marvellous stand in the Wild Garden at Wisley many years old and in the Arnold Arboretum, Boston, Massachusetts there are thousands of bulbs growing in an acreage of swampy ground and their flowering must be a beautiful awe-inspiring sight.

It has a surprisingly large range from southern New Hampshire south to Florida and Alabama, reaching as far west as southern Illinois, Arkansas and Mississippi. It is interesting to learn from Mohlenbrock that in Illinois at the two known sites the plants commonly die back before flowering. This accords with the state of the lilies found by Mrs Henry in the more southerly western states. Although she puts the problem down to grazing, it seems that this species is in any event reducing its range in the west due perhaps to a long-term change in climatological factors.

The seed is light golden-brown, well winged, 10 by 9 mm and has delayed hypogeal germination. The precise conditions of delay may vary with the original source (latitude) of the plants. The globose bulb is annual in that it forms at the end of a stout stolon growing from the mother bulb, which thereafter withers. The scales, a few of which are found on the stolon, are white, ovate and closely imbricated. The rooting stem rises directly reaching a height of 1.5 to 3 m. It is clothed with numerous whorls of lanceolate or linear-lanceolate leaves. The stem may be purplish or, with the leaves, have a greyish or light silvery sheen. The racemose inflorescence may carry as many as 40 flowers, but usually far less especially in the wild, on long bracteolate pedicels raised above the horizontal. The well recurved tepals give a turkscap flower, up to 7.5 cm across, variably coloured orange, orange-red or orange-yellow, usually crimson towards the tips and spotted dark maroon towards the throat and with a green base. The outer tepals have a raised mid-rib giving the buds a triangular section. The outspreading slender filaments carry long thin anthers with orange-brown pollen, 17-25 mm long attached 4-8 mm from the end. The curving slender style protrudes slightly and carries a tri-lobed stigma. The flowering period is from late June to the end of August, but varies much according to location and source of material. Those from the south generally flower late in the season as does the related *L. iridollae*.

Being from a large area there are not surprisingly many variations and a good selection of these have been described by Mrs Henry; those particularly interested should consult the *Lily*

Year Books and especially RHS *LYB* 1955. *L. gazarubrum* and *L. mary-henryae* belong amongst the variants.

Perhaps because of its natural inclination to live in swampy regions many gardeners are put off from attempting this glorious lily, thinking it would be too demanding for water. This is not the case. Certainly give it all that is possible, but assuming that falls far short of a swamp, then very good floriferous stems may be grown successfully, while other plants flag in the summer heat. Some shade is wanting where the soil becomes too dry. In passing it often appears that many unlikely bog and swamp plants will suffer drought conditions more readily than many plants from more moderately balanced conditions. An acid loam with plenty of humus added would be very beneficial. Propagation from seed and bulbils takes a little time and asks for some patience, but giving them the best in summer makes the young bulbs grow rapidly. Division of the young bulbs from the mother bulbs may also be resorted to where there is a vigorous clump, but the mother bulb does not flower a second time.

With its great variety and imposing grace and stature there has been, or so it appears, very little interest in crossing this lily. As already mentioned, it has successfully hybridised with *L. michauxii* and no doubt it would with *L. iridollae*, which gives the impression of being an extreme southern form of *L. superbum*. It may be possible to make worthwhile hybrids with *L. canadense*, but the first crosses will not be the best. It will be the third or fourth generation that will show the 'improvements' and this would take time.

L. szovitsianum Fischer & Avé-Lallemant (Figure 7.12)

This may be the best known and the most commonly cultivated of all the Caucasian lilies and yet should it be decided in the future that the subtle difference between this and *L. monadelphum* are not sufficiently significant to maintain them both as separate species, then the name of *szovitsianum* will sink into synonymy. It comes from three main areas. The type, that is var. *szovitsianum*, comes from Georgia at altitudes up to 2400 m along the southern side of the Caucasus. The other var. *armenum*, comes from an area around Lake Sevan and a site to the south-east in Soviet Armenia, and a number of sites along the Pontine Mountains from near Ordu in the west to near Pazar in the east. The Turkish lilies have been noted in an altitude range from 60 to 1700 m and are seen growing on acid soils at the edge of forests, in scrub and in meadows below the tree line.

Seed germination is hypogeal in warmth, following which a cold period is required before the first leaf is seen above ground.

Figure 7.12
L. szovitsianum

The bulb, whose tip is usually about 10 cm below the surface, is up to 8 cm across with very many slender scales, the outer being nearly as long as the inner. The stem may be 130 cm tall or even 180 cm with the lanceolate or linear-lanceolate leaves spirally arranged, shortly setulose on the margin and on the veins below. They are 5-14 cm long by 1-2 cm wide. The flowers appearing in June into July are 7-8 cm across, a pale yellow, 1-8 in number but rarely up to 20. They are somewhat declined or nodding and

207

the tepals are semi-recurved campanulate. There is variable spotting but sometimes none at all. The bases of the tepals are purple. The filaments are free about 5 cm long and the anthers have orange (cinnabar) pollen. The style is about 4 cm long. The scent is strong and sweet which some people find unpleasant. The var. *szovitsianum* has broader inner tepals, oblanceolate, usually obtuse and shortly tapered below, while the inner tepals of var. *armenum* are narrowly oblanceolate, acute and long-attenuate below.

This is a long-lived lily and cultivation is easy. It takes kindly to a wide range of soils, light or heavy, acid, neutral or alkaline. In southern England it has naturalised in widely differing gardens, in Gloucestershire and Essex where the plentifully produced seed has been allowed to take its chance with nature and some of the rigours of cultivation! Seed seems to be the customary method of propagation, but it takes many years to obtain a mature bulb. This can be shortened by using the domestic fridge and keeping under glass for a while trying to extend the season of growth. For those with patience a row of seed sown outdoors and kept weed free may be the simplest answer.

With a strong heart and much perseverance much might be done with this lily as a parent. Dr North has flowered the cross with *L. pyrenaicum* and raised seedlings using *L. candidum*. This latter should be done again with different clones of *L. candidum* and both ways. There is always a chance with *L. testaceum* and *L. chalcedonicum*. The initial breakthrough is what is required and that it seems takes time and a great deal of trouble. It is a challenge.

L. taliense Franchet (Plate 6)

Looking like a tall and stately *L. duchartrei*, this handsome Chinese turkscap is a prize to grow. Although found by Delavay in 1883 it did not come into cultivation until the 1930s when introduced by George Forrest who collected it some eleven times. Most of our present-day material which is far from plentiful has come by a later collection made by Joseph Rock. So far as is known this species has a small range occupying an area in northern Yunnan from Lake Tali (Erh Hai) at the southern end and Likiang and north again to Yungning close to the Szechwan boundary. It keeps to a high altitude between 2500 and 3300 m where the base rock is magnesium limestone and grows among scrub and on the margins of pine and mixed forest.

The seed is 8 × 6 mm medium brown with thin papery translucent wings and gives immediate epigeal germination. The creamy-coloured bulb up to 4.5 cm across is speckled purple, subglobose with firmly imbricated ovate scales. The stem is stoloniform (to a lesser extent than *L. duchartrei*) and rooting at the base. It then rises to 2 m or even more and carries numerous scattered dark green leaves, each with prominent mid-rib and two lesser veins, up to 12 cm long. The racemose inflorescence may carry 12, usually half this number or less, scented pendent turkscap, white, purple spotted flowers on horizontal pedicels 8 cm long. The purple colouring increases with the age of the flower. The filaments converge around the ovary and base of the style before finally spreading outwards. The anthers are purplish and the pollen yellow. The style is slightly shorter than the ovary and the green stigma large and tri-lobed. The seed capsule is 2.5 cm long by 2 cm across.

Although coming from an area of magnesium limestone, as do many fine rhododendrons, this is not to say that this lily will take kindly to chalky soils even when heavily enriched with natural humus. Possibly it would take a neutral soil or one with the pH slightly above 7, but we may expect it to prosper best in an acid loam. The situation where it may rise between rhododendrons under dappled shade should be most suitable. If it has not prospered in many gardens, it has in a few for many years and truly it may not be that difficult. Like most lilies it can fall prey to many evils and unfortunately there is so little stock in cultivation to fill the gaps when they occur. This lovely lily comes easily from seed, but it is not self-fertile (Are any of this tribe?). Possession of a clonal group from vegetative propagation, which fortunately is simple enough, is very fine, but in the end is not self-perpetuating against disease, slugs or other handicaps. Any gardeners in this position should seek pollen from other sources and duly have the joy of gathering fresh seed.

This species is not known to have produced any hybrids.

L. tigrinum Ker-Gawler

Possibly this lily has been in cultivation longer than any other and over a wider area of the globe, not because of its flower but as a source of food, or, as Ernest Wilson would have said, an esculent, referring, of course, to the bulb. Man has taken it, throughout Japan, China, Korea, into Siberia and Tibet, but then it has gone little or no further, meeting natural barriers, not surely of cultivation. Its easy spread by propagation of the stem bulbils, easily transportable and independent from the part you eat, unlike wheat or potatoes, is simple to imagine, but why did the desire to eat lilies go no farther? The physical and sociological reasons might fill another book.

The next question, and this lily poses many, is where did it originate. All the extant forms but one, the var. *flaviflorum*, are triploids and sterile. The yellow variety *flaviflorum* is diploid and comes from Tsushima, an island between South Korea and Kyushu. This is a good central point from which to suggest dispersal, but it seems these stem from cultivated stock and that a yellow form was known in China centuries ago. Miss Preston's 'Diploid' form came with *L. amabile* from Japan. Wilson considered eastern China the home of the lily and this may be a satisfactory answer, but Dr Noda concludes that the triploid arose as a result of hybridisation; and as *L. leichtlinii maximowiczii* is seen as one of the likely parents and does not occur in China, then, perhaps, Korea was the starting point of the great migration. Food for thought!

Not the final question, perhaps, but an important one is what to call this species (or hybrid)? Recently Thunberg's name *L. lancifolium* has been revived on what seem thin grounds. If Thunberg's lily was the Tiger Lily, the Ogre Lily, Oni-yuri, and he must have known it, then *lancifolium* is the earlier title and on that count valid. Yet the literature of over a century is amassed with reference to *L. tigrinum* and all its accounts as a hybrid parent are with this name. All of this is little weight, of course, until it is a matter of economics and the cost of changing a common name is assessed. We can all be inconvenienced by disruption, but money is another matter. Meanwhile the most sensible argument appears in *Lilies of the World*: 'Thunberg's description of the flowers does not fit any Asiatic lily; as the name *L. lancifolium* hort. has been so long and consistently associated with *L. speciosum* it seems best to avoid error and confusion by keeping the name *L. tigrinum* for the tiger lily.'

The white bulb is broadly ovoid 8 cm across with broadly ovate closely overlapping scales. The dark, rooting stem up to 2 m is cylindrical with small white cobwebby hairs. The numerous scattered leaves are linear-lanceolate to lanceolate 8-18 cm long and 1.5-2 cm wide. The racemose inflorescence may carry up to 40 flowers, but 12 to 20 may be expected on a reasonably strong stem. They are scentless, usually salmon orange-red with dark purple spotting, well recurved and pendent, 10 cm across. Filaments and style are reddish, anthers and stigma purplish and the pollen reddish brown.

On such a much cultivated plant it seems unnecessary to comment on how to grow it; but it enjoys a good deep acid loam in full exposure or light dappled shade. If the soil is alkaline or the shade too heavy the lily will deteriorate quite rapidly and will die out. It has to be appreciated that all tiger lilies must be considered diseased with one or more virus species, unless known to the contrary. If grown well, being so tolerant, they show little sign of disease, but they present a great menace to other lilies. In this case tiger lilies must be separated from all others and kept free of aphids. It was advocated at one time that if you wanted to grow lilies then you must exclude any form of *L. tigrinum*. Now that it is known so many Asiatic hybrids may be carrying virus this seems extreme and stringent advice. Each gardener must judge for himself.

There are a few named varieties which may have arisen by some gradual mutation, adapting to environmental conditions, other than var. *flaviflorum* (Makino) Stearn. This beautiful variety is a clean yellow with dark purple spots. It has bulbils in the leaf axils but is also fertile and it will produce seed when fertilised by suitable pollen. It is affected by virus disease and has not the strength and vigour of the orange-red kinds. From Ullung-do, the island to the east of S. Korea, came var. *fortunei* hort. which is a more woolly stemmed lily and very floriferous, salmon-orange blooming late in September. Early flowering in August is var. *splendens* Leichtlin from Japan. The flowers are large, boldly spotted of a rich fiery orange-red. Besides these and the 'Diploid' variety which, if still extant, has not the qualities of flower of those already described, is the double flowered form, var. *flore-pleno* Regel, and one with variegated foliage, var. *foliis variegatis*.

Considering that most of the varieties are triploid and sterile, it may seem surprising that the influence of the species in the hybrid world is so great. The number of hybrids with *L. tigrinum* in their blood is legion. Of course the 'Diploid' variety and var. *flaviflorum* have played a considerable part, but even so with perseverance hybridisers have crossed the triploids with other species and hybrids to obtain in each case those few precious viable seeds that have provided the breakthrough to produce a new line.

L. tsingtauense Gilg (Figure 7.13)

This is a unqiue lily in the martagon series in that its flowers are upright, also they appear the most brilliant. Another feature that sets it aside is the mottling on the young leaves which reminds one of many of the erythroniums. Fortunately this species has become well established in gardens in recent years and the confusion which besets some closely related lilies does not apply to this species. Earlier writers suggested a kinship with *L. concolor*, but this was mainly on a likeness of colour and the upright flowers.

There is still the problem of *L. miquelianum* Makino and how, in particular, it is treated by the Koreans. If *L. miquelianum* is not a synonym of *L. tsingtauense*, then it would seem to be there are two intermediate lilies between this species and *L. medeoloides* (keeping *L. hansonii* aside from this) and they would be *L. miquelianum* and *L. distichum*.

The distribution of this species is in three separated areas: Shantung province around Tsingtao, from which the lily gets its name; Cheju Do (Quelpart Island), the island south of mainland Korea; and the eastern central area of the Korean Peninsula.

Figure 7.13
L. tsingtauense

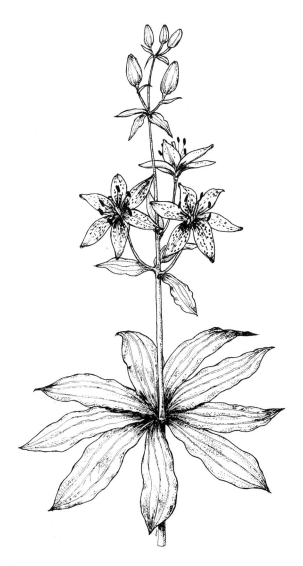

Wilson said it grew in thin woods, margins of thickets and among tall grasses, but always in moist, shady situations. Lighty found it on Mount Halla on Cheju Do amid coarse herbs and grasses associated with oaks and chestnuts.

The seed is *c.* 8 × 7 mm and of a greyish medium brown. It germinates hypogeally and growth above ground is delayed by a cold season. The white bulb is broadly ovoid with the lanceolate scales loosely imbricated, sometimes jointed. The stem is up to 1 m high but usually less. The glabrous leaves are in one main whorl with a second whorl above with fewer leaves. Immediately below the inflorescence there are 2 or 3 leaves either in a minor whorl or scattered. The scentless flowers, up to 12 but usually 3-6, are orange-red or red, spotted dark maroon, erect, flat or saucer-shaped, the tepals thick, V-shaped in section and hardly, if at all, recurved. Filaments and anthers are orange and pollen orange or orange-yellow; style straight, stout; stigma small similarly coloured. Capsule is distinctive, and sharply ribbed or shortly winged.

Two varieties have been named. They are var. *flavum* Wilson, described by Makino as yellow with dark red spots, a rare cultivated plant in Japan, and var. *carneum* Nakai which is more reddish, unspotted and has entire bulb scales. Wilson found it fairly common in rather open moist woods in the Diamond Mountains in North Korea. It would be a useful exercise to compare authentic examples of this species from its three main sources. Earlier cultivated forms would seem to be different from those we grow today as illustrations exhibit. Our present material most likely comes from Cheju Do.

Growing the good form with broad tepals now in general cultivation appears relatively easy. It is not a fussy plant, but presumably prefers an acid soil with plenty of humus. Good drainage and adequate spring and early summer moisture is necessary. *Botrytis* may easily damage the plants and ruin buds and flowers. Stunted plants may be a sign of virus infection to which otherwise the species seems reasonably tolerant.

The ability of this lily to fertilise other martagons and its erect upright flowers make this a vitally important species for the lily breeder. Development of new martagon hybrids is not a speedy process, but the current work being done in Germany, for instance, should be of considerable interest to all growers.

L. vollmeri Eastwood

This species has been called *L. roezlii* Purdy and must not be confused with *L. roezlii* Regel, which refers to a narrow-leaved form of *L. pardalinum* similar to var. *angustifolium*. The lily now under discussion comes not from the Californian Sierra Nevada or further south in that state, but from the border of Oregon and California where the Coast Range, Siskiyou Mountains and the Cascade Range tend to meet. The actual area is difficult to define, but it may be found in the very south of Curry and Josephine Counties in Oregon, most commonly in the northern half of Del Norte County, California, and again in the south of that county near the boundary with Humboldt County. Its habitat may be the wettest of any lily, frequenting *Darlingtonia* bogs where the bulbs are encased in black mud. These are areas where the water may be stagnant at the end of summer but with running water up to 60 cm deep at the end of winter. At other sites the bulbs may be in or at the edge of running water and in muddy soil under sphagnum moss. At times they may be only a few metres away from other lilies, like *L. bolanderi*, but while the latter is dry on higher ground *L. vollmeri* is entrenched in the mud.

Alice Eastwood who put the record straight and named this lily in 1948 sought comparisons with *L. occidentale* saying the two were 'closely allied and perhaps only ecological varieties'.

The seed germinates hypogeally in late autumn in cool conditions growing away directly in the spring. The bulb is rhizomatous not branching, the new scales being ivory white, the older scales yellowish. The stem grows up to 1 m high and is clothed with many narrowly elliptic-linear leaves up to 15 cm long. They may be scattered or scattered and in one or two whorls. The inflorescence in the wild may be 1 or 2 flowers or a few more in an umbel, exceptionally there may be 10, 20 or more, racemose, held on long arching pedicels. The tepals as described by Vollmer up to 8 cm long 10 mm wide, are 'reddish orange with reddish tinge along the margins near the tip, flecked with dark purple nearly black spots on the lower half of the inner surface. The fleck on the redder part of the segments is surrounded by a ring of yellow-orange.' The slender spreading filaments carry dark brown anthers up to 10 mm long, with red – or orange – brown pollen. The slender curving style has a prominent tri-lobed stigma.

The treatment for this lily may be no different to that of *L. pardalinum* and so is relatively simple. There is, however, no evidence available on lime tolerance. It does not require bog conditions nor, unless those conditions were absolutely correct, would it be wise to attempt growing the bulbs in anything but a free-draining medium. Plenty of moisture, plenty of humus in the soil and then plenty but not full sun should produce strong vigorous plants that may be raised easily from seeds in three years. Otherwise bulblets may be obtained from the scales.

It has not been used as a parent, but it may prove a suitable parent for producing dwarfer but still floriferous Pacific Coast hybrids.

L. wallichianum J.A. & J.H. Schultes

Growing at such a low altitude in the Himalayas, the tendency is to give this beautiful trumpet lily the miss, as it will not prove hardy in most of our gardens. Even the plantsmen-explorers do likewise in their race to make for higher ground. Its second failing is the stoloniform stem which makes pot culture very difficult. This species has been known for over 160 years and during most of these it has been in cultivation, due partly no doubt to its accessibility, but today, however, it must be considered rare.

Its range stretches along the Himalayas from Uttar-Pradesh in the west through Nepal (missing, as does *L. nepalense*, Sikkim and the Chumbi valley of Tibet), Bhutan and Assam. Along a narrow line this species may be found at elevations as low as 460 m, such as at Koilabas in Nepal, to as high as 1700 m which may be found over much of the range. It inhabits steep slopes of grassy stony ground, sometimes on limestone, where the drainage is so superbly good to take the constant deluge of the monsoon, during which the species grows, flowering towards the end of the season.

This species is closely related to *L. neilgherrense* from the south of India.

Although reported not to be freely produced in some forms, seed gives immediate epigeal germination. The bulb is broadly ovoid up to 9 cm across with whitish lanceolate scales. The basal stem is stoloniform wandering underground, rooting and producing stem bulblets. It emerges late in the season and grows above ground up to 2 m high, when it is clothed with numerous scattered linear or narrowly-lanceolate leaves up to 25 cm long by 1.2 cm broad. The 1-4 fragrant, horizontal funnel-shaped flowers have a slender tube 10 cm long and widely flared mouth 20 cm across. The tepals are creamy white inside and greenish outside, recurving at the tips, 18-25 cm long. The long stamens have yellow pollen. Flowering is usually in September.

Cultivation is for those with a mild climate and summer rains or having adequate glasshouse facilities to allow this sumptuous trumpet lily to perform in its own fashion. Excellent drainage is required as well as a good run for the underground stems. It is very well worth any amount of trouble and care that can be spared, such as in the make up of the compost, which should contain much sharp stone and grit in humus-rich soil. It may be lime-tolerant. A plentiful supply of water is required during the growing season which should appear to contain an inadequate quantity of nutrients. It could be very wrong to feed this lily.

L. wardii [Stapf] F.C. Stearn

This was the latest of the Chinese turkscap lilies to be found and that was 60 years ago when Kingdon-Ward first saw it in the Tsangpo valley at Gyala in S.E. Tibet. Later he was able to say its range was within a little west of 95°E to a little east of 97°E in latitude between 28° and 30°N. In 1950 he saw that it had spread south through the Lohit valley into the North East Frontier Agency in India. In altitude it could be between 1500 m and 3000 m where it inhabits scrub and pine-clad slopes sometimes so abundantly that its flowers scent the air. It was a lovely addition to this group of Asiatic lilies, the flowers being of a stronger pink than *L. lankongense*.

The medium dark brown seed (8 × 6 mm) gives immediate epigeal germination. The bulb is subglobose up to 5 cm across made of tightly imbricated ovate scales, fawn in colour and profusely speckled with red spots, the whole turning purple on exposure. The stem is normally stoloniform wandering below ground, rooting strongly where it rises erect to a maximum of about 1.5 m high. The scattered leaves cover the whole of the aerial stem to the tip of the inflorescence and are dark green narrowly-lanceolate to oblong-elliptic. The racemose inflorescence may carry nearly 40 flowers but this is exceptional and a strong stem may normally have up to 15. They are fragrant, pendent turkscap, rose-pink inclining to mauve-purple with carmine spotting, and are held on distinct long rigid horizontal pedicels except for the topmost flowers. The nectary is glabrous, the filament green, anthers purple and pollen orange. The style is long and the large stigma tri-lobed. The season is rather late starting from mid-July on into August.

The main factor inhibiting the spread of this lily in cultivation is virus disease to which it easily succumbs. This, however, must not inhibit the gardener who must take any opportunity that arises to raise this species from seed. It is only in this way that it can be conserved in cultivation, which it thoroughly deserves. Other than the stock being kept clean its other requirements are fairly modest, if we accept Kingdon-Ward's view that it is indifferent as to soil, calcareous or not. Perhaps one should add the rider, so long as it has a high humus content. Some have advocated fairly dry conditions, but the species is not from the dry plateaux, but endemic to the moderately wet pine and bracken region. So some shade is called for and a naturally organic medium loam and, as J. Comber said, with no wood ash.

This species is not known to have produced any hybrids. Dr North's attempts came to naught.

L. washingtonianum Kellogg

Under this name three Western American lilies have to be discussed. They may be thought of as one species, but the best-known variety *purpurascens* Stearn has with fairly good reason been thought sufficiently unique in a number of its qualities to merit specific rank. This is the variety that is most commonly referred to in cultivation, though it is far from common, and was in earlier days called var. *purpureum*. As this last name was confused with *L. rubescens*, which is quite distinct, the new name was necessary.

The type form var. *washingtonianum* has a distribution in the Sierra Nevada extending from the Yosemite National Park along the mountains northwards at an elevation between 1500 and 2150 m to the end of the range south of Mount Shasta. Vollmer found it in an open parklike area in the pine forest. It was covered with a most compact and dense growth of small shrubs mainly *Arctostaphylos* and *Ceanothus* and the lilies grew through these. There was a gentle slope, the soil heavy and stony with a 2-5 cm covering of leaf mould. The weather is dry from July to November and there is snow cover in winter.

The var. *minor* Purdy, the Shasta Lily, grows in one small but impressive area on the western slopes of Mount Shasta, which are covered in *Arctostaphylos* bushes and the lilies grow through these protected from deer and man. There is a layer of leaf mould 2-5 cm thick and the bulbs are normally 15-20 cm below in a yellowish sandy soil. The elevation is *c.* 1200 m. Autumn rains precede the snow which may lie 1.8 m thick in winter.

The var. *purpurascens* is the most westerly with a range commencing in the south in Humboldt County by the Mad River and spreading northward through Del Norte County into Oregon following the Cascade Mountains as far north as Mount Hood. The elevation will generally be between 750-1500 m. It will be found in open pine forests and areas of low brush where the soil is very rocky and gritty. Once again it may be growing through *arctostaphylos* bushes with the bulbs 10-15 cm below the surface where it is very dry in summer and well-drained.

The type and var. *purpurascens* have seed with hypogeal germination germinating in late autumn in cool conditions. The bulb is subrhizomatous with numerous white, lanceolate, pointed scales up to 5 cm long. The stem rises directly growing between

217

1.25 and 2.5 m high, and carries whorls of oblanceolate leaves up to 15 cm long by 3.5 cm wide. The funnel-shaped flowers from a few to 20 or more are borne horizontally and are white with purple spots in the throat, turning lilac-purple before they fade. The tepals are up to 10 cm long and may be slightly recurved towards the tips. The slender filaments bear anthers with yellow pollen. The straight style extending beyond the stamens, thickens to a tri-lobed stigma. Flowering is in July.

Var. *minor* has narrower tepals, fewer white flowers with strong purple spotting, not turning lilac-purple, the bulb smaller, more compact and rounded, and the stem slender and not so tall.

Var. *purpurascens*. The bulb, according to Purdy, is distinctive in having some of the scales jointed, even two or three joints in a scale. The stems are stout, the leaves broadly lanceolate with many in a whorl. The trumpet flower is shorter and broader, the tepals broader and overlapping towards the base. It may be pure white or white with faint purple dots, turning lavender and then wine-coloured.

As with other dryland bulbs of Western America, this species and its varieties have proved difficult in cultivation and virtually impossible to establish. Success that there has been, and great credit to the skill of the growers, has usually been with the var. *purpurascens*. Again it would appear to be the strict attachment of the species to the climatic conditions, to specific soils and, even, altitudes. We may endeavour to vary the soil, seek the best microclimate to account for altitude, but we can rarely as gardeners adapt our climate for the benefit of one or a few species. The crux of the matter must be to give them the dry period they demand from July to November, a winter preferably not too cold under the snow, and then a fast really wet growing season. The bulbs, particularly that of the type, should be treated with great care. They should go into their permanent homes at the earliest possible age (most of them do!); the first season in pots and then outside. Raising from seed is no difficulty.

One way of bringing some of the beauty of these lilies into our gardens would be to embark on a breeding programme using pollen of *L. washingtonianum*. Crosses have been made with other Pacific Coast species and results obtained. These have not become established or got into the stud book. It is unlikely that any progress was made past the first generation. The opportunity is there!

L. wigginsii Beane & Vollmer

After Miss Eastwood had nicely tied up *L. vollmeri*, it was realised there was still another lily growing on the Californian-

Oregon border without a title. It was the yellow *roezlii*. Was it an 'albino' of *L. vollmeri* or a separate species? Perhaps it was a vagrant from the Sierra Nevada and associated with *L. kelleyanum*? The answer was a new species.

The range of distribution is relatively small extending from Ashland, Oregon, along Ashland Creek south-westwards into California where its western limit is Doe Flat in Del Norte County. It is another wetland bulb and is said to occur along isolated streams and springs. At Doe Flat it is said to hybridise with *L. vollmeri*.

The seed germinates hypogeally in late autumn in cool conditions. The rhizomatous bulb is unbranching and has scales entire or 2-4 jointed. The stem, which may root at the base, rises directly and grows up to 1.25 m high carrying pale green linear-lanceolate leaves up to 22 cm long and 2 cm wide scattered or usually with 2-4 whorls or 6-9 leaves in the centre of the stem. The inflorescence may be solitary, otherwise umbellate or racemose according to whether there are few or many clear yellow, variably purple-spotted, pendulous turkscap flowers, which are subtended from long arching pedicels. The tepals are reflexed from the middle, up to 7 cm long. The filaments somewhat spreading have anthers 11 mm long with yellow pollen. The style, extending to longer than the stamens as the flower ages, has a prominent tri-lobed stigma.

Cultivation of this lovely lily should be similar to that of *L. vollmeri* and *L. pardalinum* and should be thought of as relatively easy in an acid soil with plenty of humus added, where necessary, and moisture available through to the flowering season in July. Propagation should be from seed with the bulbs taking three years to mature if the seed is obtained in the autumn. Scales will readily produce bulblets.

Cardiocrinum cathayanum (Wilson) Stearn

When Wilson named this lily as it then was he knew it to be closely allied to *C. cordatum*. Now 60 years on we may still doubt whether it is sufficiently separate to warrant being a species in its own right. We have gained very little knowledge in the intervening years, except to learn that, as might be expected, the Japanese plant is variable over its range of latitude. With that degree of variation extended just a little, it might take within its scope this Chinese plant. However, much evidence could easily be accrued if more authentic material became available, so until that time it might be best to leave things as they are.

This cardiocrinum inhabits mountains of eastern and central China, that is, Kiangsi, Hupeh, Hunan, Anwhei, Chekiang and

Kiangsu. In western Hupeh it is found at elevations between 580 and 1400 m in moist woods. Round Kuling in Kiangsi it grows in shady places, ravines and glens and here it was discovered by Père David in 1868.

The seed is dark brown with a broad membraneous translucent wing having germination which would presumably be epigeal. The bulb is whitish, yellowish on exposure, 7.5 cm high by 3.75 cm wide of rather few scales of which the outer bear petiole scars. The stem grows erect and stout to 1.3 m high the basal half naked. A third to half-way up is a false whorl of 6 long-stalked (15 cm long), dark green, oblong-obovate, net-veined leaves 20 cm long by 13 cm wide. Above the whorl are 2 or 3 scattered much smaller leaves. The flowers, horizontal or slightly ascending, may be 1-5 trumpet- or funnel-shaped, the tepals being somewhat irregular, 11 cm long, greenish white outside, creamy white inside, splashed with reddish brown. Clustered at the top of the stem in a short corymbose raceme the flowers are preceded by several persistent oblong, pointed bracts. Stamens are much shorter than the tepals, pollen yellow, style and stigma protruding beyond the anthers. The seed capsule is erect, obovoid, 5.5 cm long.

Cultivation should follow upon the lines of *C. cordatum*.

C. cordatum (Thunberg) Makino

This was the first of the cardiocrinums to be described and that was as a hemerocallis in 1784. Ten years later Thunberg changed it to that of *Lilium cordifolium*. Over the ensuing years this and the other two species were thrown and tossed backwards and forwards between the genus *Lilium* and that of *Cardiocrinum*. This was due to the reluctance of some to create a new genus when a subgenus would do. Anyway Makino pressed his point, so that in recent years *Cardiocrinum* has become generally accepted – but not by Ohwi in his *Flora of Japan* where this species remains *Lilium*!! Fortunately today the plants are looked at more broadly; it is not just a matter of the flower parts.

In distribution this is the most northerly. It is found throughout Japan from Kyushu to Hokkaido being more common towards the north. It is in Sakhalin and also the Kurile Islands. Wilson said it was widely distributed on the wooded mountains of Japan, always in cool moist situations, and that in the north it often forsook the woods for more open places. Vasak said that on Sakhalin this species 'was distributed in the warmer forests' with *Picea* and *Abies*, *Actinidia*, Hydrangea petiolaris and *Rhus orientalis*. On Kunashiri in the Kurile group it was also in primeval forest with such additional trees as *Magnolia obovata* and *Cornus controversa*. Vasak referred to these forests as 'the kingdom of the fern'. He thought *C. cordatum* the most demanding on moisture and humus, but it laid no claim to the sum.

The seed with large membraneous translucent wing gives epigeal germination. The bulb is whitish but greenish brown to brown on exposure so that the nose at soil surface is not noticeable among the woodland litter. It is up to 7.5 cm across with few thick scales showing the petiole scars at their tips. If planted too deeply or, in nature, buried it has the ability to raise a stem and form a new bulb higher up. The stem grows from 1-1.8 m, often less, and is bare of leaves on the lower portion. At a third of the length of the stem from the base there is a false whorl of leaves on long petioles. The leaves up to 30 cm across, dark bronze on emerging, are broadly heart-shaped and net-veined. A few scattered leaves of smaller size are usually found higher up the stem. The racemose inflorescence carries 4-12 (exceptionally more), tubular, irregular, trumpet-shaped (infundibuliform) horizontal creamy white flowers splashed inside with reddish streaks. They are on short, stout pedicels each with a pointed bract at the base. Stamens two-thirds the length of the tepals, pollen yellow; style slightly longer than the stamens. The seed capsule is obovoid, 5.5 cm long. Flowering is variable, July-August. The plant being monocarpic the parent bulb withers with the stem, leaving a few bulblets about the base.

Ohwi following some other authorities distinguishes a var. *glehnii*. Makino at one time separated this northern form as a separate species. Following Ohwi the distribution would be central and north Honshu, Hokkaido, Sakhalin and Kurile Islands, leaving the type coming only from Kanto district of Honshu and westward, Shikoku and Kyushu. The plants are said to be stouter, leaves broadly ovate, and flowers up to 20 on a rather long rachis. These points may not be vital, but Hope Findlay when growing the species in the Savill Gardens rightly complained that they started into growth in February when they required protection from frost and cold winds. This would be the emergence expected of a southern form and, as it did not flower until August, resembled the growth period of the southern Japanese species, *L. speciosum*. A form named *glehnii* but of actual provenance unknown, also grown in southern England, does not emerge until end March or early April, a far more satisfactory time, and flowers earlier in July. Although this species will never vie with *C. giganteum* for overall beauty and grandeur, those from the northern latitudes will make more satisfactory plants and have a place in the lily-grower's garden and not be thought of as just botanical curiosities.

The Savill Garden plants started to flower with up to 12 blooms after seven years from seed, spending the first four in seed pot and cold frame. They should be given a moist situation in shade. The soil should have a high content of leaf soil and the bulbs when planted should have their noses just covered by the annual fall of leaves and little more.

C. giganteum (Wallich) Makino (Figure 7.14)

This is the glory of the Himalayan and western Chinese forests. It is also the glory of those, who, with much patience and hope, have sown the seeds and waited through the years of expectation to the ultimate flowering of the first stem. There is nothing to match this beauty. In its grandeur it stands aloof and should be a must for all those who have conditions sufficiently suitable.

The range starting in the west near Simla passes through Himalayan India into Nepal, then Sikkim, Bhutan, southwards to the Khasi Hills in Assam, and northwards into S.E. Tibet as far as Pemako and possibly beyond for here there is the var. *yunnanense* (Elwes) Stearn to take the place of the type. This is found in Yunnan and adjoining northern Burma, Szechwan and Hupeh. The elevation in the Himalayas varies between 1500 and 3300 m, in Assam not above 2150 m, and in China between 1200 and 2750 m. In eastern Nepal Smythe found the plants growing at 3290 m on a south-facing slope in a shallow re-entrant in a conifer forest with mixed magnolia and rhododendron. On another occasion at 2790 m the species was again on a south-facing slope in mixed forest. In Sikkim just below Bakhim at 2700 m they are growing in very thick mixed forest on a steep south slope. Herklots on Shillong Hill at *c.* 1890 m found the plants 'either in the open exposed to full sun or in partial shade of pine or other trees, or in a tangle of bracken or bramble'. 'Plants were on sloping ground growing in damp, deep, black soil rich in organic matter.' Wilson obviously knew var. *yunnanense* well. He wrote of it growing 'in shady ravines and in moist woods and forests', its abundance 'on rich lower slopes' and forming colonies 'in dark recesses'. One surprising point was that he found the bulbs as low as 15-20 cm down in leaf mould and woodland soil, the plants loving a cool, moist, shady situation.

The seed which has a large, translucent, membraneous wing germinates epigeally at the end of winter often having been delayed for 12 months. The large dark greeny-brown bulb, paler

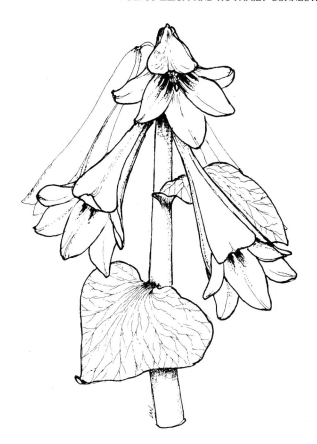

Figure 7.14
C. giganteum

below, is ovoid, up to 15 cm across, with relatively few large, thick, broadly ovate scales, showing rough petiole scars and fibres at their tips. The stem, which only grows once in the bulb's life to bear the inflorescence, is stout, erect, gradually attenuated from the base to the apex up to 4 m high, but commonly 2-3 m. The basal leaves arising from new bulb scales are long-petioled and form a rosette. The stem leaves are alternately scattered, long-petioled, up to 30 cm, broadly ovate basally cordate and can be 45 cm long by 40 cm wide. Leaves are net-veined and their size and petiole length diminishes greatly with their height. The racemose inflorescence may have up to 20 fragrant flowers or more, on short pedicels, regularly funnel-shaped, white, red-vinous striped inside, greenish without, outward-facing, but generally declining below horizontal, up to 15 cm long. They open in sequence with the lowest first from end June to early July. Stamens are shorter than the perianth, pollen yellow. The seed capsule is erect, obovoid up to 7 cm long with long fine marginal teeth to the valves.

Var. *yunnanense* is distinguished from the type by its shorter stature, being rarely over 2 m high; from its dark bronzy stem and leaves, particularly at and shortly after emergence; and from its more greenish flowers which open from the top of the stem downwards. As the flowers open very quickly one after each other this curious point may easily be overlooked. In gardens where these plants have been commonly grown for many years crosses between the two varieties have resulted and intermediate forms, therefore, do exist. Hope Findlay said var. *yunnanense* flowered usually the last week in June and the type the first week in July, though obviously there was a good overlap.

Cultivation in the woodland garden with plenty of humus in the ground is easy and straightforward. Although it grows in the wild in places where the summer rains may be almost continuous this is by no means necessary to its well-being. Certainly to obtain a good growth rate each year sufficient moisture must be available. Other factors must also be considered. Coming from relatively low altitudes the species springs into growth early in the year. This can mean frosts killing the new foliage and such a setback may result in the loss of all growth for a year. As and when necessary cover the newly emerged leaves with lightweight evergreen foliage at night, and if the garden is prone to these frosts grow the young bulbs on in the kitchen garden or somewhere where ready protection, such as Dutch Lights or other glass or plastic covers, is readily available. There are two means of propagation available, seed and the growing on of the bulblets left after the flowering of the mother bulbs, which, of course, expire. Even to the reasonably patient the first can seem a long time when seven years is mentioned as a moderately fast time to maturity. With the bulblets it is somewhat less, but you have to have a stock first or some source of supply. It is also considered that flowering plants from the bulblets are never of the size and quality of those directly from seed. Few of us on this ground are tempted to throw them away.

'Situated . . . at an altitude of 240 to 300 m, the annual rainfall is between 125 and 150 cm, most of which falls during the winter months, although thunderstorms are frequent during the summer. The humidity is high throughout the year, and night dews are heavy. The area is not subject to severe frosts, the temperature seldom falling below 30°F (-1°C) and in summer the temperature rarely exceeds 90°F (36°C). The soil in this area is a grey sandy loam, rather rocky in places – the natural rock being basalt – over a heavy clay subsoil, and enriched over the years with a copious supply of leaf mould.' If the reader has this site, as described by Dr Withers, in which to garden then he possibly will be living in the Dandenong Ranges of Australia and have no need to worry about cultivation or waiting for the first bloom, as they naturalise happily and so do it all themselves unaided.

Chapter 8
A Brief History of the
Early Hybrids

To many gardeners today the growing of lily hybrids is all important. This is an area where with care, success is assured and a beautiful display of flowers is achieved throughout the season. Some gardeners may not even require a long spell of flowers. They may be content to achieve the highest standards of cultivation with a small number of cultivars over a short period when they may be brought up for exhibition. This may not apply everywhere lilies are grown, but it is an important factor today. The business of growing hybrids is a relatively recent phenomenon, because it was not until the 1950s that hybrids were really started in gardens.

There was a snob value and possibly there still is and always will be about growing the species. This is not peculiar to lilies. But in *Lilies of the World* published in 1950 it could be said with some truth: 'Though until recently the crossing of lilies has seldom produced anything of outstanding merit, *L. testaceum* is an outstanding exception, for it is one of the choicest of lilies, an aristocrat . . .' It may be worthwhile to recall here what has happened since what has been claimed as the first lily hybrid came to light in the nineteenth century.

First, and it may be a rare thing to do, some acknowledgement has to be given to the Japanese for the lilies they have been producing for hundreds of years. The first hybrids most likely came about in a natural way as they occur from time to time now, but we may assume that the Japanese interest in floriculture brought *L. dauricum* and *L. maculatum* together and somebody noted that their progeny produced a different looking lily. Shimizu suggests this would have happened over 300 years ago as varieties of lilies were mentioned in books of the time. This lily we may call *L. elegans* Thunberg.

The origin of *L. testaceum* is unknown. Strangely it was originally thought to have come from the Fast East. It gained the name, doubtless because of the colour, of Nankeen Lily, its parentage not having been guessed at, as it was assumed to be a species. Later in the nineteenth century, crosses between *L. candidum* and *L. chalcedonicum* produced similar lilies. A back cross of *L. testaceum* on to *L. chalcedonicum* gave a brick-red lily with *testaceum* fragrance called *L. beerensii*. But it was not until 1944 that Emsweller and Stewart showed beyond doubt from cytological study the true parentage.

The next group *L. hollandicum* (syn. *L. umbellatum* hort.) also has its origins clouded in mystery as well it might, as it is considered to be a cross between *L. bulbiferum*, including *croceum*, and *L. elegans*. Wallace (1879) obviously knew them well and said they were mainly raised from seed, suggesting strains and grexes besides true clones, for which many names remain if only a few of the lilies. They most likely originated about mid-century. Most Asiatic hybrids today stem from this base.

While Wallace was revising his *Notes on Lilies*, in Boston, Francis Parkman was going to take the eye away from Asiatics to view the first ever Oriental hybrid with the now legendary name of *L. parkmannii*. From 50 or so seedlings he achieved one true hybrid from *L. speciosum* pollinated by *L. auratum*. This is something the Japanese had not done earlier, although they had no lack of opportunity, but such things are often governed by the manners of fashion and taste. The first flower was in 1869. Parkman increased his stock to about 50 and sold them to Anthony Waterer in England. When exhibited it caused a sensation and went with its First Class Certificate and virus disease to death and the pages of horticultural history. It was truly one of the landmarks. Others since are 'Crimson Queen' (1902) and 'Jillian Wallace' (1938).

The curious then set their sights on the martagon lilies. Van Tubergen in Haarlem, Holland, crossed *L. martagon album* with *L. hansonii* and produced out of the seedlings *L.* 'Marhan'. Many more have come from this clone since. That was about 1886. Baden Powell in England crossed the dark martagon with *L. hansonii* and achieved the original of the other well-known type, *L. dalhansonii*. This first flowered in 1890. Not far behind was Mrs R.O. Backhouse who at Sutton Court, Hereford, before the turn of the century, produced a range of hybrids, whose names are still well-known today. She used both var. *album* and var. *cattaniae*. As a group they are called the Backhouse Hybrids.

During the 1890s many Californian lilies were coming across to England, and by 1892 Ware of Tottenham had named a *L. pardalinum* crossed with *L. parryi* as 'Francis Fell' after his foreman. Doubtless Francis did the cross and saw it through to fruition. Similar hybrids were made by Whall, Van Tubergen and Luther Burbank, and the generic name given to these lilies became *L. burbankii*. Amos Perry continued making further hybrids with Western American lilies, but few of these made an impact. This came with the Bellingham Hybrids produced in the 1920s by Griffiths of the United States Department of Agriculture. Truly it started with Kessler who pollinated *L. humboldtii* with *L. pardalinum* and *L. parryi*. The seed Kessler passed to Purdy, who in turn passed it to Griffiths at Bellingham, who raised some 3,000 seedlings. Of the few that were finally selected 'Shuksan' still remains one of the finest Western American hybrids. In the interests of garden plant conservation those original Bellingham Hybrids still extant should be sought out and grown on as a collection, propagated and redistributed.

It is surprising how much of the basic work had been done by 1900, but it was this year that brought the flowering of a more remarkable hybrid. It did not add up to much at the time, perhaps because it became diseased without the cause being understood. The hybrid was *L. kewense* and the parents *L. henryi* and *L. leucanthum chloraster*. The buff-coloured flowers were wide open with twisting tepals recurving at the tips. More significant than the lily itself perhaps is the fact that it gave Debras the idea for his hybrid. This was *L. sargentiae* pollinated by *L. henryi*. He obtained two good seeds in 1925, one of which survived to flower three years later. This took the now famous name of *L. aurelianense*. This too became diseased but it was not destroyed before further progeny both from selfing and back crossing had been secured.

Concomitant with Debras's cross, but not in time, was that produced by Leslie Woodriff in the 1950s. He crossed *L. speciosum rubrum* with *L. henryi* and achieved the more vigorous but unfortunately sterile *L.* 'Black Beauty'. Someone may find a way around this sterility one day; if not, attempts should be made to produce a fertile cross. The interesting and most exciting part of the story is the link between the Orientals and the trumpet lilies provided by *L. henryi*. Some may challenge the necessity of this link and say we are obsessed with what we see. Yet it is not very easy with a link, but it may require a miracle without.

Before leaving *L. henryi* another important cross should be mentioned. This was Tom Barry's pollination in 1933 of *L. sulphureum* with supposedly *L. tigrinum*, but which turned out to be *L. henryi*. The lily was named 'T.A. Havemeyer' and is the forerunner of many hybrids.

It is all a question of crossing frontiers, breaking down barriers and destroying images in the mind. There is also much tenacity and resilience required throughout years of patient work to which you have to return each season or waste much you have done before. Charles Robinson thought of the cross between *L. candidum salonikae* and *L. monadelphum* in the mid-fifties and first saw something of the achievement in 1969. It was then a new breakthrough. Since then he has crossed a longer bridge with 'Prelude', a hybrid between *L.* 'June Fragrance' and *L. bulbiferum croceum*. This seems a little far-fetched at first, but not on second thoughts. Cooper at the Royal Botanic Garden, Edinburgh, produced hybrids from a cross between *L. croceum* and *L. monadelphum* during the 1940s.

In 1901 Gertrude Jekyll published her *Lilies for English Gardens* and devoted a chapter, but of few words, to hybrid lilies. It was a time of great activity. There was the first Lily Conference, a Conference on Hybrids and another on Genetics. She wrote: 'It is probable that the efforts of those who are now hybridising Lilies, will end by producing just a few excellent things and a large number of confusing nondescripts, much worse as garden plants than the types from which they are derived.' 'Still, though it is difficult to imagine it, there may be potentialities of beauty undeveloped in the Lily family.' There is a touch of Lady Bracknell in all this, especially, when her practical sense appears in the last paragraph. 'A hybridist who could get the grand substance of the tender Indian Lilies into hardy garden plants of good constitution would indeed be a benefactor to horticulture.' May you draw your own conclusions.

Chapter 9
Horticultural
Classification and
the *International*
Lily Register

Horticultural
Classification

In the previous chapter mention has been made of the early crosses and their resulting hybrids in the breeding of groups of lilies. Purposely each significant group, with one exception, was taken in turn acting more or less chronologically.

Following upon the publication of the first *International Lily Register* by the Royal Horticultural Society in 1960 with a hundred pages of lily names and by most standards incomplete, it became patently obvious that in a short while this orderly publication would be chaos itself without some reasonable form of classification. On the other side of the Atlantic the North American Lily Society was going from strength to strength aided by competitive exhibitions. Similar situations applied in Australia and New Zealand, but not so in the UK. Commercial exploitation of lilies was also big business and, if customers were to comprehend readily one type of lily from another when there were possibly hundreds or even thousands to choose from, then some simple classification was necessary.

So in January 1963 a sub-committee of the Lily Committee sat down, with Jan de Graaff as a visiting member, under the chairmanship of the distinguished gardener, E.B. Anderson. It seems they did a good job, because during the past 20 years it has required very little revision. Perhaps at the stem roots – rather than 'grass roots' – close to the show bench it has had to withstand the customary strains that human emotions engender. Even so the classification should prove to be adaptable when the time comes. It may be under some pressure at the edges, with the gradual breaking down of barriers between different types of lily, but even the extreme cases can be contained within the present system and there is no need for revision yet.

Strictly the classification is for all lilies, both species and hybrids. It should be appreciated that it is not a botanical classification, but, as originally stated, a horticultural classification specifically designed for 'registration, show and catalogue purposes'.

There are in all nine major divisions. There was to have been a tenth to cover cardiocrinums, but it seems never to have been used. Division IX contains all the species and the previous eight Divisions cover the hybrids. The divisions themselves are, as required, broken down into sub-divisions mainly on the basis of shape and position of the flowers.

The classification as it appears in the current *International Lily Register* 1982 is as follows:

The Horticultural Classification of Lilies

DIVISION I	Hybrids derived from such species or hybrid groups as *L. tigrinum*, *L. cernuum*, *L. davidii*, *L. leichtlinii*, *L.* × *maculatum*, *L.* × *hollandicum*, *L. amabile*, *L. pumilum*, *L. concolor* and *L. bulbiferum*.
I(a)	Early-flowering lilies with upright flowers, single or in an umbel, such as 'Enchantment', *L.* × *hollandicum* or 'Joan Evans'.
I(b)	Those with outward-facing flowers, such as 'Prosperity', 'Valencia' or 'Brandywine'.
I(c)	Those with pendent flowers, such as 'Lady Bowes Lyon' (Plate 13), 'Edith Cecilia' or 'Palomino'.
DIVISION II	Hybrids of Martagon type of which one parent has been a form of *martagon* or *hansonii* such as 'St Nicholas', the Backhouse Hybrids or 'Achievement'.
DIVISION III	Hybrids derived from *L. candidum*, *L. chalcedonicum* and other related European species (but excluding *L. martagon*) such as *L.* × *testaceum*, 'Ares' or 'Apollo'.
DIVISION IV	Hybrids of American species, such as the Bellingham Hybrids, 'Shuksan' or 'Sunset'.
DIVISION V	Hybrids derived from *L. longiflorum* and *L. formosanum*, such as 'Formobel', Formolongi g. and Florosanum g.
DIVISION VI	Hybrid Trumpet Lilies and Aurelian Hybrids derived from Asiatic species including *L. henryi*, but excluding those derived from *L. auratum*, *L. speciosum*, *L. japonicum* and *L. rubellum*.
VI(a)	Those with trumpet-shaped flowers, such as Golden Clarion g., 'Sulphur Queen' or 'Black Dragon'.

VI(b)	Those with bowl-shaped and outward-facing flowers such as Heart's Desire g., 'Gwendolyn Anley' or 'New Era'.
VI(c)	Those with pendent flowers such as the Golden Showers g., 'Summer Song' or 'Christmas Day'.
VI(d)	Those with flat, star-shaped flowers such as the Sunburst g., 'T.A. Havemeyer' or 'Mimosa Star'.
DIVISION VII	Hybrids of Far Eastern species such as *L. auratum*, *L. speciosum*, *L. japonicum* and *L. rubellum*, including any of their hybrids with *L. henryi*.
VII(a)	Those with trumpet-shaped flowers.
VII(b)	Those with bowl-shaped flowers, such as 'Empress of India', 'Pink Princess' or the Opal Hybrids.
VII(c)	Those with flat flowers, such as 'Jillian Wallace', 'Lavender Princess' or 'Aurora'.
VII(d)	Those with recurved flowers, such as the Potomac Hybrids, 'Journey's End' or 'Electra'.
DIVISION VIII	To contain all hybrids not provided for in any other division.
DIVISION IX	To contain all species and their varieties and forms.

Earlier publications had shown Division IX to be broken down into eight sub-divisions. Although to those interested in botanical classification the breakdown may have shown some expediency, it may still with its faults be worth showing for the guidance of those who have to contend with the organising of shows and the judging of exhibits.

DIVISION IX

IX(a)	Those of martagon form with reflexed flowers, but excluding those of American origin, such as *L. martagon*, *L. chalcedonicum*, *L. monadelphum*, *L. hansonii*, *L. duchartrei*, *L. wardii*, *L. henryi*, *L. davidii* and *L. cernuum*.
IX(b)	Those with upright flowers such as *L. bulbiferum*, *L. dauricum* and *L. tsingtauense*.
IX(c)	Those of American origin.
IX(d)	Forms and polyploids of *L. longiflorum*, *L. formosanum* and *L. philippinense*.

IX(e)   Those with bowl-shaped or trumpet flowers, but excluding those mentioned in IX (d), such as *L. regale, L. candidum, L. sulphureum* and *L. sargentiae.*

IX(f)   Asiatic lilies with short trumpet or slightly recurved pendulous flowers such as *L. primulinum, L. nepalense* and *L. bakerianum.*

IX(g)   Forms and varieties of *L. auratum* and *L. speciosum.*

IX(h)   Asiatic lilies which are usually dwarf and which have affinities towards *Nomocharis* such as *L. henrici, L. mackliniae, L. nanum* and *L. sherriffiae.*

Fortunately there is nothing obligatory about this system. It is no enviable task judging spikes of *L. henryi, L. monadelphum* and *L. cernuum* in the same class. Show secretaries may not see the need to separate the few hybrids in Division V from their species and forms, which may be far more numerous, in Division IX (d). Are all American species so much alike? Some would fit aimably with the hybrids in Division IV on the show bench, others would look completely out of place. But these are minor points that, perhaps, seldom arise and it is up to those involved at the local level to interpret their needs as they arise. A task of which they are surely quite capable.

Reverting to the *International Lily Register*, it is now in its third edition (1982) and has increased much during the intervening years. It was at the Fifteenth International Horticultural Congress in 1958 that the Royal Horticultural Society was appointed as the International Registration Authority for the names of *Lilium* cultivars. Such a task is not to be undertaken lightly and is an onerous burden. It involves a great deal of painstaking work and a devotion to precision and exactness. The light-hearted relief may come through the detective work in searching for the almost unknown in a sea of casual errors. The duties of a registration authority are to compile a list of the past names and to get current and new names registered by their breeders or introducers. As this is done on an international basis which is becoming more broadly based as the years go by, it is not without complications of language and commercial interest on the one hand and the tiresome frustration of indifference on the other to suggest a few thoughts that come to mind.

A few moments reflection will bring home to anyone the need

The International Lily Register

for a register of lily names. This is not the same as every lily requiring a name, which is nonsensical and quite out of the question. Only those that deserve a name should be named and at the same time properly registered. Even as it is the *Register* is full of dead wood – or dead bulbs – but this itself is not to put off raisers doing the right thing.

There is a code for the naming of plants and the registrar is able to guide people in their choice of names along the right lines. The rules are rather obvious and one of the main features is to guard against duplication or even apparent duplication of names. Quite considerable detail is requested of each new cultivar's history and description, which is easy enough if the raiser, as he or she should, keeps the records straight and works systematically. In such circumstances it does not appear tedious or a nuisance. These descriptions may indeed play a large part in the future conservation of garden plants. Today, many of the problems and, perhaps, why many plants are lost, is because of totally inadequate descriptions left us in nurserymen's catalogues. There is too much 'beautiful red with yellow centre to 4 feet in July' which may be no better than no description at all. None of the work of registration can be accomplished without cost, and so a fee is levied. This involves small international monetary transactions which are a nuisance, and usually expensive and, perhaps, national societies might find a way out of this by acting as collecting agents.

So it behoves anyone from Georgia, USSR, from Georgia, USA, or from somewhere between here and New Georgia, to register the names of their lilies. All that is required in the first place is a request for the appropriate forms with a mention of the names to be used to find out whether they might be appropriate. Letters should be addressed to:

The Director,
The Royal Horticultural Society's Garden,
Wisley,
Woking,
Surrey GU23 6QB,
England.

Chapter 10
Hybrid Review

There is no shortage of hybrid lilies and yet has the one we so desire been produced? To many the species provide the answer, but since some of the most beautiful are difficult to maintain in our gardens there is still the possibility that the hybrids may be able to take their place. For this reason and for many others new hybrids turn up every year, while others fall by the wayside, casualties in some marathon march of progress.

To satisfy the purists there are two perfectly good reasons for continuing the supply of new hybrids. The first is simply that it keeps the pressure off the species. The state of the latter in the wild is certainly not such as to support a growing leisure industry like garden horticulture. Unfortunately this does not always work. The florists' cyclamen and the new more acceptable hybrids have not taken the pressure off the species of cyclamen even with conservation controls. But it is working and can continue to work with lilies, which are happily more easily produced vegetatively. Secondly, producing hybrids has told us a great deal about the genus we would not otherwise have found out or so easily. More knowledge indeed may come from the hybrids we cannot produce than the ones we do as man delves more deeply into the causation of sterility.

Division I

By far the most important Division is that devoted to what are called the Asiatic hybrids. There are more hybrids being produced in this group than any other and the situation is unlikely to alter in the future. The reason behind their great popularity is possibly first and foremost their ease of culture. They can be easily propagated by division, stem bulblets and, with many cultivars, leaf axil bulbils. The small bulbs in healthy clones have a good vigour and soon reach maturity. Many are stout plants and far from fragile, allowing them to be put on the show bench or in the florist's window as if they have been cut but half an hour ago. This good condition lasts, making them suitable for decoration. The flowers may be upright, outward or pendent or a combination of these, and vary much in shape from crocus or tulip-form to turkscap. They may be spotted or unspotted, monochrome or bicoloured with the colour range as broad a spectrum as the genus *Lilium* allows. Although the colours may be harsh, lacking in clarity or poor in substance, others have brilliance and great depth. In newer cultivars there may be subtle shading or tinting. They are normally unscented. Certain combinations have produced sterility in some lines, but there has always proved another one to follow.

Comparing all lilies together, the Asiatic hybrids are not considered the most beautiful. This view stems from the rigidity of early upright-flowered varieties of the *elegans* school and the cramped flower heads of 'Enchantment'. Whether attitudes change before the pinks and whites, such as 'Twilight' and 'Juliana' from the Oregon Bulb Farms, Mrs Koehler's 'Hawaian Punch' and 'Snowlark' from Wadekamper remains to be seen, but the North hybrids, involving *L. langkongense* and *L. davidii*, both elegant species in the form, say, of 'Theseus', dark red, and 'Iona', a pale fawny pink, almost demand that they should be considered amongst the most beautiful of lilies. The other group of Asiatics we will continue to see a great deal of is the spotless type made famous by Stone & Payne. There are now cultivars like 'Wattle Bird' bred by Hayler in Australia, 'Marilyn Monroe' by Parsons in England and 'El Paso' by Ewald in Germany. The first two are yellow and the third red and orange.

The Asiatics seem to have been most successful in the United States, Australia and Germany. All are countries enjoying continental climates. There is no doubt about the hardiness of this group and, as well as any lilies, they revel in hot summers. They are affected by virus diseases usually showing a considerable degree of tolerance other than becoming less vigorous and going into a slow demise. The North hybrids with *L. langkongense* parentage are standing up well to virus disease, which is a little surprising, because *L. langkongense* easily succumbs and shows it. Obviously some gene dominance from, say, *L. davidii* is proving most beneficial.

Division II

Division II is devoted to the hybrids of the true martagon lilies. These lilies comprise the species *Ll. martagon* and all its subspecies and/or varieties, *hansonii*, *distichum*, *medeoloides* and *tsingtauense*. They form a unique group. There has been much debate respecting the relationship between them and the American lilies. The lily 'Kelmarsh' is recorded as having the

236

parentage *martagon* × *kelloggii*. It is hoped to resolve the problem as to whether it is a hybrid by cytological means and this is under investigation now. *L. medeoloides* on morphological grounds would seem to have the closest affinity to the American lilies while also retaining today the most acceptable geographical distribution.

The origins of the martagon hybrids have been discussed in the historical survey in Chapter 8. These hybrids are just as important today as when they were first introduced and still make an important contribution to our gardens. Other growers have produced very similar lilies in more recent times, particularly Jan de Graaff with the Paisley Hybrids. Many fine specimens are grown at Quarry Wood where the unique clone *L*. 'Ellen Field' was produced from *L. hansonii* × *martagon cattaniae*. From its silvery green buds come glistening rich red green-centred flowers with yellow anthers. It was presumably the work of Ellen Field and outlives her as a fitting monument to her great interest in lilies as Walter Bentley's gardener. Wyatt, besides 'Kelmarsh', also produced the lovely 'Pink Starfish', presumed to be a seedling from 'Ellen Willmott' × *martagon*. Not only is it a lovely magenta-rose colour, but it is aptly named as the tepals hardly recurve, making it a striking and beautiful plant.

But with the availability of *L. tsingtauense*, the upright-flowering bright shiny red martagon, others saw that the limited range could be broadened. Edward Robinson in Canada used *L. dalhansonii* and produced a new line with names such as 'Hantsing' and 'Dalhense'. Further generations and back crosses have been produced since, particularly in West Germany where these lilies may be expected to grow well. Beutnagel has gone a stage further introducing *L. medeoloides* into his breeding programme, as has Ewald, recalling Grove's *L. marmed* (*martagon album* × *medeoloides*) of 1915. Petruske in East Germany has introduced his own line *L. martagon cattaniae* × *tsingtauense* with 'Theodor Haber', a characteristic dark shiny red, and the Komet grex of more complex breeding with orange and orange-yellow shades.

These lilies do not pop up overnight and are not what are described as great commercial successes. They require the devoted attention of a number of amateurs over many years to produce the best hybrids from these species which are surely yet to come.

Division III

Division III is more limited initially in its scope than even the last group, the martagons. It is based primarily on *L. candidum* and

237

its hybrid, *L. testaceum*. The other parent *L. chalcedonicum* was brought in again to make the back cross. This was done most successfully by Wyatt producing 'Ares', 'Artemis', 'Apollo', 'Hephaestus' and 'Zeus'. Little is seen of them today, but two or more of the clones are still in the land of the living. They do show what is possible just with this one cross. Now a few enthusiasts are reviving an interest in this Division and re-makes and more adventurous pollinations may be expected. There are a couple of drawbacks, which can be overcome. If the crosses are to be made in England, some excellent summers are required, because warm or hot conditions seem to be essential to obtain much viable seed. Chaff is plentifully produced. Secondly *L. candidum* is early to mid-season, while *L. chalcedonicum* is late. So the amateur has either to save his pollen, cold and dry, for the later lily or better still, grow *L. chalcedonicum* under glass, forcing it a little. Using the latter method is more likely with extra heat to ensure good fertilisation and well-ripened seed. Zalivsky produced seedlings from *L. ledebourii* × *candidum*, but they were lost during the 1939-45 war. Charles Robinson produced 'June Fragrance' from *L. candidum salonikae* × *monadelphum*, and North made a cross between *L. szovitsianum* and *L. candidum*, but it was obviously weak and died before flowering. Here is considerable scope, especially if *L. testaceum* can be brought into the picture.

The advantages these hybrids offer are many. They may be reckoned hardy except in the most extreme conditions and prefer hot summers, though adapting not unwillingly to cooler, damper conditions. They are lime-tolerant and do not demand a deep soil. They offer a rather restricted colour range, but in a less common area of muted pale shades. There is future scope for exciting new flower shapes and placement from the combination of characteristics in the species. Doubt may be expressed on disease resistance as *L. candidum* is easily troubled and very troublesome in this respect. The Caucasian lilies, however, and even *L. chalcedonicum* are less easily afflicted.

Division IV

Division IV is almost exclusively a tale of the West Coast American lilies. Only Showalter has seen some real success with crossing East Coast lilies followed up with an East-West hybrid. Today's situation is far less exciting unfortunately. Gone are the days when Oregon Bulb Farms marketed the San Gabriel Strain and the Del Norte Hybrids. Now, so it is said, none of this class is available (I was to have added 'commercially', but is this necessary?) in the United States and presumably Canada. They are very uncommon in Australia, and most likely in New Zealand, where they should be better received. They can grow on the Continent of Europe, but there they are hampered by lack of availability. Only in the United Kingdom do they find anything of a haven. They are produced only in a few gardens and mainly in that of the author.

It so happens that some of the most beautiful lilies of our time are West Coast American hybrids based on the floral qualities of species like *L. parryi* and *L. kelloggii*. One has only to study lilies like 'Oliver Wyatt' and 'Lake Tahoe' to appreciate that quality and constitution go hand in hand. There are possibly a few parts of the lily-growing world where some West Coast hybrids are of borderline hardiness, but for most of us that should be no problem. The majority of hybrids are a mixture of wet and dryland bulbs adding considerably to their adaptability. Most if not all contain the genes of *L. humboldtii* giving them the ability to withstand both heat and a dry atmosphere. Although generally thought of as acid lovers, they are proving as years go by, perhaps because of the use of *L. bolanderi* and *L. pardalinum*, not only a tolerance of lime but some additional benefit when grown on alkaline soils. All of which makes it a little confusing why they have not become more popular.

The best hybrids today, other than those mentioned above, include one of the originally selected Bellingham Hybrids, *L.* 'Shuksan' which is as good today as it was over 50 years ago; the Monterey Hybrids produced by Mayell on the Pacific Coast; the Bullwood Hybrids and the selected clones produced here in Hockley, Essex (Plate 15); 'Coachella' another lovely yellow *parryi* hybrid and 'Lake Tulare' a beautiful deep pink and white flower with partly recurving tepals (Plate 16). There are others on the way, besides the benefit of seed that will yield pink lilies galore.

Some gardens may not offer the advantages of a little shade and others may be too exposed for the tall stems, resilient though they are, so some improvements can be bred into these lilies for the future. Their disease resistance is a little unpredictable but overall it is better than for most hybrids. It would still be a great benefit to this Division if there was a little competition among growers and a welcome opportunity exists if someone on their home ground in California would take up their cause.

Division V

Division V hybrids have little opportunity to lord it over the other groups. As presently seen only three species, *L. longiflorum, L. formosanum* and *L. philippinense* are usable as parents. Hybrids from these have been obtained and satisfactory though they may be have not proved to have advantages over the dominant species, *L. longiflorum*. The tetraploid form of the latter, 'Tetrabel', crossed with *L. formosanum* produced at the John Innes Institute the triploid 'Formobel'. Superior though such lilies are they have not taken a position in the florists' trade to which this class seems to have been irretrievably cast. Apparently they are too good, or anyway too large. The best of the numerous varieties of *L. longiflorum* can hold their own against hybrids and, as and when necessary, new varieties may be raised from this variable and fertile species.

Division VI

Division VI includes the many forms of the trumpet lilies and the associated Aurelian Hybrids and as shown in the previous chapter is divided into four sub-divisions in order to cater for all grades from the truly funnel-shaped to the flat star-shaped Aurelian. It looks as if everything happened at once. There was one great big explosion and out fell a galaxy of different coloured trumpet lilies. That was well over 30 years ago. A recent glossy highly coloured pamphlet advertising lilies showed six hybrids from Division VI. They were all famous names. Four were established by 1950 and the other two were re-makes that appeared by 1960. Kept apart they can be reproduced as seedling strains for years to come. There can be improvements by careful selection, but it is most likely minimal. It is possible, therefore, for anybody who wishes to produce excellent forms of most of the trumpet kinds. The seedlists admit this is the situation: one golden trumpet × another golden trumpet = just another golden trumpet. But, in fact, all are very good garden lilies, while the best are prize winners on the show bench.

While not denying that the judicious and keen eye may still select and the breeder choose which stigma takes pollen, the way ahead may be to return to the beginning on one side of the parent line. By the beginning is meant obtaining new seed of the species, such as *L. brownii* and *L. leucanthum* and their varieties, from China.

It is heartening even so to see that a few, like Wadekamper in the United States and McPherson in Australia, are endeavouring to pick out the best from those currently available. In Germany new clones and new grexes are being produced and what is refreshing is that it is possible to obtain good quality white trumpet lilies. The cooler shades still and always will have an important place to fill in any good garden in high summer.

These trumpets and aurelians fit happily into large or small sunny borders. If the soil is kept clean of pests the bulbs may last well and have to be replanted rather than replenished. Sometimes they can fail miserably due to basal rot or similar disease even though drainage is good and soil in an apparently sweet condition. These lilies may usually be considered lime-tolerant even though one or two of the species in their background are not. Although accepting some shade they demand sufficient light to perform well, otherwise they will linger on and never prove their worth. Raising new supplies from seed is the best way to defeat disease as it is so easily managed. There are no medals to be gained by having the longest-lived trumpet lily. Clever cultivation in this category may well mean reproducing your favourite again by suitable parent selection.

Division VII

Division VII covers what are generally known as the Oriental hybrids. Again there are four sub-divisions, ranging from trumpet-shaped flowers – a category that may not have been correctly used yet, but would apply to a flower shape like *L. japonicum* – to recurving flowers like *L. speciosum* such as 'Journey's End'. As with the trumpet lilies many of those offered commercially are hybrid grexes produced consistently from seed with considerable constancy of characteristics. They are not showing the individuality which marks many of those produced as clones over the past 40 or so years, but they are gloriously beautiful lilies, none the less. One must pay a tribute to those in New Zealand and Australia who have become legends in producing and cultivating superb lilies in this class. There are still qualities to achieve in the *parkmannii* hybrid and anyone coming new to the game should try their hand, but the real frontiers are now beyond the graceful trumpet species, *L. japonicum* and *L. rubellum*. There is still much to be gained by reproducing more of these kinds, because it is not only flower characteristics which are important. There is the overall size, the plant's disposition, and the flowering season for a start. Then there are the two white lilies. Mrs Ruth Clas made her 'Easter Bunny' from *L. alexandrae* and *L. speciosum*. If you then consider the upright-flowering of *L. nobilissimum* and all the combinations these two may make with all the others there is a marvellous wealth of opportunity awaiting lily fanciers in the immediate future.

But for those who want to start well the standard kinds that come your way, whichever country you live in, take some beating. Care should be taken over the cultural requirements: acid gritty soil with leaf mould, deep planting outside only when the basal roots are growing well again, perfect drainage and plenty of water in spring and through most of the growing

241

season, some shade across the mulched soil and the lily's head in the open, isolation from other lilies and regular spraying against aphids with a systemic insecticide. Is it worth it? Yes.

Some of the standard types are briefly described below. The species *L. auratum* and var. *platyphyllum* are bowl-shaped with spotting and gold bands down the centre of each tepal. The basic changes produced by *L. speciosum* are to flatten the bowl, to recurve the tips to a greater extent and to add more pink/red colouring to the flower, whose overall size may be less.

Type (a) is the whitest form with the gold bands absent or almost so and the spotting only light. De Graaff calls this Imperial Silver VII(c).

Type (b) is similar to var. *platyphyllum* having strong gold bands and plentiful spotting. De Graaff calls this Imperial Gold VII(c).

Type (c) has the gold band substituted by a red band and are called Red Band Hybrids VII (b).

Type (d) has the red band expanded across the petal, but still allowing a fairly broad white edging. The depth of colour is variable and they may be called Imperial Crimson VII (c).

Type (e) has the red often very deep colouring across the face of the flower allowing only a narrow white margin. De Graaff called this Jamboree VII (d). The influence of *L. speciosum* is far more noticeable in this type.

Before finishing this section attention must be drawn to the pollinations that looked the other way. Gordon raised a hybrid from *L. auratum virginale* × *henryi*, bearing a similarity to the pollen parent, *L. henryi* and being almost sterile. Woodriff produced his cross between *L. speciosum rubrum* and *L. henryi* in the mid-1950s and called it 'Black Beauty'. It is still an exceptionally good lily and vigorous. Besides that and the sterility problem, they show what should be done or done again. On some future occasion the result may turn out differently and we may look forward to a marriage between the Chinese trumpets and the Japanese Orientals.

Division VIII

Division VIII is meant to contain all those hybrids not otherwise provided for and stands virtually empty. The long shots occur most infrequently, perhaps every ten years, and they do not always make the record book. There has been a tendency to push the oddities into a well-known Division so that they will not look uncomfortable alone.

In 1914 Michurin produced a cross between *L. szovitsianum*

and *L. thunbergianum* (syn. *L. elegans*). It will never be known which particular Asiatic hybrid was used or even whether it was a hybrid. The resulting lily was called 'Fialkovaya' and is described in the RHS *Lily Year Book* 33 (1970), when considered to be on the point of extinction. It suggests that possibility of a cross between *L. dauricum* and a Caucasian species. The Russians do not claim to have achieved such a hybrid, but Tsvetaeva got nine seedlings to the flowering stage of 'Fialkovaya' × *L. dauricum* in 1940. Further work in the USSR moved on towards the more easily produced Asiatic hybrids rather than back crossing on to the Caucasian lily again. Perhaps it was tried, but without success. With Charles Robinson's 'Prelude' ('June Fragrance' × *bulbiferum croceum*) now in being, a success between a Caucasian lily and *L. dauricum* looks more likely. If not that directly, 'Prelude' or 'June Fragrance' might be tried not with one, but with a number of the cultivars, under the *L. hollandicum* hat.

Chapter 11
Making New Hybrids

A little pollen dabbing is simple to do. It is a lovely summer's day in July (or January) and in the south border the Super Yellow Pendent Lily purchased last fall is flowering well, a real picture. As we go round the garden it looks as though the Stalwart Red, that is not stalwart any more, has a little brick-red pollen on a drying anther. We take the anther off between our fingers and on our way back dab it on the stigma of the SYPL while something else catches our eye. A month later and the ovary of the SYPL is not swollen. It does not matter, we have forgotten about it anyway. Or it is swelling and going to be full of plump viable seeds. It does matter, but we have forgotten what we did. Is this the one we pollinated with the Orange Outward at the back? No. Or was it? Goodness knows! We cannot bother with it, waiting all those years from seed to flowering bulb when we cannot remember what it is. Send it to the club seed exchange marked '?Liliaceae col. Nei Mongol 1527 m'!!

It is far better to work to a plan, which may be worked out beforehand. Making plans are what dreams are used for. The plan need not be so rigid as to exclude adjustment, but if you are that sort of person you should write it down. Progress is slow so it is good to have a number of plans going at once.

The gardener, the grower or the lily enthusiast will know what lilies he has available to work on, both as female parents, the seed parents and as male parents, the pollen parents. Some parents, especially if they are hybrids, may be poor in producing seed or poor in producing pollen. If the would-be hybridiser has other lily growers within a reasonable distance or convenient to a speedy postal service then the number of pollen parents available to him or her may be greatly increased. If all this information has not been logged and sorted by the mind already, consciously and subconsciously, then it can easily be assembled on paper. It may be a good exercise in any case, because schemes may then become apparent which had not awoken earlier in the mind. Accidents and disappointments may easily occur during the growing season so make due allowance for this.

All pollinations will have to be recorded, detailing all the relevant facts and conditions. Their main place will be in a permanent record book – a computer is not essential at this stage! A secondary record may be kept, say, as the pocket notebook used in the garden. The third record, a temporary one, will be the label on the pollinated flowers.

The information to be recorded should consist of a numbering system; the name of the seed parent further identifying description if it is one of a grex; the name of the pollen parent and further description if necessary, and source and age if foreign to the garden; the number of flowers pollinated; conditions (weather, etc.) at the time of pollination, and the date. Further columns may then be left free to add when seed collected, when sown, etc. if this is not tabulated in a further book with a final space for remarks, such as FAILED or when first flowered.

The numbering system may be very simple, like '1 up', or it may be managed as a complex code. Take the last two numbers

of the year	83
the classification Division of the parent (trumpet)	6
the number of the cross between trumpets that year (third)	3
If a number of female parents of a grex are being used then an oblique stroke and a further number may be used to indicate each individual parent	/4
	8363/4

When the time comes to sort out the various seedlings then a further oblique stroke may be added and a further series of number used   8363/4/12

This type of code, which may be varied in many ways to suit the hybridiser, should only be adopted if it is going to be useful. As time goes on it is helpful to know straightaway the year or how old a pot or bed of seedlings may be. When sorting out pots of seedlings and memorising the urgent jobs it is extremely helpful to recognise immediately from a numbered label what type of lily you are handling. On any kind of label writing soon becomes difficult to decipher so plain codes are a boon, so long as we understand what they mean.

Some small tools and equipment may be found useful. They may include little jars with screw-on lids for storing pollen. These should hold calcium chloride for absorbing moisture and keeping the pollen dry, which should be covered over with cotton wool. Little glass or plastic phials may be just as handy to use, but they

245

must be easily labelled. The little plastic phials can be used for sending pollen to friends. A small pair of scissors are useful. The blades should be narrow and pointed and preferably curved. They may be used for emasculating the buds, especially of smaller lilies. For obtaining and holding anthers with dehisced pollen small tweezers can be used preferably not too stiff and having small spade ends. A brush is often recommended, but for lilies it is of doubtful usefulness. If the pollen bearing anthers are collected on to cotton wool, then using the tweezers again the pollen can be directly rubbed on to the stigma. The pollen is so sticky that the most direct transfer to the stigma is to be recommended. Even so at times some applicator may be required and cotton wool 'buds' will be found handy to use and easily disposed of afterwards in a plastic bag. Where a number of different pollinations are to be done at one time then the hands should be kept free of pollen and methylated spirits used to decontaminate them and, of course, any equipment such as the scissors and the tweezers. So a jar of methylated spirits with a suitable tight lid should be kept for this job. Labels are another essential and they should not be too heavy and bulky. The white price tag type with fine cotton string are very suitable. A fine fibre-tip pen with permanent ink is suitable both for numbering the label and writing up the garden pocket book record.

No plant could be easier to fertilise than the lily. All the parts are large and clearly visible. The procedure to adopt should be as follows. Let us assume the male parent flowers early. When the flowers are open and the pollen free on the anther, we take the jar, or desiccator, with calcium chloride and cotton wool, to the plant. If the flowers are dry, with the tweezers pick off sufficient anthers, remembering a little pollen goes a long way, and place them in the desiccator on the cotton wool. Screw on the lid and mark the label suitably with name and date or code. Place the desiccator in the cool section of the refrigerator. The pollen will keep alive for a few months under these conditions. If storage is only required for a few days refrigeration should not be necessary, but keep the jar in a cool place.

Keep a close eye on the female parent especially when the flower buds begin to turn colour. They eventually reach a stage when they have not begun to open, but the tepals are free enough to be prised apart. At this stage pull them sufficiently open to be able to see the stamens. Being very careful and having located the style and delicately held it to one side out of harm's way remove the six anthers. The flower is now emasculated, but the stigma could still be at risk from cross pollination and so it should be given a capping of light gauge aluminium foil or silver paper. In 24-48 hours time the stigma will have become viscid and receptive for pollen and a good covering may be given, taking care not to do any harm during the removal of the foil capping. If the stigma is well coated with pollen the hybridiser may risk not re-capping the stigma as fertilisation will have occurred in a few hours. As protecting the stigma in the way suggested is a very delicate operation bagging the flower may be better, using paper bags peppered with pin pricks. The latter will prevent excessive damp inside the bag. The day following pollination the bag should be removed.

The risk of pollen contamination with many lilies is not very great, but unless you know your lilies and your circumstances and possible pollinators well it is best to cover the stigma, otherwise you cannot be sure of the outcome. If you are to be in control of the situation you must make certain of what is happening. To judge the end result years later and to be able to be guided by it you must be sure of what happened in the past.

If the cross has worked the pedicels will, if they are not already, turn erect and the capsules start to fatten. After some weeks they will be ripe and ready for picking. Before this keep an eye on them because in some areas birds may ruin your work by pecking out the seeds for food.

It must not be assumed that because the stigma was receptive, the pollen looked good and then the pod swelled up that new hybrids are about to be born. Some lilies are notoriously difficult to fertilise, some impossible that they will not perform except to their own kind. However tempting the beginner should not consider outlandish crosses. Open the mature pod and out falls chaff. The most difficult crosses achieved have often followed the unsuccessful patient work of previous seasons. In the end through the combination of unpredictable circumstances a few viable seeds have been produced.

In some cases where species have presumably grown apart for millions of years apparently good seeds are produced, but no normal germination takes place because the embryo is detached from the endosperm, or an acid is formed killing the embryo. In other circumstances the embryo grows normally but the endosperm is found to have aborted, leaving it without sustenance when germination is meant to be taking place. Dr North found that if the embryo of *L. lankongense* hybrids were excised they could be raised on simple agar nutrient medium and grown on to become normal vigorous plants. So where embryos are found to be normal plants may be raised if satisfactory aseptic laboratory conditions are available.

It is one thing making new hybrids, but in looking forward to the results we should have aims and standards. Some of the purposes of having hybrids have already come out in the text and it would be right to list those and more here:

(a) To have more good garden plants.
(b) To be easier to grow than species.
(c) To keep healthier in gardens than species.
(d) To maintain their vigour in gardens.
(e) To be more floriferous.
(f) To show a greater range of colours.
(g) To have larger flowers.
(h) To have stronger stems.
(i) To have shorter/taller stature according to need.
(j) To be easier to propagate than some species.
(k) To take the strain off the demand for the species.

We cannot judge by looking at it whether a lily is easier to grow or going to be healthier, but if the facilities are available we could put it on trial. For lilies this has not been found to be fair, so there is no other way, except growing them in our gardens alongside all other plants which really means they have been accepted, at least, for a life. We can judge whether a flower is larger, is a different colour or brighter and because of this we should be thorough in our criticism. Less immediately obvious points should be watched carefully as they often do make for better lilies.

Let us look at the flowers. Broader petals make for more substantial flowers. The petals look more graceful if they are not tightly recurved. The flowers are set off better if the pedicels arch or curve and are inclined at an angle and not straight, horizontal or too close to the vertical. More flowers in the inflorescence are an advantage if the rachis is tall enough and each flower is seen individually to be well-placed, otherwise more flowers are a disadvantage. Similarly if the pedicel bifurcates to give two flowers this is good as long as there is ample room for both flowers. Flowers without spots have a cleanness and a brilliance of colour; spotted flowers may show more character and even a bizarre appearance. Both spotted and unspotted can have advantages one over the other. If a too tightly rolled flower is a poor characteristic so is too flat a flower. Flatness may be relieved by the curving tips; colour variation along the median line of the tepal, by papillae spotted or unspotted, by the turn of tepals towards the base showing nectary furrows and a contrasting green ovary, by the strength and size of the stamens and pistil.

Aspect or direction of the flowers counts for a great deal. It has done in the species for millions of years. There are reasons why *L. tsingtauense* and *L. philadelphicum* look up and why *L. martagon* and *L. canadense* hang down. Flowers should give of their best naturally. The upright should not hang down and the pendent type should not look up. What of some of the outward-facing Asiatic hybrids? Combined with upright-facing flowers they can look well in the inflorescence, but they should be screened by a critical eye.

Remember that the new lily with the slightly different slant will catch the eye of the beholder and raise the interest of the curious gardener. The flower that flouts convention is harshly criticised and deemed an outrage. It is so with lilies. Read what has been said about double lilies before now, and it must be noticeable they get hardly a mention in these pages.

Sometimes when surveying the future scene it is possible to take a narrow blinkered view. So much has been done in the past to little effect. All those pages of hybrids created, and where are they? Either in the dust or some sodden field; they are certainly, but for a very few, not in our gardens. But that does not matter, we can go on creating new ones and enjoy them while they survive. The one per cent or one in a thousand will be left to soldier on and show what was done in this age.

In some divisions there is much to be done. In the field of Division IV without even trying to involve the Eastern American species the scope is tremendous. There are some good red, good pink and good yellow lilies of beautiful shape and carriage, but the latter still lack that necessary stamina. When that is achieved it is the time to transfer the pink and red colours to the excellent *parryi* shape without forgetting that the fine scent must be retained at all costs. The foliage should have the strength of *L. pardalinum*. *L. parvum* would seem to come in most of the basic colours, orange-red, yellow, red and pink, and white (or colourless) with a touch of green, so they can be played about with endlessly. But the flowers must be enlarged without loss of their unique form and have built in the chance to withstand damper atmospheres. If *L. parvum* and its stocky brother on the waterfront, *L. maritimum* have not been put to use, then *L. washingtonianum* has not been tamed one little bit in any of its varieties, and neither has the lovely *L. rubescens* with its differing form and more upright flowers. Even *L. bolanderi* has not made its full impact yet.

So there are all these opportunities in one slice of Division IV and normally without the problems of sterility or incompatability. The commercial venturer is unlikely to stray into this area. They are inclined to keep to Divisions I, VI and VII. So the field is open for the amateur with the perseverance not just to tackle the first generation crosses, with which so many of us are willing to content ourselves, but to go on to the second, third and fourth generations when the best results will be achieved.

In those Divisions – and across them too – where incompatibility abounds again commercial enterprise is unlikely to play a dominant role. It will be here that universities, research establishments and such national institutions will need to play an important part, mainly because they have the tools and equipment suitable to the task. What, however, is vital to the success of any schemes put in train is the utmost co-operation among amateurs, scientists, technicians and commercial growers filled with a similar strain of enthusiasm.

Chapter 12
Lilies for Special Uses and Situations

The following lists of species and hybrids are set out as a simple and quick guide. They are obviously a personal choice and other Lily growers could argue for the exclusion of many of the lilies and inclusion of their own favourites. Nevertheless, these should prove useful to many readers. Lime-tolerant species are listed on p. 43 and hybrids having a lime-tolerant parent may themselves be expected to have reasonable tolerance.

Lilies for Beginners

L. dauricum
L. pumilum
L. pyrenaicum rubrum
L. regale
L. 'Black Dragon'
L. 'Connecticut Yankee'
L. 'Enchantment'
L. 'Green Magic'
L. 'Hornback's Gold'
L. 'Imperial Crimson'
L. 'Marilyn Monroe'
L. 'Theseus'

Easy Lilies

L. columbianum
L. dauricum
L. hansonii
L. martagon
L. Bellingham Hybrids
L. 'Beckwith Tiger'
L. 'Black Beauty'
L. 'Bright Star'
L. 'Eros'
L. 'Golden Splendour'
L. 'Orestes'
L. 'Wattle Bird'

Easy Lilies from Seed

L. amabile
L. cernuum
L. concolor
L. dauricum
L. davidii
L. formosanum
L. longiflorum
L. maculatum
L. pumilum
L. regale
Asiatic hybrids
Trumpet hybrids

Lilies for Specialists

L. bolanderi
L. carniolicum albanicum
L. henrici
L. kelloggii
L. ledebourii
L. leichtlinii
L. maculatum bukozanense
L. nepalense
L. ponticum
L. taliense
L. wardii
L. washingtonianum
    purpurascens

Lilies for Cottage Gardens

L. bulbiferum croceum
L. candidum
L. dalhansonii
L. maculatum luteum
L. martagon
L. martagon album
L. pyrenaicum
L. szovitsianum
L. testaceum
L. Bellingham Hybrids
L. 'Ellen Willmott'
L. 'Viking'

Lilies for Open Situations

L. bulbiferum chaixii
L. candidum
L. chalcedonicum
L. humboldtii
L. maculatum
L. pomponium
L. regale
L. testaceum
L. Fiesta Hybrids
L. Mid-Century Hybrids
L. 'Saint Keverne' and other
  Cornish Hybrids
L. 'Maxwill'

Lilies for Woodland Gardens

L. amabile luteum
L. canadense
L. mackliniae
L. pardalinum fragrans
L. tsingtauense
L. parkmannii hybrids
L. 'Lake Tahoe'
L. 'Lake Tulare'
L. 'Oliver Wyatt'
L. 'Shuksan'
C. giganteum
C. giganteum yunnanense

Lilies for Pots

L. concolor coridion
L. formolongi
L. formosanum
L. longiflorum
L. sulphureum
L. parkmannii hybrids
L. Little Fairies
L. Moonlight (VIa)
L. 'Black Dragon'
L. 'Connecticut King'
L. 'Juliana'
L. 'Little Lavender'

Lilies for Mild Gardens

L. brownii
L. formolongi
L. formosanum (and cultivars)
L. longiflorum (and cultivars)
L. neilgherrense
L. nepalense
L. philippinense
L. primulinum
L. speciosum
L. sulphureum
L. wallichianum
L. 'Sulphur Queen'

Lilies for Cold Gardens

L. amabile
L. canadense
L. cernuum
L. dalhansonii
L. dauricum
L. pumilum
L. tsingtauense
L. 'Brenda Watts'
L. 'Jasper'
L. 'Marhan'
L. 'Sonnentiger'
L. 'White Princess'

Dwarf Lilies

L. cernuum
L. concolor
L.c. jankae
L. maritimum
L. nanum
L. oxypetalum
L. pumilum
L. rubellum
L. Little Fairies
L. 'Girls Only'
L. 'Red Carpet'
L. 'Rusty'

Tall Lilies

L. auratum platyphyllum
L. henryi
L. leichtlinii maximowiczii
L. leucanthem centifolium
L. pardalinum giganteum
L. superbum
L. taliense
L. tigrinum splendens
L. Bellingham Hybrids
L. Bullwood Hybrids
L. 'Viking'
C. giganteum

Lilies for Rock Gardens

L. bulbiferum chaixii
L. cernuum
L. concolor
L.c. albanicum
L. duchartrei
L. formosanum (very dwarf form)
L. maritimum (very dwarf form)
L. nanum
L. oxypetalum
L. pomponium
L. rubellum
L. sherriffiae

253

Appendix I
Lily Societies

The societies play an important part in fostering an interest in all matters relating to the true lily. Some have a broader role espousing all or many liliaceous plants, but all are good for the novice and the expert alike and for those just interested in or loving lilies.

The main societies known to the author are given below together with the names and addresses of their secretaries.

Australia

The Australian Lilium Society
  Mr. J.H. Young
  24 Halwyn Crescent
  West Preston
  Victoria, Australia 3072

Canada

Ontario Regional Lily Society
  Mrs Gordon Brown,
  RR1
  Harley, Ontario N0E 1E0

The Canadian Prairie Lily Society
  Dr E.A. Maginnes
  University of Saskatchewan
  Saskatoon
  Saskatchewan

Germany

The 'Fachgruppe Lilien' is part of the Gesellschaft der Stauden-freunde EV
  Martel Hald
  Dörrenklingenweg 35
  D 7114 Pfedelbach-Untersteinbach
  West Germany

254

New Zealand

The Auckland Lily Society
  Mrs B. Gross
  34 Maungakiekei Avenue
  Auckland

New Zealand Lily Society
  Mr John Gover
  P.O. Box 1394
  Christchurch

Otago Lily Society
  Miss D. Aldous
  15 King Edward Street
  Dunedin

South Africa

South African Lilium Society
  Mrs Eileen Stiemens
  P.O. Box 3082
  Pretoria 0001

Sweden

There is no formal Lily Society, but those interested meet and
keep in touch. Contact:
  Mr Kenneth Lorentzon
  Nordanvindsgatan 2D
  41717 Gothenburg

United Kingdom

The Royal Horticultural Society Lily Group
  Mrs A.C. Dadd
  21 Embrook Road
  Wokingham
  Berkshire RG11 1HF

USA

The North American Lily Society Inc.
  Mrs Dorothy B. Schaefer
  P.O. Box 476
  Waukee, Iowa 50263

Other Societies in the USA include:

Michigan Lily Society
Mrs R.H. Briggs
21615 Oxford
Farmington, Michigan 48024

New England Regional Lily Group
Mrs K. Yates
70 Spring Street
Shrewsbury, Mass. 01545

North Star Lily Society
Marsha Hartle
RR4 Box 14
Owatonna, Minnesota 55060

Ohio Lily Society
Mrs L. Hinman
29449 Pike Drive
Chagrin Falls, Ohio 44022

USSR

There is no Lily Society as such, but in more general societies there are often lily groups. The Moscow Naturalist Society (MOIP) has a large Lily Section.

Appendix II
A Simple Bibliography of Books and Papers on Lilies

Adams, H.S. (1913) *Lilies*, New York

The American Horticultural Society (1939) *The American Lily Year Book*, Washington, DC. Also published in 1940, 1942 and 1946.

—— (1941) *Lily Bulletin*, Washington, DC

Botanical Magazine, Curtis' (1790-) London. Contains numerous coloured plates of lilies

Craig, W.N. (1928) *Lilies and Their Culture in North America*, Chicago

Duchartre, P.E. (1870) *Observations sur le genre Lis*, Journal de la Société centrale d'Horticulture de France, Paris

—— (1872-5) *Observations sur les bulbes des Lis*, Annales des Sciences Naturelles, Paris

Eastwood, Alice (1948) *From Studies of Pacific Coast Lilies*, Leaflets of Western Botany, **5**, San Francisco. (See also RHS LYB **12** (1948))

Elwes, H.J. (1877-80) *A Monograph of the Genus Lilium*, London

Evans, A. (1974) *The Peat Garden and its Plants*, London

Feldmaier, C. (1970) *Die Neuen Lilien*, Stuttgart

Florist and Pomologist. The (1862-84) London. Contains numerous coloured plates of lilies

Fox, Helen M. (1928) *Garden Cinderellas*, New York

Franchet, A. (1892) *Les Lis de la Chine et du Thibet dans l'herbier du Museum de Paris*, Journal de Botanique, **6**. Paris

Garden, The (1875-1906) London. Contains many coloured plates of lilies

Gerarde, J. (1597) *The Herball or general Historie of Plantes*, London

Gilmour, J.S.L. *et al.* (1980) *International Code of Nomenclature of Cultivated Plants*, Utrecht

Graaff, Jan de (1951) *The New Book of Lilies*, London

Graaff, Jan de & Hyams, Edward (1967) *Lilies*, London

Grove, A. (1911) *Lilies*, London

257

Grove, A. & Cotton, A.D. (1933-40) *A Supplement to Elwes' Monograph of the Genus Lilium*, Parts 1-7, London

Jekyll, Gertrude (1901) *Lilies for English Gardens*, London

—— (1983) Reprint of *Lilies for English Gardens*, introduced and revised by G.S. Thomas, Salem, NH

Leeburn, M.E. (1955) *Lilies and Their Cultivation*, London

Macfie, D.T. (1939; rev. 1947) *Lilies for the Garden and Greenhouse*, London

Macneil, A. and Macneil, Esther (1946) *Garden Lilies*, New York

Marshall, W.E. (1929) *Consider the Lilies*, 2nd edn and Supplement, 1930, New York

Matthews, Victoria (1984) 'Lilium pyrenaicum – a Complex Species', *The Kew Magazine*, **1**, Part 1, pp. 36-43

Maxwell, Alice C. (1953) *Lilies in Their Homes*, London

Mohlenbrock, R.H. (1970) *Flowering Plants Lilies to Orchids*, Illustrated Flora of Illinois, Carbondale & Edwardsville

Munz P.A. with D. Keck (1968) *A California Flora*, 4th edn, Berkeley and Los Angeles

North American Lily Society (1948) *The Lily Yearbook of . . . . Number one (1947-8), edited by G.L. Slate, Geneva, NY to Number 35 (1982), edited by Norma Simoni, Westwood, Ma.*

—— *Bulletin* Vol. 1 to Vol. 37, No. 3 (Sept. 1983)

Ohwi, J. (1953) *Flora of Japan*, Tokyo. Republished in 1965 by the Smithsonian Institute, Washington, DC

Parkinson, J. (1629) *Paradisi in Sole Paradisus terrestris*, London

Preston, Isabella (1929) *Garden Lilies*, New York

—— (1947) *Lilies for Every Garden*, New York

Purdy, C. (1919) *Pacific Coast Lilies and Their Culture*, Journal of the International Garden Club, **3**, New York

Redouté, P.J. (1812-13) *Les Liliacées*, Paris

Redouté, P.J. & Mathew, Brian (1982) *Lilies and Related Flowers*, London

Royal Horticultural Society, *Journal of the* (1901) Lily Conference Report and Papers, **26** (also contains reprint of 'Experiments in Plant Hybridisation' by Gregor Mendel), London

—— *Journal of the* (1946) 'Recent Developments in Lily Cultivation', H.D. Woodcock, **71** Part 11, London

—— *Journal of the* (1947) 'Unfamiliar American Shrubs and Plants', Mrs J.N. Henry, **72**, Part 10, London

—— (1956) *Dictionary of Gardening*, 2nd edn, **3**, Oxford

—— (1969) *Supplement to the Dictionary of Gardening*, 2nd edn, Oxford

(1973-) *Lilies and Other Liliaceae* (1973, 1973/1974, 1974, 1975, 1976, 1977, 1978/9), London

—— (1982) *International Lily Register*, 3rd edn, London

Royal Horticultural Society Lily Committee *Lilies and Allied Plants 1972*

Royal Horticultural Society Lily Group *Bulletin 1981* and *1982*

—— *Lilies and Related Plants 1984/85*

Sealy, J.R. (1950) *Nomocharis and Lilium*, Kew Bulletin, London

Slate, G.L. (1939) *Lilies for American Gardens*, New York and London

—— (1972) *Diseases of Garden Lilies and Their Control*, NALS

Smith, W.W. (1922) *Notes on Chinese Lilies*, Transactions and Proceedings of the Botanical Society of Edinburgh, **28**, Edinburgh

Stern, F.C. (1960) *A Chalk Garden*, rev. 1974, London

Stewart, R.N. (1947) *The Morphology of Somatic Chromosomes in Lilium*, American Journal of Botany, **34**, Burlington, Vermont

Stoker, F. (1943) *A Book of Lilies*, London and New York

Synge, P.M. (1961) *Collins' Guide to Bulbs*, London

—— (1973) *In Search of Flowers*, London

—— (1980a) *Lilies*, London

—— (1980b) '*Some Newer Hybrid Lilies*', The Plantsman, **1**, Part 4, London

Taylor, G.M. (1947) *Lilies for the Beginner*, London

Turrill, W.B. (1960-2) *A Supplement to Elwes' Monograph of the Genus Lilium*, Parts 8 & 9, London

Tutin, T.G. *et al.* (1980) *Flora Europaea*, **5**, Cambridge

Wallace, A. (1879) *Notes on Lilies and Their Culture*, 2nd edn, Colchester

Wang Fa-tauan & Tang tsin (Liang Sung-yun) (1980) *Flora Reipublicae Popularis Sinicae*, **14**, Liliaceae Lilium, Beijing

Watson, S. (1879 & 1885) *Californian Lilies*, Proceedings of American Academy of Arts and Sciences, **14** & **20**

—— (1879) *Revision of the North American Liliaceae*, **14**, Boston, Mass.

Wherry, E.T. (1947) *A Key to the Eastern North American Lilies*, Bartonia, **24**, Philadelphia. (See also RHS *LYB* **12** (1948))

Wilson, E.H. (1925) *The Lilies of Eastern Asia, a Monograph*, London

Woodcock, H.B.D. & Stearn, W.T. (1950) *Lilies of the World, Their Cultivation & Classification*, London

Index

(Excludes lilies and cardiocrinums listed in Chapter 12)

260